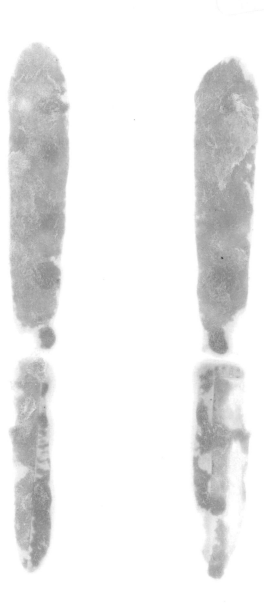

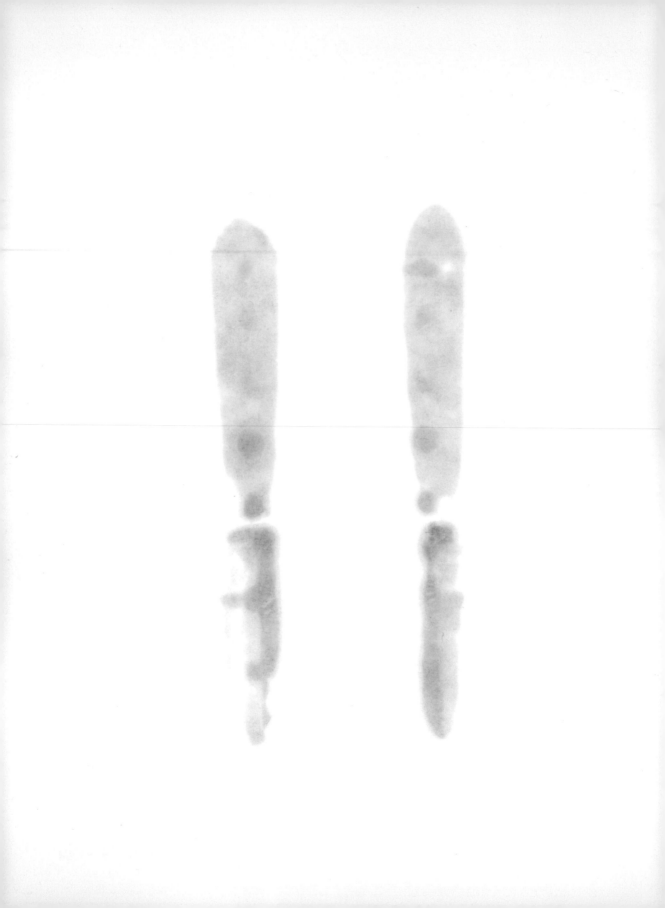

EUROPE,
CENTURY
BY CENTURY

EUROPE, CENTURY BY CENTURY

Stephen Usherwood

DRAKE PUBLISHERS INC NEW YORK

ISBN 87749-355-3

Published in 1973 by Drake Publishers Inc
381 Park Avenue South
New York, N.Y. 10016

Printed in Great Britain

Contents

page

List of Illustrations   7

Introduction   11

ONE   *The Centuries before Christ*   13
Pre-history—Europe breaks away from Asia—Sparta and Athens—
Religion and Philosophy—Athenian Democracy—The Empire of
Alexander the Great—The Rise of the Roman Empire

TWO   *The Early Centuries 0–AD 1000*   27
The Founding of the Christian Church—The Founding of the Barbarian
Kingdoms—The Viking Invasions—The Great Princes of Kiev—The
Kingdom of Germany

THREE   *The Eleventh Century*   44
The Kingdoms of Hungary and Croatia—The Conversion of the Vikings—
Papal Supremacy—The First Crusade—The Norman Conquest of England

FOUR   *The Twelfth Century*   55
Feudalism and Monarchy—Monasticism and the Crusades—The Rise of the
French Monarchy—The Career of the Emperor Frederick Barbarossa

FIVE   *The Thirteenth Century*   68
Pope Innocent III and Francis of Assisi—The Tartar Invasion of Russia—
Gregory IX and the Dominican Order—Louis IX and the Development
of Gothic Architecture—The Emperor Frederick II and the Downfall of the
Hohenstaufen—The Sicilian Vespers—The Hanseatic League—The
Reconquest of Spain and Portugal

SIX   *The Fourteenth Century*   81
The Beginning of the Hundred Years' War—Denmark and the Hanseatic
League—The Rise of Poland and Lithuania—The Conquests of the
Ottoman Turks in Europe—The Russian Church and the Princes of
Moscow—The Suppression of the Templars—The Avignon Popes
The Swiss Confederation—Giotto and his Patrons

page

SEVEN   *The Fifteenth Century*   94
    The Fall of Constantinople—The End of the Hundred Years' War—
    Heresy in Bohemia—Ivan III, Tsar of All Russia—The Expansion of France—
    Portugal, Spain and the Ocean Route to India—The Italian Renaissance—
    The Invention of Printing

EIGHT   *The Sixteenth Century*   107
    Progress with Gunpowder—The Affairs of Italy—Reformation and
    Counter-Reformation—The Habsburgs and Hungary—Philip II and the
    Netherlands—The French Wars of Religion—Copernicus, Kepler and
    Brahé

NINE   *The Seventeenth Century*   121
    The Thirty Years' War—The Affairs of Russia, Poland and the Jews—
    The Frontiers of France—John Sobieski and the Relief of Vienna—
    Galileo and the Progress of Science

TEN   *The Eighteenth Century*   132
    The Reign of Tsar Peter the Great—The War of the Spanish Succession
    —Artists in Porcelain—Books and Despots—Habsburg and Hohenzollern
    —Taxation and Revolution—The Early Career of Napoleon Bonaparte
    —The Partitions of Poland

ELEVEN   *The Nineteenth Century*   148
    Nations in Arms: the Napoleonic Period—Italy: Campanilismo and
    Liberty—Bismarck and the Second Reich—The French Impressionists—
    The Prevention of War

TWELVE   *The Twentieth Century*   162
    Nations in Arms: The Liberal Period—Art in Russia—Nations in
    Arms: The Fascist Period—Scientific Progress—A Declaration of
    Independence

Index   182

List of Illustrations

Bison: Stone Age cave sculpture (*Commissariat Général au Tourisme*)   13
Greek fighting Amazon (*British Museum*)   15
Triptolemos bowl (*British Museum*)   17
Roman aqueduct near Nîmes (*Commissariat Général au Tourisme*)   25
Pantheon, Rome (*Paul Popper Ltd*)   26
Antonia (*British Musum*)   28
The Amphitheatre, Pula (*Yugoslav Government Tourist Office*)   30
Sculpture from the Antonine Column, Rome (*Author's Collection*)   31
Porta Nigra, Trier (*Mansell Collection*)   32
Ivory diptych of Christ's Miracles (*Victoria & Albert Museum*)   33
Santa Sophia, Istanbul (*Paul Popper Ltd*)   36
Evidence in Italian, AD 960 (*Ralph Usherwood*)   40
The iron crown of Lombardy (*Author's Collection*)   42
Viking stone from Gotland (*Author's Collection*)   45
Henry IV at Canossa (*Author's Collection*)   48
Sant' Angelo, Rome (*John Freeman*)   49
Islamic symbol (*Author's Collection*)   51
Falaise Castle (*Commissariat Général au Tourisme*)   54
Mosaic of Roger II of Sicily (*Mansell Collection*)   56
Interior of the Church of the Martorana, Palermo (*Mansell Collection*)   57
'Le Moulin Mystique', Vézelay (*Commissariat Général au Tourisme*)   58
Vézelay, Burgundy (*Commissariat Général au Tourisme*)   59
The return of a Crusader (*Author's Collection*)   60
Frederick Barbarossa (*Author's Collection*)   64
Chartres Cathedral (*Author's Collection*)   73
A window in Chartres Cathedral (*Victoria & Albert Museum*)   74
Amiens Cathedral (*William Crush*)   74
Beauvais Cathedral (*William Crush*)   74
Walls of Visby (*Radio Times Hulton Picture Library*)   77
Castle of the Teutonic Knights, Marienburg (*Paul Popper Ltd*)   79
Interior of the Alcazar, Seville (*William Crush*)   80
A crossbow (*Wallace Collection*)   82
The Schifferhaus, Lübeck (*Paul Popper Ltd*)   84
Arrest of Knights Templars (*British Museum*)   88

Florence as a walled town (*John Freeman*) 91
The prophet Haggai by Pisano (*Victoria & Albert Museum*) 92
Sultan Mahomet II (*National Gallery*) 95
The town and harbour of Rhodes (*John Freeman*) 96
The Kremlin, Moscow (*John Freeman*) 99
Lagos harbour, Portugal (*J. Allan Cash*) 101
The Alhambra, Granada (*William Crush*) 102
Page from the Gutenberg Bible (*British Museum*) 105
Arquebus and pistol (*Victoria & Albert Museum*) 107
Calvinist cartoon (*John Freeman*) 109
Geneva (*Author's Collection*) 111
College of the Jesuits, Rome (*John Freeman*) 113
Rotterdam harbour (*Author's Collection*) 115
The Escorial, Spain (*William Crush*) 116
Ecclesiastical cope (*Victoria & Albert Museum*) 117
Jousting scene by Dürer (*British Museum*) 118
Tycho Brahé's observatory (*Science Museum*) · 120
Prague (*Author's Collection*) 121
Stockholm (*Author's Collection*) 123
A 17th century Dutch sword (*Victoria & Albert Museum*) 124
Gunner's linstock (*Wallace Collection*) 127
'The Polish Horseman' by Rembrandt (*Frick Collection*) 129
Galileo's drawings of the moon (*Science Museum*) 130
The Old Admiralty, Leningrad (*Author's Collection*) 132
Louis XIV and his family by N. de Largillière (*Wallace Collection*) 134
Harlequin in Meissen porcelain (*Victoria & Albert Museum*) 136
Moritzburg, near Dresden (*Tourist Office of the German Democratic Republic*) 137
Frederick the Great and Voltaire (*Author's Collection*) 139
French peasants (*Author's Collection*) 142
Paris as a walled city (*Author's Collection*) 143
Schönbrunn, Austria (*Austrian National Tourist Office*) 148
The Empress Josephine by J. Chinard (*Victoria & Albert Museum*) 150
Dobrente Castle, Hungary (*Keystone Press Agency*) 153
Jews of Russian Poland (*Forward Agency*) 156
'Les Parapluies' by P-A. Renoir (*National Gallery*) 157
Mobilisation of French Army, 1914 (*Radio Times Hulton Picture Library*) 162
German cavalry in a Russian village, 1916 (*Radio Times Hulton Picture Library*) 164
Russian supply column, 1916 (*Radio Times Hulton Picture Library*) 164
President Masaryk enters Prague, 1918 (*Radio Times Hulton Picture Library*) 166
Backcloth for the ballet *Les Contes Russes* by Larionov (*Victoria & Albert Museum*) 169
Benito Mussolini (*Keystone Press Agency*) 171
Barter trade in Germany, 1923 (*Atlantic Photo*) 173
Moscow monument to space exploration (*Author's Collection*) 177

The surface of the moon photographed by an unmanned satellite (*US Information Service*) 178

Budapest and its bridges (*Keystone Press Agecny*) 180

The frontier between East and West Germany (*Keystone Press Agency*) 181

Introduction

Human beings are not born free; however far from their place of birth or upbringing ambition or fate may take them, they remain bound to it by chains as light as air but strong as iron, remembering its hills and skies, the scent of forest, plain or river and the sound of their mother tongue spoken in the streets. These senses, far more powerful than the intellect, exert magnetic forces that have influenced history at every stage. Europe, being a western peninsula of Asia, broken into many great promontories and fringed with islands both large and small, has provided new homelands reminiscent of the old to a constant stream of migrants both in ancient and modern times. Peoples from Asia found in the hot sun and snowy mountains of Spain a land so like home that they did not hesitate to build palaces that would not have seemed out of place in Damascus or Aleppo. Until AD 1000 the Atlantic ocean was the only geographical barrier to delay the westward wanderings of the barbarians, and then the Vikings reached North America.

The myths, legends and history of Europe evoke the imagery of dark forests infested with bears and wolves, the thunder of hooves on the grassy steppe, mountains that hold up the sky and life-giving rivers pouring across fertile plains. All these mingle in the folk stories of the nations, arousing an extraordinary conflict between affection for an ancestral home and the desire to explore what lies beyond the farthest hill and over the most distant horizon.

The absence in northern latitudes of any insuperable barrier between the Pacific shores of Asia and the Atlantic coasts of Europe is a fact, but the presence of mountains, seas and rivers has always had a double effect upon men's minds, producing on the one hand a sense of awe and fear, and on the other inspiring them to cross the forbidding waters and seek roads between the rock-strewn peaks. Great rivers like the Danube and the Rhine were at one period regarded as 'natural frontiers' to be kept under constant watch, and at another developed as highways of water-borne commerce. High mountains like the Pyrenees were no obstacle when the enchanted horn of Roland, calling from the pass of Roncesvalles, tempted men to conquer Spain, nor did the Alps prevent the medieval German emperors from aspiring to the kingship of Italy.

In addition to these geographical influences with their strange sensual effects, Europeans in historic times received a rich mental and spiritual inheritance from three peoples of the ancient world, the Greeks, the Romans and the Jews. Often, like the spoiled children of rich families, they have wasted these assets or allowed an exaggerated enthusiasm for the past to be a substitute for fresh creativity. 'We are all children of Hellas'—so begins a famous English history of Europe. We are nothing of the sort—only descendants of barbarians who broke into and destroyed the homes and cities of the Roman empire and, not knowing what to do with the splendid literature and science stored in their libraries, imitated only the militarism of the former owners and their devotion to false visions of the divine. A re-descent to barbarism is a prospect never far from modern politics, and nothing but a recognition of this danger, and the relighting of those torches by whose light Europe was once before led away from paganism, can restore what two world wars destroyed.

CHAPTER ONE

The Centuries before Christ

Pre-history

The knowledge that until about 25000 BC the greater part of Europe was covered by a thick sheet of Arctic ice was not available until recent times. Geologists in the early nineteenth century did not recognise in the gorges of the middle Rhine or the valleys of the Harz the marks of glaciers just as powerful as those that now carve out valleys in Norway and Switzerland. As the ice receded, grasslands appeared on its southern edge and from the direction of the equator a great army of forest trees, pines, larches, oaks and birches, advancing from the north coast of Africa, crossed the Mediterranean and conquered Germany, Poland and Russia.

As the weather grew warmer, fish and game of every kind multiplied, providing the scattered tribes of stone age hunters with inexhaustible stores of meat. In lands of such plenty they had no need to live as nomads following the seasonal migrations of their prey like Lapplanders or Eskimo; but large animals like mammoths, bison and bears

Bison sculptured on the clay wall of a cave about 10000 BC. Discovered close to the banks of the river Tarn near Montauban in 1952

B

could not be overcome with weapons of stone unless the hunters were highly trained and disciplined. Traps had to be set and watched. In some places deer were stampeded towards precipices overhanging a river gorge and, being killed in falling, were recovered from the water below. Rock carvings on the face of cliffs occasionally recall such exploits, and give glimpses of a life that can be imagined with extraordinary vividness. At Dolni Vestonic in Czechoslovakia, for example, figures of animals, modelled in clay and baked in an oven, have been found which date from as early as 23000 BC. Their 'truth to life' is conveyed with an economy of effort and an artistic sense until recently associated only with artists belonging to highly civilised communities. Later paintings, found on the walls of caves, include animal drawings, hunting scenes of great vivacity and even inter-tribal battles. With each new discovery of this kind the mysterious origin of man's intellectual powers becomes more, rather than less, baffling, and the old assumption that the Greeks and Romans were, of all the peoples of the ancient world, supreme in art and architecture can no longer go unquestioned. It was their military prowess that enabled them to impose ideas and erect temples over such vast territories. Their rectilinear buildings, for instance, may excel in beauty, but not in inventiveness or design, the much earlier curvilinear buildings such as the constellation of round towers at Su Nuraxi in the south west of Sardinia.

Between 2000 and 1500 BC the use of bronze, an alloy of tin and copper, began to replace stone in the manufacture of tools, drinking vessels, arms and armour. The search for supplies of tin and copper required men to make long sea voyages, and to use the stars to guide them. The straits of Gibraltar no longer marked the world's end, and along the western coasts of Spain, Portugal, France and the British Isles grave mounds, or barrows, on capes and headlands were left by people almost certainly of Mediterranean origin. Further inland are the remains of temples that were in effect astronomical clocks, huge monoliths erected in gigantic circles, aligned to mark sunrise at the solstices. Such monuments are to be seen at Carnac in Brittany, Stonehenge, which dates from about 1500 BC, and Callanish in the isle of Lewis. No written records of the builders exist, but the length of their voyages is sufficient evidence of their genius.

The remains that archeologists have collected do not cast such a brilliant light on the pre-history of Europe as the royal tombs and ruined palaces throw upon that of Egypt and Iraq. Excavated sites, if plotted on a map of the continent, give it the appearance of a patchwork quilt; if those few sites where rich finds have been made are marked in colour, there are still great areas of blankness and many places where tantalisingly little has been recovered. It is clear, however, that the advance of primitive communities who relied on hunting or herding for their livelihood depended much on their skill in domesticating wild animals. Their first friends were dogs, who were invaluable for the chase, and soon learnt to herd cattle and sheep. Their bones have been unearthed on most of the earliest sites. Man's next friend was the horse, probably first tamed on the borders of Europe and Asia, but not put to its full use until comparatively late in history. The reasons for this are mysterious. Bridles with metal bits, a pre-historic invention, marked the first great advance, but in war driving probably came before riding. The ever quarrelsome tribes of Celts who spread right across northern Europe about 400 BC harnessed their small horses to chariots, presumably with the aid of yokes. The animals' backs were not strong enough to carry armed men any great distance, and fighting on horseback was not easy until the invention, about AD 400, of the saddle and stirrups.

The ancient Greeks loved riding and racing horses for sport, but did not favour them in war, the strength, discipline and skill of their heavily-armed infantry were sufficient

A Greek fighting an Amazon, 4th century BC. A bronze shoulder-piece from a cuirass, embossed and chased; the figure of the Greek is only 11cm high

to give them victory. The heroes of Homer's epics used chariots but fought on foot, as did the soldier-citizens of Sparta and the men of the Athenian republic. Philip of Macedon, and his son Alexander the Great (356-323 BC), developed cavalry and without such a force would not have been able to destroy the empire of the Persians. The Roman legions fought on foot but their commanders recruited large forces of cavalry from among the barbarians whom they conquered. In 53 BC an army of the Roman republic met the mounted archers of the Parthians in Syria without cavalry of its own, and was utterly defeated.

To fight on horseback is not easy without saddle and stirrups and the failure of such gifted people as the Greeks and Romans to invent them is possibly explained by the

15

poor opinion that they had of those who earned their living by the work of their hands and by the conservatism of those who taught riding. Devices that might have made it easier to learn were probably frowned upon. Nor could Roman blacksmiths shoe horses; the shoe nailed on to the hoof was not known till the eleventh century AD. The Romans knew only the hoof-boot and the rigid yoke.

The full power of the draught horse's shoulders was not utilised in western Europe until the introduction, about the tenth century AD, of the stiff horse collar. The soft collar previously employed interfered with the arteries of the horse's neck and with his breathing. The stiff collar, held in position by a breast strap, left the neck unhampered. Harness of this type brought about a peaceful economic change of even greater consequence than the stirrup. Draught oxen, though less expensive to keep, were exceedingly slow and obstinate; the horse, with his high intelligence and quick movements, brought more and more land under the plough every season. Yet the cost of two collars to replace one wooden yoke delayed the use of horse-drawn ploughs and waggons in some parts of Europe until the present day.

It is impossible to trace with certainty the steps by which a knowledge of iron smelting reached western Europe. While meteoric iron that has fallen from outer space is rare, the various ores (oxides) of iron are liberally distributed over the earth's surface, though to obtain good metal from them is not easy, especially when they contain an admixture of phosphorus, as a majority do. The necessity of having an oven of the retort type to reduce ore was probably discovered by accident when a piece of haematite (blood-coloured ore) was left in a potter's kiln. Some of the earliest iron foundries, those in the Anatolian plateau in Asia Minor, were kept secret by the rulers of the Hittite empire who dominated the area about 1100 BC. When they were overthrown, iron smiths travelled in search of new employment and some may have reached Europe through Scythia, as the land lying to the north of the Black Sea was called. In some areas tools of stone or bronze were not exchanged for those of iron until Roman times. The expressions 'stone age', 'bronze age', 'iron age' may therefore be misleading, especially as the craft of the blacksmith made available many different articles of iron, a comparatively soft metal, but only very small quantities of steel. Iron, not steel, was the metal with which the Romans equipped their army. From about 320 BC the legionaries were each armed with a short stabbing sword and two javelins 1.8 metres long with iron points, called *pila*. These were hurled from a range of 20 metres; their points bent on impact; and before the enemy could recover the legions charged upon them with their swords. Countless victories were won by this combination of fire-power and sword-power.

The art of making steel by hammering red-hot iron till all the carbon in it was burnt away, and then adding sufficient carbon to harden it without reducing its tensile strength, was a guarded process of the Franks, who used long two-edged swords. The temper of Roland's sword was legendary and Charlemagne, his master, strictly prohibited the export of swords. The Vikings stole Frankish swords when they could, for their own were not reliable. One Norse saga describes them pausing in battle to straighten their blades.

Europe breaks away from Asia

Because Europe is but a promontory of Asia there were many occasions when its inhabitants were in danger of becoming incorporated in an Asiatic empire, and that part of the continent's history recorded in writing begins with the struggle of the ancient Greeks to repel the armies of Persia. Their poets and writers present this struggle as one fought by a civilised and democratic people, small in numbers but superior in breeding and intelligence to the 'barbarian' hordes. In fact, both the Asians and the Europeans

Attic red-figured bowl, 490-480 BC, showing Triptolemos, a corn god, seated in a winged chariot drawn by serpents, entertained by Demeter, the earth goddess, and her daughter Persephone. The Triptolemos myth signified the introduction of corn-growing and its communication from country to country

were of mixed race and both were of 'white' or Aryan descent. The struggle began along the coasts of Asia Minor where Greek colonies, ruled by monarchs no less autocratic than the kings of Persia, built up trade connections spreading westwards to Sicily and beyond.

The prosperity of the Greeks who came down from the north to the coasts of the Aegean about 800 BC sprang up with the invention of money. Trade by barter is cumbersome; with money, calculations become simple, and credit easily arranged. Traditionally the kingdom of Lydia under Gyges (678-652 BC) was the first to have a widely accepted coinage. Soon the towns of Miletus and Ephesus on the coast of Asia Minor and the offshore islands of Chios and Samos were issuing coins of electrum, an alloy of gold and silver, and a century later Croesus, the king of Lydia whose name is still a byword for wealth, had a bimetallic currency of pure gold and silver. On the other side of the Aegean the earliest known gold coins come from the island of Aegina. As iron had previously been much used as barter, the names of two Greek coins of low value, the obol and the drachma, originally meant an iron ingot and a handful of ingots.

The archipelago that bridges the Aegean from east to west formed an ideal nursery for seamen and shipbuilders. The sea, constantly changing in mood, now calm, now mounting high under the strong north wind, was mastered by captains whose ships were propelled by both oars and sails. During the long summers of clear weather mariners were seldom out of sight of land for more than a few hours, while in the pellucid water, free from sand and seaweed, look-outs could detect the presence of sunken rocks and reefs. Ships, the only bulk carriers available to man before the invention of railways, could transport large cargoes of grain, wine, olives, cattle or textiles, and, as they passed from cape to cape and island to island, not only found innumerable havens when storms threatened but carried man's most precious possession, ideas, from one port to the next. Yet, out of all the inventive races that in turn dominated the Mediterranean, none ever designed a sailing vessel to match in speed and seaworthiness those that after AD 1500 brought the peoples of the Atlantic seaboard world supremacy. Perhaps human life was never put at a value high enough for any to feel the need to save the labour of galley slaves.

Most of the ancient Greek sea ports on the eastern side of the Aegean now lie in ruins, the great marble cylinders that formed the columns of their temples tossed in every direction by the seismic undulations of many an earthquake. Their once busy harbours, buried under silt and fringed with pines and olives, hold nothing but stagnant pools filled with noisy frogs. In some places the towns were built on steep slopes that could be defended against raiders from the sea or invaders from the interior. If a precipitous rock offered a site, a citadel or acropolis was constructed where a garrison could defend the treasure deposited there by citizens who had taken temporary flight. The political life of such places, sometimes praised as nurseries of democracy, was often turbulent and on occasions murderous. In intellectual matters, on the other hand, there was in the sixth and fifth centuries BC a remarkable ferment of ideas. Learned men, to all of whom the Greeks gave the name philosopher, ceased to accept the explanations of natural phenomena offered by the priests of polytheistic religions, and began the search for a single and universal principle, an order in the physical universe knowledge of which might put an end to the chaotic superstitions of the majority.

Thales of Miletus, a place regarded as a sister state by the Athenians, put forward the theory that life had begun in the sea, fish being created before land animals, and all things being derived from water. He was also able to predict, with knowledge of astronomy probably acquired from Babylon, the eclipse of the sun that occurred on 28 May 585 BC. A fellow citizen of Thales, Anaximander, to whom tradition attributed many original scientific ideas, held that the earth floated in space without visible support. This interest in astronomy continued and in Athens, two hundred years later, Anaxagoras of Clazomenae in Ionia, a friend of Pericles and Euripides, discovered that the moon shone by reflected light. Heracleides of Pontus in Asia Minor proved about the same time that the planets Venus and Mercury revolve round the sun and the earth rotates on its axis every twenty-four hours. Aristarchus of Samos (310-230 BC) taught that not only the planets but the earth also revolves round the sun, and so anticipated the discoveries made by the Renaissance astronomer Copernicus in the sixteenth century AD.

These and other intellectual achievements, brightly as they shine against the black ignorance of subsequent centuries, were nonetheless incapable of supplying the spiritual understanding needed to sustain men in time of trouble. Polytheism played so powerfully upon human hopes and fears that the incidence of war, famine and disease were still confidently attributed to 'the anger of the gods', not to lack of political prudence. When the Persians under Darius the Great, the conqueror of Babylon, overran the kingdom of Croesus in 546 BC, the philosopher Bias of Priene, a Greek city state not far from Miletus, proposed that all the Ionians should migrate to Sardinia. More sensibly Thales suggested they should form a political league with a common headquarters. Neither of them found any support.

Such insights into the mentality of the Greeks posterity owes to an historian of genius, Herodotus of Halicarnassus, a town near the modern port of Bodrum in south-west Turkey, famous for the tomb of Mausolus, one of the seven wonders of the ancient world. To him history was an inquiry or inquest into the past, and being one of the most widely travelled men, having visited Babylon and Egypt to collect material, he went to Athens to present his findings in the form of lectures which have survived in writing.

Athenians were immensely proud of the part their ancestors, some of them well-remembered personalities, had played in repulsing the Persians and as the climax to his work Herodotus described how the Ionian city states had revolted against Persian rule in 499 BC, how the Athenians had gone to their aid, marched inland and burned the town of Sardis and then returned home. In reprisal Darius, King of Persia, destroyed Miletus; transplanted some of its citizens to the mouth of the Tigris, a thousand miles away; and began preparations for a punitive expedition against the Athenians. In 490 BC a large Persian force landed north of Athens; there was nothing to oppose their southward march but a small force, mainly of Athenians, stationed in the hills at Marathon overlooking a narrow plain and the bay where the Persians had landed. The Athenian commander, Miltiades, did not wait to be attacked but led his infantry down to the plain and, in a dawn charge upon the enemy camp, forced them back to their ships in panic. According to Herodotus, the enemy losses were 6,400 against 192 on the Greek side. The Athenians were astonished at their deliverance.

For ten years the Persians made no further attempt at invasion, and in the interval Darius died. In 480 BC his son and successor, Xerxes, having assembled from many parts of his empire a large and unwieldy army, led it across the Dardanelles on a double bridge of boats and advanced round the north coast of the Aegean. He was accompanied by a fleet of transports and warships, mainly recruited from the Greek cities of Ionia. This time the European Greeks were better prepared. The Athenians and the Spartans, whose troops were the best in the peninsula, were well led and acted as allies. Xerxes, approaching Athens by the east coast of the Aegean, found that the pass of Thermopylae, a narrow passage between the mountains and the sea, was held by about 7,000 under the command of Leonidas, a famous Spartan general. While they waited, the Persian scouts reported, some were doing athletic exercises and others combing their hair. 'Xerxes did not guess the truth, that these men were getting ready to be killed, and, so far as they could, to kill.' So comments Herodotus, who in that one sentence depicts the horror not of one battle, but of every war in which young men in their prime, superbly trained and proud of their cause, have gone down to dusty death.

The first Persian assaults failed, but part of their force found a way through the hills and so outflanked the Greek position. Leonidas sent back all but 300 Spartans and died fighting. In the long struggle over his corpse most of his comrades perished. The Asian host swept on towards Athens. There the Athenian leader, Themistocles, had persuaded the inhabitants to take refuge in the Peloponnese and on the island of Salamis. In the narrow waters that separated the island from the mainland he mustered the galleys of the Athenians and their allies, intending to fight where the enemy could not bring their superior numbers to bear. The Persians set fire to Athens, and their ships approached Salamis expecting the Greeks to avoid battle. A long conflict ensued and after heavy losses Xerxes withdrew most of his ships and his troops to Asia Minor, where a year later they were again defeated. An army he left to winter in northern Greece was also beaten and, though the war dragged on in Asia, European Greece was able to enjoy for the next fifty years a fair measure of peace and prosperity.

Sparta and Athens

The architects, sculptors and writers of Greece created in the exultation of victory a multitude of beautiful things. To walk today on lonely hillsides among the half-visible remains of once proud cities is to realise how little has survived of the total Greek achievement; yet the fragments of temples, theatres and law courts, the rare manuscripts with their passionate lyrics, profound and intricate tragedies, outrageous comedies and penetrating histories, re-read with new eyes since the fifteenth century, have inspired both artists and politicians of every complexion, not only in Europe but throughout the world.

Yet the Greek legacy has not been wholly beneficial. Over the bodies of the dead at Marathon the Greeks raised a great mound and a stone whose inscription read:

> Go tell the Spartans, thou that passeth by,
> That here, obedient to their laws, we lie.

The laws of Sparta required death rather than surrender and were unique for their militaristic rigour. In the seventh century BC life in Sparta had been much more free. The Lydian poet Alcman, for example, taken there as a slave and given his liberty by a discerning master, became famous throughout Greece for the sensuous power of his verse, but in the next century those who considered themselves the descendants of the original invaders began to live a life apart, treating with contempt the rest of the inhabitants of that secluded valley in the Peloponnese, ringed in by mountains, which was their homeland. Agriculture, industry and trade were left to non-citizens and helots. If a male child born to one of the Spartan élite showed any physical defect, he was left to die by the wayside. This type of infanticide was common in other states, but in Sparta its object was to ensure that every boy who lived to the age of seven could then be trained to bear the hardships of a military life, living in a barrack apart from his family and serving in the army until his thirtieth year, when marriage was permitted. Spartan girls were brought up as athletes in the hope that they would bear strong sons to fight for Sparta. Visitors from other states were usually excluded, so that paiderasty, the chief vice of the system, was overlooked and the country's constitution won admiration even from the Athenian philosopher Plato. Its failure to produce any major work of art was ignored.

By contrast, the sea-empire built up by the Athenians in the fifth century BC made possible artistic achievements for which they are still universally acclaimed. Fortunate in acquiring silver and gold mines, they made their currency acceptable all over the Aegean. The richest mineowners employed as many as a thousand slaves. Athenian warships dominated the whole region. A memorial to the members of a single family, or 'tribe', killed on active service in the year 459 BC recalls that they had fallen 'in Cyprus, in Egypt, in Phoenicia, at Haleis, in Aegina, at Megara'. During a long war with Sparta (431-404 BC) all the men and boys on the small island of Melos, which had sided with the enemy, were massacred and all the women and girls sold into slavery. This incident took place in 416 BC and was recorded with righteous anger in a contemporary history of the war written by Thucydides, an Athenian aristocrat who lived in exile rather than risk imprisonment or death for his political opinions. The next year the dramatist Euripides boldly produced in the theatre of Dionysus his play *Trojan Women*, nominally about those enslaved after the fall of Troy, but vibrating with the pity and terror of the Melos tragedy.

Religion and Philosophy

High on the Acropolis of Athens, dominating the plain below and visible far out to sea, was a bronze statue of the maiden goddess Athene, armed with helmet, shield and spear. Another statue of her, executed in gold and ivory by the sculptor Pheidias, stood in the dimly-lit interior of the Parthenon. There too was kept the ornate throne from which Xerxes had chosen to gaze down on the battle of Salamis, so certain had he been of victory. There were other temples and shrines, frequented, like those of Athene, for private devotions, but not designed for corporate worship. Public respect for the gods was shown in an annual round of processions and sacrificial ceremonies which took place in the streets and places of assembly, including the theatre. Due attention to these rituals was regarded as essential to the political and economic welfare of the state.

The ethical content of the old cults was so slight that the more intelligent attended the 'schools' of the philosophers and sophists, or teachers, in search of some objective moral doctrine. The Greek word from which 'school' is derived had the double meaning of leisure and discussion, and nothing more pleasant for young men can be imagined than the pursuit of knowledge in cool riverside glades or under the colonnades of some magnificent temple. Such delights could not, however, be enjoyed without risk. In 399 BC the conservative forces of the old religion struck against one beloved teacher named Socrates, condemning him to death for impiety in not worshipping the gods of the city, for introducing strange gods, and for corrupting the youth. The conviction was carried by not more than six votes in a court of five hundred, and one wealthy young pupil, an aristocrat nicknamed Plato because of his broad shoulders, watched while the man whom he described as 'the wisest and most just and best who ever lived' took the cup of deadly hemlock from the executioner. Deeply shocked, Plato, who was thirty years of age, went into voluntary exile in Sicily and Italy, and then returned to teach philosophy in Athens from about 385 BC until his death at the age of eighty-two.

Socrates told his judges that he was 'a sort of gadfly given by God to the state, all day long and in all places fastening upon you arousing and persuading and reproaching you'. He left nothing in writing, but Plato's works, composed in dialogue form, developed and greatly extended his teaching. The conversations that Plato attributes to Socrates are highly polished reconstructions; they demonstrate that men commit many evil deeds through ignorance and argue that knowledge is the prerequisite of a virtuous life; if men perceived what was good they would do it. The fact is that some men, born with every advantage socially and intellectually deliberately choose to do evil rather than good, and others, though desperately poor and uneducated, succeed by an effort of will in living the lives of saints. Nevertheless that part of Plato's work in which he analyses four cardinal virtues, prudence, moderation, justice and fortitude, became an invaluable model for all subsequent moralists.

The most serious criticisms of Plato's philosophy came from a man forty-four years his junior, a Macedonian named Aristotle, who at the age of seventeen came to study under him in Athens and remained there teaching philosophy until Plato died. Master and pupil admired and loved one another, but Aristotle's spirit was of a quite different kind. He based his ideas on observation and in many different fields accumulated and recorded a vast number of facts, particularly about birds, beasts and fishes. It is characteristic that in describing the great variety of constitutions existing among the Greeks, he should state 'Man is by nature a political animal'. In ethics he insisted on the importance of heredity, training and habit. He saw every virtue as a golden mean between two opposing evils; courage, for example, stood between foolhardiness and cowardice, and temperance between sensuality and coldness; and a man's true happiness lay in the exercise of the highest virtue within his power.

Athenian Democracy

The Athenians called the system of government which formed the background to their intellectual and artistic life, and was inseparable from it, democratic, because it demanded the active participation of all free men. Its rule applied to a population of about 300,000, of whom 100,000 were slaves. Without the slaves the free men would not have had the time or the means to undertake the many official duties demanded of them. All were expected to attend the Ecclesia, or Assembly, which was called together about forty times a year and voted on all major questions of policy. To carry on the business of the state between sessions of the Assembly a Council of Five Hundred was chosen by lot. Its members, who had to be at leasty thirty years old, served for a year, but even this body was too large, and in practice the ten men elected to command the army and navy played as large a part in non-military as in military affairs. These generals were also elected to serve a year, but could be re-elected any number of times, and it was in the office of general that outstanding leaders such as Pericles wielded continuous power.

The hill-side amphitheatre where the Assembly met had seats for about 18,000, and sometimes, when the subject under discussion was dull, the police took a cord dipped in paint through the streets and roped the citizens in. None liked to be marked as reluctant, and Pericles, who was in power from 443 until his death in 429 BC, proudly declared:

> When it is a question of putting one person before another in positions of public responsibility, what counts is not membership of a particular class, but the actual ability which the man possesses . . . . We do not say that a man who takes no interest in politics is a man who minds his own business; we say that he has no business here at all.

It cannot be said that this democracy was notably more successful than other forms of government either in maintaining law and order at home or in promoting peace with neighbouring states. The noisiest speaker rather than the best leader was not infrequently chosen and given tasks which he was ill-equipped to perform. Torrents of oratory too often drowned the voice of reason, and even in these early times democracy won a bad name for fickleness and delay.

The Empire of Alexander the Great

The endless strife between the Greek city states did not cease until each in turn had yielded to the Macedonians, whom they regarded as barbarians. In 338 BC the King of Macedonia, Philip, and his eighteen-year-old son Alexander defeated the combined armies of the Athenians and the Thebans, a battle won largely by Alexander's impetuosity and courage. The prince was endowed not only with immense physical strength but also great intellectual power. From Aristotle, one of his tutors, he probably acquired the breadth of vision and mastery of detail that enabled him to overcome not only his enemies in Greece but the armies of the Persian empire, which included many thousands of Greek mercenaries.

In 336 BC, at the beginning of his reign, Alexander undertook a series of campaigns against his neighbours in Europe, destroying Thebes and forcing the Greeks to appoint him as their leader against Persia, the ancient enemy. When he died at the age of thirty-two, he had not only conquered the Persian empire, which stretched from Asia Minor to the borders of India and included Palestine and Egypt, but had also founded a chain of cities modelled on those of Greece. Everywhere he encouraged the spread of Greek culture.

The rich fountain of ideas that sprang from his restless brain had an indirect but profound effect on European history. Many of the non-Greek races of western Asia acquired a working knowledge of Greek and for some it became the language of literature and science. The Egyptian port of Alexandria grew to be the capital of a powerful kingdom under the Ptolemies, descendants of one of Alexander's generals, and there a vast library of over half a million volumes was built up. Here the carefully preserved books of

Jewish history and prophecy which became the nucleus of the Christian Bible were translated into Greek and found a far wider readership than they would ever have acquired in Hebrew. Eratosthenes, one of the astronomers working in Alexandria in the third century BC, made the calculations on which was based the calendar called Julian after Julius Casear, who inaugurated it in 45 BC. It remained in general use until the sixteenth century and in Russia until 1917.

The Rise of the Roman Empire

The Romans, whose power originated in the fifth century BC from their skill as farmers and hardihood as citizen-soldiers, were by 300 BC the foremost military power in Italy, already a country inhabited by people of many different races. The Romans gave the name *socii* (allies) to those who acknowledged their supremacy and to a few among them extended the privileges of citizenship.

Up to this point the Romans had felt no need for mastery at sea but now, in Sicilian waters, they met the warships of the Carthaginians, based on the fortress and harbour of Carthage in north Africa, but operating also from friendly ports in Sicily and Spain. They were manned by mercenaries, and the Romans, in order to use their superior land-trained forces, developed a technique of ramming the enemy ships and dropping on to their decks a kind of drawbridge for the boarding parties to swarm across. After a long war (265-242 BC) they expelled the Carthaginians from Sicily.

The metal mines of the Iberian peninsula were another source of the Carthaginians' wealth and in 218 BC their forces in Spain came under the command of Hannibal. With great daring he led an army into the Rhone valley and over the Alps. Having defeated the Romans first in the north and then in the south of Italy, he won for a time support from the southern Italians and Sicilians. The ruler of Syracuse, fighting on Hannibal's side, defended himself against the Romans for three years before surrending. The Greek scientist Archimedes, who lived there, aided the defence with powerful catapults and other devices of his invention. He was killed by a Roman soldier in the confusion at the end of the siege. Later in the same war Scipio, a young Roman aristocrat commanding in Spain, drove the Carthaginians out of the country and by 201 BC they made peace, giving up all their overseas possessions to the Romans. In a third war the Romans attacked Carthage itself, an almost impregnable fortress near the present site of Tunis, and in 149 BC razed it to the ground.

Eastwards the Romans watched Greece and Macedonia with mingled envy and contempt. They had produced nothing in science, literature, art or architecture to compare with the Greek achievement. In 146 BC they intervened, not for the first time, in one of the wars which continually racked the peninsula, captured Corinth, massacred all its male inhabitants and sold all its women and children into slavery. From that time both Greece and Macedonia came under Roman control. By 133 BC Asia Minor, and by 62 BC Palestine and Egypt, had also been subjugated (a Latin word meaning 'brought under the yoke', which referred to the Roman custom of humiliating their defeated enemies by marching them under an ox yoke suspended as a symbol of conquest).

In the last years of the Republic Julius Caesar, perhaps the greatest of Roman statesmen, subdued the Gallic tribes in what is now France and Belgium and attempted the conquest of their kinsmen in Britain, who twice repulsed him. Southern France had been a Roman province for many years before Caesar's campaigns, but after them Italy itself was not more Roman.

Roman aqueduct built across the river Gard in 19 BC to supply Nîmes with water. It is 48.6m high and the largest of its three tiers has 35 arches and is 440m long. Clean city living required ample supplies of pure water, but the art of making a pipeline in metal capable of withstanding pressure at its joints had not been discovered; colossal structures of this kind were therefore necessary in order to lead water gently downhill in open conduits

In 49 BC, to overawe the Senate, Caesar, having led his army back to Italy and across the Rubicon, insisted that he should be granted supreme powers. Then, after victories over his rival Pompey and his allies in the east, he returned to Rome, clearly intending to keep the right to appoint both civil and military officials in his own hands. Under the Republic there had been a system of checks and balances intended to prevent such a military dictatorship.

The assassination of Caesar in 44 BC was followed by a long and bloodthirsty struggle for power between his former friends and enemies. In 29 BC Caesar's heir, an adopted nephew, emerged victorious, and became head of state with the title Caesar Augustus. Until his death in AD 14 at the age of seventy-six he and a small group of rich and powerful friends worked ceaselessly to establish peace throughout the dominions of Rome. To avoid hurting republican sentiment he did not call himself *Imperator* (Emperor), but the result was an empire admired throughout the world for its size, strength and permanence. From Asia to Gaul, architects, assisted by the writings that Vitruvius dedicated to Augustus, began to construct temples, bridges, aqueducts and theatres whose massive style after nearly 2,000 years still gives their ruins the air of buildings nearing completion. The poets Virgil and Horace, whose patron was Maecenas, one of the chief men at the court of Augustus, wrote with enthusiasm of the peace that had fallen upon the Roman world after so many wars. Both fitted their verses together with the precision of Roman masons building an arch and then polished them to a gem-like perfection, happily convinced that their work would be as Horace said, 'more durable than bronze'.

The Pantheon, Rome, built by Agrippa in 27 BC as a temple of Mars, Venus and the deified ancestors of the family of Julius Caesar. The dome is 43.2m in diameter and in height, a triumphant demonstration of the strength of Roman concrete. It was dedicated as a church in AD 608

CHAPTER TWO

The Early Centuries 0-AD 1000

The Founding of the Christian Church

When Christians of the eighth century first began to date documents from the time of Christ's birth and not, as previously, from the supposed year of the foundation of Rome, 753 BC, they chose well. No records of the ancient world are better authenticated than those concerning Christ and the early Church. The four brief accounts of Christ's life known as gospels date from the first century after his birth. Those of Matthew, Mark and John, though notably different in character, are written from a Jewish point of view; that of Luke, who also compiled the Acts of the Apostles, shows the critical outlook of a Greek. He tells part of his story in the first person, having been in all probability an eyewitness. Writing of Christ after the crucifixion, he says: 'He showed himself to these men (his disciples) after his death and gave ample proof that he was alive; over a period of forty days he appeared to them and taught them.' Ever since that time the core of the Christian faith has been 'Christ lives', and the immediate and rapid growth of the Church is proof of its reality. Yet few historians accept the New Testament as reliable and many have attempted to explain the evidence away. By far the simplest and most likely explanation is that what the writers said happened did happen. Their words have the ring of truth.

For the earliest converts no gospels were necessary. They already knew by oral tradition that Christ had illuminated and expanded the ancient doctrine of the Jews, requiring them to treat 'the stranger within their gates' with the same humanity as their own kinsmen. The disciples who had known Christ in the flesh remembered that he had not ministered only to devout Jews, but mixed freely with both rich and poor, showing compassion to Roman officers and tax gatherers equally with outcasts, lepers and madmen. This had puzzled them at the time, but afterwards they gladly imitated him, subordinating their religious rules to the new simplicity of his law—to love God and their neighbours. This way of life, strange yet homely, happy yet demanding, at once attracted thousands upon thousands, most of whom were not, as the disciples were, Jews by upbringing. The hostility of orthodox Jewry to the new faith caused Christians to migrate to Asia Minor, Macedonia, the Aegean islands, Greece and Italy.

Among the earliest converts was Paul of Tarsus, whose life work it became to establish Christianity firmly in Europe. He had inherited the rights of Roman citizenship

27

from his father; Greek was his mother tongue, but he was brought up an orthodox Jew. As a young student in Jerusalem he witnessed the first Christian martyrdom, that of Stephen. Immediately after this he was sent to persecute the Christians in Damascus. On the road he had a vision of Christ, which remained with him all his days. Naturally the Jews regarded him as an apostate and on five occasions administered their customary

Antonia, daughter of Mark Antony and mother of the Emperor Claudius, who incorporated Britain in the empire. A marble bust made in her life-time

punishment of thirty-nine lashes, yet he probably never gave up hope that they would be converted. Among non-Jews he was very differently received, winning from people unaccustomed to monotheism and the strict moral discipline of the synagogues lasting love and devotion. Many modern critics argue that by the very force of his intellect and personality he caused the faith to lose its early simplicity. There is no substance in this; everywhere he insisted that he spoke not for himself but for Christ, and that the mark of the faithful was that they should have that mind which was in Christ.

Towards the end of his life Paul exercised his right of appeal to the imperial courts. Saved by a Roman cohort from a Jewish mob and brought before the governor of Judaea, he pronounced the fateful words *Provoco ad Caesarem* (I ask to be called before Caesar) and was sent as a prisoner to Rome. His ship was driven by a storm on to a lee shore in Malta and the guards asked for the usual permission to kill their prisoners to prevent their escape through the waves to land. Permission was refused, and Paul at last reached Rome. There, about AD 64, while he was still waiting trial, he was martyred.

The first pagan historian to describe the Christians was Tacitus (AD 55-120), a Roman aristocrat whose works are famous for their epigrammatic style and passionate denunciations of Roman cruelty. He states that in AD 64 a great fire occurred in Rome, half the city being burned down, and popular rumour began to attribute the disaster to Nero, the much-hated Emperor, who, to divert attention from himself, arrested a large number of Christians. They were convicted on charges not of arson, which could not have been proved, but of 'hating the human race', a charge apparently arising from their declared belief that the end of the world and the return of Christ were at hand. The victims were either crucified or burnt alive to entertain Nero's guests. Such punishments would not have been inflicted on those holding Roman citizenship; probably the majority were artisans or slaves. Fortunately for the other churches, this persecution did not spread beyond the capital.

The fact that so many converts were slaves did not mean that they were without education or influence. Among the large number of male and female slaves in every wealthy Roman household there were usually one or two whose standard of education excelled that of their masters and they were in consequence frequently trusted with important family and business affairs, but in general the social and economic evils inherent in slavery produced a race of servants who were lazy, dishonest and lascivious, as the surviving texts of Roman comedies show. When such people were converted into honest, hard-working retainers, it must have been startling and, as more information about them accumulated, the authorities became anxious. Pliny, a learned and very wealthy man, who had been made governor of a province in Asia Minor, wrote about them to the Emperor Trajan (reigned AD 98-117) with whom he was on friendly terms, saying that he had executed several Christians brought before him on charges made anonymously, and had sent others, who held Roman citizenship, to Rome for trial. He had also put two female Christian slaves to the rack in order to get evidence. In an empire where any form of association, even a local fire brigade, came under suspicion as a possible form of political conspiracy, Pliny noted that on certain days the Christians met before going to work and sang hymns to Christ as to a god, and after work shared an evening meal. They also bound themselves to commit no crime of any sort and to keep all promises. The only fault he could find in them was 'excessive and perverse superstition'. The Emperor replied in a 'rescript' that Christians were not to be sought out, and not to be arrested on charges made anonymously, but, if publicly accused and convicted, should be punished (in what way he did not state).

For a long time after Trajan's death the terms of this rescript were observed; Christians

C

were liable to police action, but enjoyed in practice a fair degree of immunity. The constantly growing congregations were centred in towns; the very word pagan originally meant villager or country-dweller. By the end of the first century the church in Rome was already regarded with special reverence and affection by Christians everywhere, for it sent out advice and help, including money collected in the capital, to the poorer brethren of the hard-pressed churches of Asia and Africa.

The policy of the Romans towards subject races whose religion was different from their own is sometimes described as one of tolerance. This is a misuse of language; their overriding concern was with the maintenance of law and order. Rivalries between cults,

Roman amphitheatre seating about 23,000 people at the Adriatic port of Pula, 60km south of Trieste

they found, were a perpetual source of disorder and riots, and any faith claiming, like Christianity, to be universal was bound to impinge on the worship of local gods. On the other hand the Romans were exceedingly superstitious themselves and much concerned with foretelling the future. Oracles and soothsayers were in constant demand; astrology, the most sophisticated and bogus of all methods of prediction, flourished, and any pagan priest or fortune-teller, faced with an unforeseen disaster, was likely to point to the Christians as scapegoats. Christian writers were well aware of this; in denouncing the

Carvings on the column in Rome commemorating the victories of the Emperor Marcus Aurelius Antoninus (AD 161-180) over the German tribes. The two men without helmets, standing in the middle of the legionaries, are standard-bearers

emptiness of superstition, they did not minimise its enormous and ever-present grip on men's minds. Tertullian (AD 155-225), a Christian living in Africa, wrote: 'If the Tiber has left its bed, if the Nile has not poured its waters over the fields, if there is an earthquake, if famine or pestilence threatens, the cry immediately arises, "The Christians to the lions!"' In the same period Celsus, a pagan writer in Alexandria, complained that the aim of the Christians was to convince 'only idiots, slaves, poor women and children— we see (among them) wool-carders, cobblers, washermen'. On the other hand the great physician Galen, who attended the Emperor Marcus Aurelius (reigned AD 161-180), admitted that Christians despised death, led chaste lives and were as zealous in their pursuit of virtue as true philosophers.

The last and worst assault on the Christians occurred between AD 303 and 305. Imperial decrees were issued by Diocletian ordering the demolition of churches, the

Porta Nigra, Trier, built in the reign of the Emperor Constantine (AD 323-337) whose father had chosen this town on the Moselle as his administrative capital for Britain, Spain and all the lands between the Rhine and the Atlantic

confiscation of the rolls of papyrus on which the gospels and other sacred writings had been copied, and the torture of priests who refused to sacrifice to pagan gods. Diocletian was a soldier and administrator of exceptional ability, whose will met with far more general obedience than usual. In the previous seventy years the empire had suffered greatly. The burden of taxation had grown intolerable; the lines of forts, walls and ramparts, built to prevent invaders from the north and east crossing the Tyne, the Rhine and the Danube, could not be maintained at a reasonable cost, and garrison duties lowered the efficiency and morale of the legions. Yet in spite of civil war, foreign invasion and the disruption of trade, Christian congregations had everywhere grown in size and numbers. Bishops had on occasion succeeded in obtaining peace where soldiers had failed. It was their power and influence of which Diocletian and his military friends were jealous, for all autocrats fear those whose ideas and methods differ radically from their own. After two years the persecution in the western provinces, where there were far fewer Christians than in Asia Minor and Egypt, ceased, Diocletian abdicated and, worn out by his labours, retired to a magnificent villa near his birthplace in Illyria, where his parents had lived in poverty, probably as slaves. He had made Nicomedia in Asia Minor his capital, not Rome.

A civil war followed the Emperor's retirement, and one of the generals who emerged

Ivory diptych, probably Roman, AD 450-460, showing six miracles of Christ: feeding the five thousand, healing the blind man, the man sick of the palsy, the raising of Lazarus, the wine at Cana, and healing the leper

victorious was Constantine, who was first named Emperor by the legions in York. He attributed his success to the Christian god and, having seen the sign of the cross in the sky on the eve of one of his victories, he issued an edict granting the Christians toleration. The sign, from which much good and much evil ensued, was probably a manifestation of the *aurora borealis*. After AD 323, Constantine, having become supreme over the whole empire, showed great favour to the churches but little understanding of Christianity, postponing his own baptism until he was on his deathbed. Only a minority of his soldiers were Christians; the faith was nowhere that of the majority of his subjects; he had no wish to offend pagan feeling unnecessarily. On the other hand his many gifts to the churches were made with a purpose. He hoped that the bishops would make a much larger contribution to the political unity of his empire than any pagan priesthood could. In addition they were stronger and more numerous in Asia and Africa than in western Europe. Having decided, like Diocletian, that Rome was too far to the west of the geographical centre of his dominions, he chose to make Byzantium *Nova Roma*. The name did not last; the aura of the Italian city could not be transported; Byzantium became known as Constantinople.

The organisation of what later became the Orthodox Church began with the emperor's urgent encouragement. The bishops were called together at Nicaea, not far from the new capital, and formulated in his presence a definition of the nature of Christ. This was a task of great difficulty. For more than a century Christian leaders had attempted to adapt the language of Greek philosophy to the elucidation of mystical ideas that were Hebrew in origin. No two tongues could be more different, and in the loquacious, argumentative atmosphere of the Hellenic cities over which the emperor ruled differences had inevitably arisen in Christian doctrine, especially as persecution had made formal gatherings of bishops from different areas impossible. At the Council of Nicaea the followers of Arius were at odds with those of Athanasius. The formula of Athanasius was eventually accepted as orthodox, but that of Arius had been widely used by missionaries working among the barbarians on the northern boundaries. When their converts eventually invaded the empire they founded Arian churches and only after many struggles were these brought back to accept the creed agreed at Nicaea.

The Founding of the Barbarian Kingdoms

To speak of the decline and fall of the Roman Empire, as the eighteenth century historian Gibbon did when he chose the title of his life's work, assumes that at some period the empire rested upon a plateau of power from which it subsequently descended. The metaphor is misleading; autocracies are never at rest, never dependable; too often they provide only tyranny mitigated by assassination. From beginning to end the Roman system depended on the personality of the emperor; a man of the highest quality might bequeath the throne to a monster, as in AD 180, when Marcus Aurelius was succeeded by his son Commodus, and he, murdered after twelve years of misrule, was followed by a succession of four emperors in less than two years. An aggressive regime might add a province here or a defensive wall there, only to give way a generation later to a weak government incapable of holding what had so recently been gained. Soldiers and ad-

34

ministrators alike looked back with envy upon a mythical past which Roman historians and poets had combined to glorify, deceiving both their contemporaries and posterity about the true state of affairs. In the past, they implied, men always did their duty even at the cost of their lives; therefore the same methods and the same weapons as those used by Julius Caesar were the only means capable of accomplishing the task described by Virgil in the lines

> *Tu regere imperio populos, Romane, memento . . .*
> *Parcere subiectis et debellare superbos.*

Remember, citizen of Rome, to rule the nations with imperial might . . . spare those who submit to your yoke and bring down the proud by war.

The empire employed a professional army of about 400,000 men recruited from many different races and, as the pressure from the Goths and other barbarians outside the borders increased, more and more tribes were accepted as auxiliaries. By AD 400 the Goths beyond the Danube had found in Alaric a powerful leader intent on winning by force of arms appointment as commander-in-chief under the emperor in Constantinople. In AD 409 he invaded Italy and threatened to sack Rome. To buy him off the citizens handed over 5,000lb of gold, 30,000lb of silver, 4,000 robes of silk, 3,000 pieces of fine scarlet cloth and 3,000lb of pepper corns. The pepper, imported from India, was a favourite spice and proved the most difficult part of this useless ransom. A year later Alaric returned and his troops sacked Rome. The act horrified every country over which the Romans had once ruled; it seemed as if the end of the world had come. A year later Alaric died suddenly in southern Italy. His funeral is said to have been celebrated with barbaric cruelty and splendour. The Goths, having forced slaves to divert a river, buried his corpse in its bed, together with the spoils of victory. Afterwards they restored the stream to its course, and in order that no enemy might be able to find the tomb, massacred the slaves.

Just before his death Alaric attempted to invade Rome's richest province, north Africa, but after losing many ships in a storm, his men lost heart. In AD 455 a bolder and more adaptable race, the Vandals, surrounded Rome. Pope Leo I persuaded them not to burn and kill, but for three days they pillaged the churches and palaces. For a century the people of Rome had given the affectionate name *Papa*, father, to their bishops, and Leo was named the Great for his services in mitigating the distress of the times. From the word *Papa* the title *Pope* is derived.

From Italy the Vandals crossed the sea to Carthage and there set up a powerful, but comparatively short-lived, state, relying upon piracy mixed with commerce to maintain their position as a ruling race. Like the Goths, they were Germanic in origin and at no time formed more than a minority in a population that remained Christian. In AD 527 the imperial throne in Constantinople was taken by Justinian, a man of megalomaniac ambition. Prompted by a ruthless wife, Theodora, he ordered his bodyguards to rid the city of his political enemies; 30,000 of them were surrounded as they watched the chariot races and killed.

The Cathedral of Santa Sophia, Istanbul, built by the Emperor Justinian (AD 527-564), on a hill overlooking the Bosphorus. The dome is 34.5m in diameter and 53.4m high. The four minarets were added after the Turkish capture of the city in 1453, when the church was converted into a mosque

His next objective was the restoration of the empire in the west. There was no doubt in Justinian's mind that it was his Christian duty to win back north Africa. He sent out an army in which the most ferocious troops were barbarian cavalrymen clothed in mail and armed with lances and bows. They were commanded by an outstanding general, Belisarius, and his success was immediate; for a time the authority of the emperor was recognised again both in Carthage and Italy.

The confusion and misery caused by the military adventures of barbarian leaders moving across the continent with their women and children and all their possessions, continued until late in the eleventh century. By AD 500 most of Europe had been divided between three Germanic peoples, the Franks, who had recently extended their power till it included northern France and western Germany; the Visigoths who held southern France and Spain; and the Ostrogoths in Italy and the mountains between the Danube and the Adriatic. In the subsequent history of Europe the most important of these kingdoms was that of the Franks. At Christmas AD 496 their ruler Clovis and 3,000 Franks were baptised at Rheims. As a pagan Clovis had previously made an advantageous marriage to a Catholic princess; without giving up his former methods of force and fraud he found that as a Christian he could rely on Catholic bishops to support his government. He also chose Paris, a former Roman settlement, as his capital, giving future kings of France a town with formidable defences, since its heart was an island in the Seine, yet easily accessible by water and road. Communications at this time were so slow and uncertain that they severely limited the authority of kings. The pursuit of criminals was far from easy and news of incipient rebellion came through so late that only a military campaign could quell it and those who had openly rebelled were, if defeated in battle, treated with open brutality in order to deter others. By ancient custom the barbarians preferred to set wrong right by the blood feud, the relatives of a wronged man holding themselves responsible for exacting an eye for an eye, a tooth for a tooth, a life for a life. To prevent feuding, kings, with the approval of the Church, put a price on murder, instituting fines regulated according to the dead man's rank in society, a system that, when imposed by a strong monarch, gained slow acceptance.

In the eighth century a threat from Asia and Africa seemed likely to put an end to the barbarian kingdoms in France, Spain and Italy. In Spain the Visigoths had, like the Franks under Clovis, been at times united by kings who fought to bring the whole land under their rule, but the mixture of races and religions had proved one of contrasts so great that foreign conquerors found it easy to divide and rule. Spain had been the most Romanised province of the empire, and when Christianity replaced paganism as the religion of the state, a bitter quarrel developed between Arians and Catholics. The numerous Jewish population also suffered, and the majority of Jews, to avoid persecution, went through a form of forced conversion, while maintaining their faith in a clandestine fashion until AD 711, when they welcomed an invasion of Moslems from north Africa. These were Berbers, who landed by the rock which still bears the name of their leader, Gibraltar, (Gebel Tariq, Mount Tariq). On 19 July he overwhelmed Visigoths who had mustered to expel him. The Moslem conquest of Spain had begun. When Tariq moved northwards, only two towns, Seville and Merida, attempted to withstand him. The invaders required only surrender, and interfered little with local life. They paused some time before penetrating the northern regions where the olive trees would not grow. This beautiful tree, celebrated as the symbol of peace, encouraged idleness throughout the Mediterranean countries. It fruits prolifically with scarcely any cultivation and yields oil to the most primitive presses. A small plot with a few large trees seemed to millions of possessive and narrow-minded peasants the one insurance against poverty and starvation. Young men, eager to see the world and acquire riches, could join in some distant piracy or brigandage, knowing that when all else failed they could return to the ancestral olive grove.

The vast extent of Moslem conquests and the speed with which they were executed has astonished the world unnecessarily. They were not the fruit of a superior culture, but the triumph of barbarism and religion. Moslem princes acquired a reputation for learning, but only after two centuries of rapine and aggression in every land from France to the Persian Gulf.

Mahomet, the founder of their religion, was born in AD 570 or 571. His parents belonged to the Arab tribe which guarded the building under which lay the sacred Black Stone of Mecca, a block of meteoric iron. Close by was the spring of fresh water which had made the spot an important staging post on the caravan route to Basra, where spice-laden ships came in from India. He grew up to be a camel driver, unable to read or write, for Arabic at that time was a spoken language with virtually no literature. At the age of twenty-five he married a rich widow of forty and began a life of prayer and meditation, learning much from the teachings and practices of Jews and Christians. He determined that his doctrines should, like theirs, be preserved in a holy book, and so dictated the nucleus of the Koran to a secretary. At the age of forty-five, he led his followers to their first military success. He had fled to Medina to escape his enemies in Mecca and from there attacked a Meccan caravan. At this time he broke with both Judaism and Christianity, appointing Friday, not Saturday or Sunday, as a sabbath, instituting an annual fast of one month, Ramadan; the pilgrimage to kiss the Black Stone in Mecca; and a ban on all idols. In AD 632 he returned to Mecca in triumph, smashing the idols to which the tribesmen were much devoted, but died in the same year.

The succession to the prophet's position was not settled without much quarrelling. After his first wife's death he had married nine times, but his son Ibrahim had not survived him, and it was his father-in-law who seized power in Mecca and urged the faithful to make war on their neighbours. The title of caliph was given to the prophet's successors and with it the right to declare a *jihad* or holy war. The belief that death in battle ensured eternal bliss in the next world made the caliph's soldiers formidable foes. Using the desert as navies use the sea to make surprise attacks from many different directions, they soon conquered Syria and Mesopotamia. Alexandria, a seaport to which the emperor in Constantinople sent help, held out until the Arabs, seizing Greek ships, gained command of the sea. They proved excellent sailors and their word *amir*, general, when adopted in the west, came to mean admiral. Carthage was held by the Arabs after a fierce struggle with Berber tribesmen from the desert, who soon afterwards accepted Islam and joined in a lucrative traffic in slaves, especially women, for which the Arab markets in the east provided an inexhaustible demand.

In AD 714 a Moslem army, recruited from many different races, crossed from Spain into France, and in AD 721, advancing by way of the Rhône valley, besieged and captured Autun, a town to which an amphitheatre and other splendid buildings still gave the air of a Roman capital. Central France was troubled for eleven years by constant Arab raids, until, in AD 732, the Franks in the north were persuaded to intervene. Their leader, Charles Martel (the Hammer) met the Moslems between Tours and Poitiers (the exact site of the battlefield is unknown). The Moslems failed to break the Frankish line, and eventually fled, leaving behind them tents piled high with loot. After this decisive defeat the south of France, once more under Christian rule, suffered only from Arab sea-raiders and slave-hunters.

In AD 778 an opportunity occurred for a counter-attack in Spain. Charlemagne, a grandson of Charles Martel, who had been crowned King of Franks at the age of twenty-six by Pope Stephen IV, was persuaded by the Moslem ruler of Barcelona to come to his aid in a dispute with the Caliph of Cordoba, who regarded himself, not the Caliph in Baghdad, as the rightful ruler of Spain. Charlemagne with his usual efficiency organised two armies and these converged by different routes on Barcelona, which he captured. The Franks then left Spain by way of the Basque country, where they did much destruction before withdrawing through the Pyrenees. In the pass of Roncesvalles their rearguard under Roland, Prefect of Brittany, was ambushed by the Basques and massacred. This disaster, minimised by Frankish chroniclers, an eleventh-century poet transmuted into one of the most bewitching stories of medieval chivalry, the *Chanson de Roland*, giving the part originally played by the Basques to the Moslems. Barcelona and the country of the Catalans with their distinctive language and culture never returned to Moslem rule.

The Franks, though united in war, were already divided between those who spoke French, a language derived from the Latin of Roman Gaul, and the German-speaking majority to which Charlemagne himself belonged. For many years he campaigned against the pagan Saxon tribes of central and northern Germany, and for this reason moved his capital eastwards from Paris to Aachen. The Saxons had been partially Christianised by the saintly Boniface (AD 680-754), a Benedictine monk from England, who, backed by papal authority, established the famous monastery at Fulda, but the Franks insisted on forcible conversion.

The fulcrum of Charlemagne's power was an army of a new kind, a cavalry force armed with lance, sword and bow and protected by helmets and shirts of leather sewn with metal rings. These knights, though not professional soldiers, were obliged to answer a royal summons to war if their holdings in land amounted to about 100 acres or more. Usually they served from the time the grass was green enough to provide horse fodder until autumn. Attached to the cavalry was a smaller force of infantry trained to batter down walls and build bridges of boats. These travelled on horseback and were called *fantassins*. The mobility and skill of these troops gave the Franks a decisive advantage.

Charlemagne was a man of commanding height, handsome and dignified, noted in a nation of heavy drinkers for his sobriety, unable to read or write until the end of his life, but eager to listen at meal times while musicians played or such books as St Augustine's *Civitas Dei* were read to him. His personality was a perpetual source of wonder to the poets and scholars whom he attracted to his court and shines in their writings like light through a dioptric lense. Bishops and monks served him as judges, ambassadors and administrators, receiving orders from him as from the Pope. He consciously aspired to the title of emperor, and this eventually came to him unexpectedly on Christmas Day AD 800. Having already made himself King of the Lombards, a Germanic people who had settled in the valley of the Po, he was on a visit to Rome. During mass in St Peter's Church Pope Leo III placed a coronet on his head naming him *Imperator Romanorum*, an act that for centuries was a matter of controversy. Leo had recently been treated by personal enemies with gross brutality and in part he was making a gesture of gratitude to Charlemagne for protecting him; he probably also wished to assert his independence from the emperor in Constantinople. Monastic writers, with their enthusiasm for elaborate similes and high-pitched rhetoric, had been presented with an almost inexhaustible subject. One theory, based on a passage in Luke's Gospel, held that the office of pope conveyed a spiritual jurisdiction over the whole of Christendom which was his alone, and a temporal jurisdiction which he could delegate to an emperor, enabling him to claim supremacy over all other kings and princes. These powers were symbolised by two swords, a spiritual and a temporal. Certainly on that Christmas Day no sword in western Europe dared challenge that of Charlemagne, but after his death in AD 814

Sao ko kelle terre, per kelle fini

I know that those lands, and those boundaries containing

que ki contene, (t)renta anni

them, have belonged to Saint Benedict for thirty years

le possette parte sancti Benedicti

These are the earliest known words in Italian; they were inserted in the Latin evidence taken in AD 960 during a lawsuit concerning land at Capua belonging to the monastery of St Benedict at Monte Cassino

none could control so vast an area. In AD 843 three of his grandsons, Lothar, Louis the German and Charles the Bald, divided the empire between them. Each made warlike moves to secure the biggest share for himself, but each was afraid of an alliance between the other two. After some fighting it was agreed that the eldest, Lothar, should be Emperor and take Italy, the lands round Aachen and the mouth of the Rhine and a corridor between them; that Louis the German should have the territory to the east of Lothar's lands; and Charles the Bald central and southern France and Catalonia. Ecclesiastical writers of the time bemoaned this fragmentation of Christendom, as they regarded it. They need not have done so. A civilised Europe could only evolve from the unimpeded local activity of townspeople and country-dwellers adapting their way of life to the soils and climates of an infinitely varied terrain. The ambitions of men pursuing the ghost of the old Roman empire were irrelevant to the struggle to provide, with only the most primitive mechanical aids, enough food, clothing and shelter for all.

The Viking Invasions

Just as the Roman empire had been viewed with jealous greed by its northern neighbours the Goths, so in the ninth century that of the Franks attracted sea robbers called Vikings from Norway, Denmark and Sweden. Modern archeological studies have revealed that their ancestors had lived in Scandinavia for some 10,000 years and, though poor, had by AD 800 developed many skills in agriculture, house construction and shipbuilding. Their religion was polytheistic; Odin, the king of the gods, held court in Valhalla, to which all warriors killed in battle ascended by a rainbow bridge to live a life of eating, drinking and eternal leisure. As pagans they had no respect for the many Christian monasteries which had been founded in isolated places, and particularly on coastal islands. They could not believe their good fortune in finding stores of church plate and other treasure watched over by men whose religion forbade them to fight. Their diplomacy was as treacherous as their spirits were wild. One old Viking, who found that Christians would pay a high price if he accepted their faith, boasted that he had put on a white sheet and been baptised sixteen times.

The reason for the sudden and widespread movement of the Vikings is not mysterious. At first they did not migrate and settle in new lands; they preferred to make summer raids, or sometimes to camp for a winter or two near a harbour or river estuary from which they could terrorise the country before returning home with the silver they had collected in tribute and cargoes of women and slaves. They developed a keen eye for trade, and, being masters of the sea, eventually prospered more by commerce than by piracy.

The numerous atrocities that the Vikings committed all over north-west Europe, including the British Isles, made them so feared that whole populations would flee in terror at the news of their approach, leaving everything behind them. In AD 834 they ravaged Dorestad in Holland, a flourishing place during Charlemagne's reign; in AD 856 they burnt Paris; and three years later a Viking fleet entered the Mediterranean and plundered Provence and Tuscany.

Three ships dating from this time have been recovered from the shores of Oslo Fiord, where they were interred under mounds of peat for use in the next world by the princes and princesses whose bodies lay in them. The ship found at Gokstad in 1880, nearly a thousand years after its burial, was built entirely of oak. She was long and narrow, about 23 metres overall, 5 metres broad and in section 2 metres deep. She had sixteen oars on either side each with two rowers. Her mast of pine, probably 12 metres high, was mounted amidships and carried a single large lug sail. The keel, stem and stern post were each hewn from a single piece of timber and the ribs were covered with sixteen rows of planking, nine of them below the waterline, giving the ship considerable elasticity. No rudder had yet been devised, but a large steering paddle over 3 metres long, also carved from a single timber, was strapped to the starboard quarter. Through the neck of this paddle passed a tiller, giving the helmsman easy command of the ship in all weathers. To men in vessels of such shallow draught the many navigable rivers of Europe were highways to fame and fortune.

In the tenth century, Vikings, tired of fighting in Britain and in France against soldiers and sailors whose quality had risen to match their own, began to form permanent settlements. They had no taste for war from which there was no spoil to be won. In AD 911 Rollo, the Danish leader of the Norwegian Vikings based at Rouen, accepted baptism in return for the cession of land, and later extended his dukedom from the Seine valley to the borders of Brittany. These Northmen, or Normans, soon learnt to speak French and became generous patrons of the Church.

Vikings from Sweden set up their first trading posts in Russia round Lake Ladoga and Lake Onega in the north and under Rurik made Novgorod (new town) the capital of a princedom. These Swedes, previously known as Varangians, were called Rus by the native Slav population, and so gave their name to the whole country. In AD 839 they sent ambassadors to the emperor in Constantinople, seeking to establish a trade route to the south by way of the Dnieper valley. They already had a fort at Kiev, where high cliffs overlook the broad meandering river. Here during the winter trappers brought in furs and sold slaves, for travel was easy and quick over the frozen plains. Each spring a huge armed convoy set off to the south, and, after bartering away their winter collections in the sunny markets of Constantinople, returned home before the autumn rains.

The Great Princes of Kiev

The genius of a comparatively small number of Vikings, by organising the Slavs and other tribes between the Baltic and the Black Sea, turned the waterways of Russia into the trade arteries of a new military empire. In AD 907 their leader Oleg, having made himself master both of Novgorod and Kiev, attacked Constantinople, but was repulsed.

The iron crown of Lombardy, whose wearers bore the title, so much coveted by the German emperors, 'King of Italy'

His son Igor, attempting another siege, was driven off by flame throwers using an inflammable compound known as Greek fire. His widow Olga made peace, and was baptised in the presence of the emperor, but her successors were pagans who continued to war on all their neighbours, and none did so more successfully than Vladimir, who became Great Prince of Kiev in AD 980, having murdered his brother to do so. Coveting

42

Cherson on the southern shores of the Crimea, which was ruled by Basil II, the Emperor in Constantinople, he arranged to marry Basil's sister Anne, and promised in return for her and this territory to be baptised. He insisted that thousands of Russian nobles should also accept Christianity and invited architects and craftsmen from the imperial court to beautify his capital with its first churches. In this way he linked Russia with the rest of Europe and permanently separated his princedom from the nomadic tribes of Asia who constantly threatened its eastern frontier.

The Kingdom of Germany

A century after the death of Lothar, son of Charlemagne, there was no emperor in the west. His 'middle kingdom' had been greatly reduced; the northern part, known as the dukedom of Lotharingia, stretched from Strasbourg to the Frisian islands. To the east of it lay the German dukedoms of Saxony in the north, Franconia in the centre and Swabia in the south. A fifth, Bavaria, commanded the Danube as far east as Linz.

In AD 936 Otto, Duke of Saxony, was elected King of Germany. A man of high ambition and outstanding gifts, he immediately had himself crowned at Aachen. The Archbishop of Mainz officiated in the cathedral Charlemagne had built and the four other dukes acted as his chamberlain, steward, butler and marshal, offices symbolic of their status as officials appointed by him. Otto did not find his claims universally accepted and was busy for some years putting down rebellions and extending his dominions eastwards. In AD 952 he took an army over the Alps, intending to make himself King of Italy, but troubles in Germany caused him to withdraw. Ten years later he re-entered Italy, was received in Rome and crowned emperor by the Pope and reigned as Otto I until AD 973, bringing peace and comparative prosperity to all central Europe. The ideal of a Christian empire, first grasped at by Charlemagne, had been successfully revived and did not wholly die until the nineteenth century.

CHAPTER THREE

The Eleventh Century

The Kingdoms of Hungary and Croatia

After some dreadful primeval earthquake the volcanic mountains of Moravia on the left bank of the Danube blocked the river's flow to the east and forced it to turn south. Near this point, at Esztergom, was born the man who in 1000 became the founder of modern Hungary, Istvan (Stephen). Esztergom had been a border fortress in Charlemagne's time, marking the eastern limit of his empire, and Stephen's people, the Magyars, were then pagan nomads of Asiatic origin, speaking a language unlike any other in Europe except Finnish. On their long wanderings across Russia, before they settled west of the Carpathians, they had come into contact with the Turks, who called them 'the ten tribes' and Hungary is a word derived from their Turkish name. In the tenth century they made devastating raids into Germany, France and Italy, but in 955 their swiftly moving columns of horsemen had been trapped at the Lechfeld near Augsburg by Otto I and so severely beaten that they never came westwards again.

Stephen, having come under the influence of Czech missionaries from Bohemia, was baptised and in 1000 recognised by Pope Sylvester as king and 'apostle'. According to legend, the pope sent him a holy crown named after St Stephen, the first Christian martyr, and coronation ceremonies came to have a mystic significance for Hungarians. At the time, however, the title of king conferred much of practical value. It allowed Stephen, modelling himself upon Charlemagne, to hold mass baptisms and appoint bishops in almost imperial style. Esztergom became the seat of an archbishop recognised as primate of Hungary. Such a sudden change could not have been accomplished without German aid. Stephen employed Bavarian knights against recalcitrant pagans and, through his wife Gisela, strengthened the ties that bound him to the rest of Christendom, for she was a sister of Henry, Duke of Saxony, who became emperor and reigned from 1002 to 1024.

At this period a man did not, on receiving the title of king, acquire a ready-made machine of government and officers trained to carry out his commands. He was expected to create these for himself, and at the same time to travel from place to place dispensing justice in person, for he had no permanent headquarters—no one countryside could produce food enough for more than a few weeks. A messenger ordered to report the presence of some enemy on the frontier had first to discover where the king was. Fear

Odin, the King of the Gods, after riding over land and sea on his eight-legged grey horse Sleipnir, gallops into Valhalla, a building with a domed roof. Above him floats a dead warrior still clutching his sword. Below, a Viking ship in full sail with armed men on board. An engraved stone from Gotland

was the deterrent on which monarchies relied, both in war and peace, and for this life had to be taken, often many lives. Stephen, for his success as a king at a time when the maintenance of law and order were a rare blessing, was canonised.

After his death in 1038 there were two great pagan revolts among those Magyars who resented the break-up of their tribal organisation under the impact of foreign and Christian influences. Christianity was not re-established until the last quarter of the century, when Lazlo (1077-1095), a strong king, subsequently canonised, was succeeded by an equally able ruler, Kalman the Booklover (1095-1116). In Kalman's reign Hungary saw the passage of the first crusading armies as they pushed eastwards towards Constantinople and the Holy Land. This invasion had many drawbacks, but was beneficial in opening fresh trade along the whole length of the Danube valley.

The country to the south of Hungary from the Sava to the Adriatic was much disputed during the eleventh century between the native Croatians, whose homeland was round Zagreb, the Venetians and the emperors in Constantinople, who had always

D

claimed Italy and all the land northwards as far as the Danube as theirs on the ground that the emperors in Rome had done so. The Venetians wished to command the Dalmatian coast for three reasons: to use its beautiful wooded hills as a source of timber for ship-building; to stop pirates hiding among its many inlets, bays and islands; and to prevent the Byzantines, their greatest trade rivals, from coming further west.

Between these powerful enemies the Croat kings could not long prevail. Under Peter Kresimir (1058-1074) they extended their rule to include the Dalmatian coast as far south as the border of Montenegro, and northwards to the river Sava, but after his death the kingship was much disputed. In 1097 the last king of Croat blood was killed and Kalman accepted an invitation to become King of Croatia on condition that he left the people free to keep up their own customs and parliament. The Croatian churches, like those of Hungary, recognised the supremacy of Rome.

The Conversion of the Vikings

In Sweden, Olaf, the first Christian king, came to the throne in 993 and reigned until 1024. His country had received missionaries two centuries earlier but paganism had remained strong until his time, when it seems to have faded away without any of the forcible conversions common in other countries. In Denmark the contest between pagans and Christians had been equally slow and obstinate, but Canute, who ruled Denmark and England from 1017 to 1035, gave the Church, as the custom was, great gifts of land. After his time Denmark was, in name at least, Christian.

The first Christian king of Norway, Olaf Tryggvason, who came to the throne in 995, perished in a sea-fight against the Swedes and the Danes in 1000. Before his accession he had been a noted Viking, but was converted by a hermit whom he met in the Scilly Islands. The English bishop Alphege, who confirmed Olaf's baptism, was later captured by the Danes and murdered because he refused to raise a ransom. Olaf favoured compulsory baptism both in Norway and in the Norwegian colonies in Iceland and Green-land, where he sent missionaries in the year of his death. Fifteen years afterwards another Olaf, a man of similar character, became king after having been a Viking from boyhood. He too terrorised those of his subjects who were still pagan into accepting the faith. In 1028, when Canute conquered Norway, Olaf fled to Russia, where he was made welcome and offered the governorship of the heathen Khazars east of the Volga. He preferred to wait for a chance to return to Norway, where he led a revolt in 1030 and was killed in battle. Five years later his son Magnus was successful, and set his country free. Minstrels were soon composing sagas in praise of 'Olaf the Saint', telling for example, with what cunning he had destroyed belief in pagan idols and how, before his last fight, he had given 'soul-mulct' in order that masses might be said for the souls of those whom he might kill, while refusing to give any money for those who died for his cause, saying that they would certainly be received in heaven. Such epics about dead heroes flourished particularly in Iceland, whose people were Norwegian in tongue and custom.

The structure of Scandinavian society accounts in part for the obstinacy of its paganism. The free peasant farmers were intensely conservative, and imagined their lives to be hemmed in by witchcraft and malignant spirits. In every action they looked for omens of good or evil. Yet in other respects they were free men, and did not become tenants either of the nobles or of the Church until the eleventh century, much later, that is, than peasants elsewhere. They were also accustomed to conduct their own local 'things', or parliaments. Even kings preferred not to take important decisions without formal consent from their companions in arms following free and outspoken discussion reminiscent of the ancient Greeks. Some Viking raiders were once asked by their opponents. 'Who is your leader?' The reply was 'We have none. We are all equals'. This proud boast was of course untrue. Victory in war cannot be won without a chain of command strictly followed, but the Scandinavians nonetheless upheld an ideal of liberty much admired elsewhere in Europe. On the other hand the pursuit of blood-feuds among them was considered praiseworthy until Christianity and royal justice, coming hand in hand, offered a more peaceable way of life and, from about 1050, encouraged Dane, Norwegian and Swede to live as neighbours.

Papal Supremacy

Outside certain strict monasteries the Christian ideal seemed so remote from reality in 1000 that the coming of the millenium was by many confidently expected to bring an end of the world and the Day of Judgement. No institution had fallen into greater disgrace than the papacy. Elections to this supreme office were accompanied by intrigue, bribery and intermittent street fighting in which the Roman mob contended with the noble Roman families whose sons were commonly made bishops and cardinals, sometimes in their twenties. Popes were chosen not as examples of righteousness but as likely to act as the puppets of those who voted for them. In 1046 an autocratic and wildly ambitious emperor, Henry III, having entered Rome to receive the imperial crown, set aside three men claiming to be popes and appointed a German. Neither the new pope nor his German successor lived for more than a year, but Henry, intervening a third time, chose Bernard, Bishop of Toul in Lorraine, who took the title of Leo IX and immediately began to reorganise the Church. The impulse towards reform had been kindled over a century before by the teachings of the monks of Cluny in Burgundy and the new monasteries planted throughout western Europe under their inspiration insisted upon an ascetic life and observance of the rule requiring poverty, chastity and obedience.

Three scandals needed to be removed—disorderly papal elections; the practice of simony, or sale of church appointments; and clerical concubinage. Leo IX began by appointing as cardinals, and therefore as future electors, men of ability from outside Rome, the most outstanding of whom was a young Tuscan named Hildebrand. Henry III was then requested to put a stop to the scandalous behaviour of Norman soldiers of fortune in southern Italy where, under the pretence of defending the rights of legitimate rulers, they were carving out large estates for themselves. The Emperor prudently refused, knowing the Normans to be the best fighters in Europe, but Leo persisted. Having failed to get help from the Patriarch in Constantinople, though there were many Byzantine churches in the south, he gathered an army of his own. The Normans defeated and captured him in the first battle. They always professed extreme devotion to the Church, and so, kneeling as penitents before him, they extracted consent to all their demands. This humiliating surrender on Leo's part, which was followed a year later by his death (1054), deeply offended the Patriarch, and the breach between the eastern and western churches was never afterwards healed.

In 1059 a Church Council was held in the Lateran in Rome and a decree issued restricting the vote in papal elections to the cardinals. As they were appointed by the pope, this was obviously intended to create a self-perpetuating oligarchy and caused fourteen years of dissension and civil war in Italy. The Milanese clergy, many of them married, were bitterly opposed to the reformers, but they could expect no help from Germany, for Henry III had died in 1056, leaving a child heir, the future Henry IV, and the country was ruled, or misruled, by the Archbishops of Cologne and Bremen, who had charge of the boy king. They were afterwards blamed for allowing him to grow up a villain, but, as was once said of the tutors whom Marcus Aurelius chose for his infamous heir Commodus: 'The power of instruction is seldom of much efficacy except in those dispositions where it is almost superfluous.'

Hildebrand, who was elected pope in 1075 with the title Gregory VII, held a council

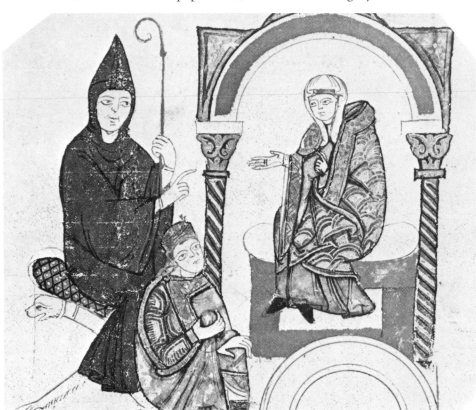

Henry IV at Canossa. The emperor on bended knee begs the Abbot of Cluny and Matilda, the ruler of Tuscany, to intercede with the pope on his behalf

in Rome which issued decrees denying monarchs the right to invest the bishops of their choice with the symbols of office, the ring and crozier. This was one means of preventing simony and the appointment of men who had wives or concubines. A righteous pope had declared his intention of refusing recognition to bishops whom he considered unworthy. A righteous emperor could have had no reasonable objection, but Henry IV, a vicious youth who had 'come of age' at sixteen, saw Gregory's policy only as an affront to himself. To show his authority over Lombardy he defiantly deposed the Archbishop of Milan and substituted one of his supporters. In response Gregory threatened to depose the emperor and he in turn declared Gregory deposed. For this he was excommunicated, thereby releasing his subjects from the obligation to obey him. Italian bishops were

Veduta del Ponte e Castello Sant'Angelo.

Rome, showing on the right of the Tiber bridge the papal castle of Sant'Angelo, once the marble-encrusted tomb of the Emperor Hadrian, and in the distance the dome of St Peter's

accustomed to such action and took little notice, but in Germany bishops were terrified and rebel dukes delighted. They informed the emperor that if he had not within a year

49

reconciled himself with the pope they would renounce their allegiance and elect another king. At the same time they closed the eastern passes of the Alps to prevent Henry from meeting the pope. They forgot what a cunning and determined man their overlord was. In mid-winter through deep snow he crossed by the Mont Cenis pass and reached the castle of Canossa where Gregory was waiting for an escort before joining his German allies. For three days the emperor, clad in the white sheet of a penitent, stood barefoot on the icy pavement at the castle gate asking for admission. The pope's friends, including the Abbot of Cluny, urged him to grant Henry absolution, something that could not justly be withheld from one who appeared so repentant. Gregory yielded to his councillors and Henry returned to Germany, fought a successful civil war with his enemies, and then marched on Rome, where he appointed an anti-pope who crowned him emperor. During the ceremony Gregory remained safe behind the walls of Sant' Angelo, a castle close to the Tiber, waiting for the Normans from the south to come to his rescue. When they did so, they destroyed a large part of Rome, making Gregory so unpopular with the citizens that he had to leave, going virtually a prisoner to Salerno where he became mortally ill. As he lay dying the words of the 45th Psalm came into his head and he said: 'I have loved righteousness and hated iniquity'. Bitterly he added: 'Therefore I die in exile.'

Though it seemed to Gregory that he had laboured in vain, the papal court, which as a young man he had seen so degraded, had become a place to which men from all over Europe looked for leadership and approval not only in politics but in many other activities. Gregory, like most men bred in the world of books and able to retain in the memory most of what they read and hear from men similarly nurtured, had ideas far beyond practical reach, but, unlike most intellectuals, he possessed the willpower and energy to pursue them in the world of affairs. He saw, or thought he saw, how to achieve political unity in Europe by a short cut, just as Henry IV, with equal arrogance, strove to bend every princeling in Germany to his will. For centuries their successors attempted to succeed where they had failed.

The First Crusade

At the beginning of his pontificate Gregory VII received an urgent message from the Emperor Alexius Comnenus, who had succeeded to the throne shortly after the imperial forces had been overwhelmingly defeated by a new enemy from Asia, the Seljuk Turks. These rough soldiers, whose families were shepherds, not farmers, had occupied the whole of Anatolia. In 1071 they captured Jerusalem and threatened to attack Constantinople. Gregory replied to Alexius sympathetically, but his long dispute with Henry IV prevented him from taking any action. Another appeal from Constantinople reached Pope Urban II in 1094 and he, being appalled at the internecine fighting going on in Europe, saw an opportunity for a holy war in which Europe might unite. It is doubtful whether any of his advisers were able to provide the geographical information required before a plan of war could be made, but this Urban's great oratorical gifts concealed. Having assembled a council of bishops, abbots and nobles at Clermont he pleaded for the recovery of the Holy Land; *Deus vult*! should be their watchword (*it is God's will*); the cross should be their badge; and heaven would be the certain reward of those who lost their lives on the campaign. He was astounded at the enthusiasm that his words aroused, especially among the high-born youth of France. The monarchs of Europe watched while some of their most troublesome subjects chose a new outlet for their energies. By various routes separate contingents reached Constantinople, where they took an instant dislike to the emperor and to the Greeks, whom they considered shifty and effeminate. The Greeks, finding the Crusaders unable to read or write and totally ignorant of the eastern empire, regarded them as barbarians. The emperor, disturbed by the numbers and manners of his new allies, obtained from them an oath of allegiance and dispatched them across the Bosphorus, where they captured Nicaea and, after a most arduous march across Asia Minor, Antioch. They then found that deep dissensions between the Moslem princes had opened the road to Jerusalem. Having stormed the city and massacred its inhabitants, most of the Crusaders then went home, but a handful of French and Norman knights stayed, and with the flimsiest resources began to organise a chain of princedoms along the coast to which they gave the name Levant, the land of the rising sun. Of these the kingdom of Jerusalem lasted less than a century, being overrun by the Moslems in 1187.

This campaign had not been an isolated conflict between Moslem and Christian; it

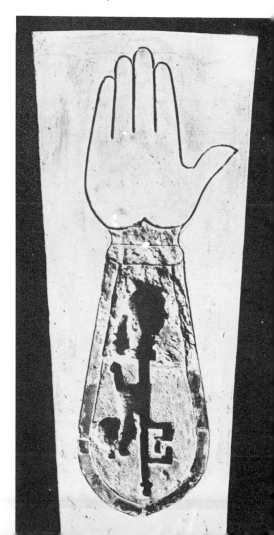

Keystone with Islamic symbol. The open palm signifies the five articles of the creed and five duties imposed on all Moslems: belief in God, in angels, in the revealed books, in the prophets, and in the day of judgement. The duties are to recite the creed, say prayers, pay tithe, keep the fast of Ramadan, and make a pilgrimage to Mecca

was merely the first to have papal encouragement and to bear the romantic name of crusade. Moslem and Christian had long been engaged in hostilities in the Mediterranean. The grandfathers of the Crusaders from Provence knew well how Arab raiders had penetrated as far north as Burgundy, carrying off the Abbot of Cluny, and in the Alps had robbed traders passing through the Great St Bernard pass. The seamen of Genoa and Pisa, self-governing ports each wealthy enough to maintain fleets of war galleys, had combined in 1016 to prevent a Moslem prince from Spain conquering Sardinia and had helped in recovering Sicily from the Arabs. French and Norman knights, fighting for Christian states in northern Spain, had captured Toledo from the Moors in 1085.

The Seljuk Turks were more intolerant than other Moslems and treated Christians more harshly than their predecessors, but had not banned their entry. Pilgrims, most of whom hired ships from Italian ports, had landed on the coast of Palestine ever since the Moslem invasion in the seventh century. It was Urban II who propagated the idea that the mere presence of a non-Christian ruler in Jerusalem was an affront to Christendom. The Crusaders rejected compromise on pilgrim traffic as unworthy and, once fighting had started, sought victory and spoil with an ardour worthy of their Viking ancestors. The motive for war is usually robbery and, while men beggared their estates in the west to get passage money to the east, many did so on the calculation that the adventure would amply repay them. Opposed to them were Moslem warriors who looked for a profit from every jihad.

The Norman Conquest of England

Robert, father of William the Conqueror, became sixth Duke of Normandy in 1026 when Duke Richard III, his eighteen-year-old elder brother, died suddenly after a reign of less than two years. He and his brother had been feuding at the time and, when Richard's infant son was put away in a monastery, Robert was suspected by some to have committed fratricide. After an interval of confusion he succeeded, with the help of an uncle, the Archbishop of Rouen, in restoring order in the duchy. The Archbishop was a married man who had sons to provide for and therefore good reason to support his nephew's cause. Less than ten years later, the young Duke announced his intention of going on pilgrimage to the Holy Land. This was a method popular among prominent men for showing that they repented their sins and desired forgiveness. Robert, though his decision outraged his advisers, who foresaw civil war in his absence, set off with a retinue so magnificent that even the Emperor in Constantinople was astonished by it. Having visited the holy places he was on his way home through Asia Minor when he fell ill and died.

In Normandy he had left behind an eight-year-old son, William, whose mother, the daughter of a Falaise tanner, had subsequently married Count Herluin and borne him two sons, Odo, who was made Bishop of Bayeux at the age of nineteen, and Robert, Count of Mortain. Normandy was at once rent by factions; one party nearly succeeded in murdering William, but by the age of thirty he had by sheer fighting ability made himself master of the whole duchy. He also considered that he had a strong claim to the throne of Edward the Confessor, King of England, whose mother had been the sister of

Duke Richard II. Edward, who before his accession had been a refugee in Normandy for many years, was childless and William was his nearest male relative. In the first week of 1066 Edward died at Westminster after a long illness. No invitation to assume the throne reached William. Instead, the English crowned Earl Harold, son of Godwin, the richest landowner in the country.

Duke William began preparation for invasion. He gave out that Harold, in accepting the crown, had committed perjury. The story is told in the pictures of the Bayeaux tapestry, embroidered about twenty years after the events it portrays. They show the English earl embarking at Bosham and landing in the territory of Guy, Count of Ponthieu, who takes him to William in the ducal palace at Rouen. There Harold addresses the enthroned duke, possibly on the latest news from England about the succession, and then goes to war in William's company in Brittany. As a reward for his services he is knighted, accepting arms from the Duke as his overlord. According to a Norman chronicler, William of Poitiers, writing about five years afterwards, the Duke then asked Harold in the presence of witnesses to give him a solemn oath that he would ensure his succession to the English throne, placing Norman garrisons in Dover Castle and such other castles as the Normans might specify. The Bayeux tapestry shows the Earl with his right hand on a reliquary containing a saint's bones and his left on an altar bearing the host. There is no suggestion that the oath is being obtained by trickery, as some later Norman accounts state. On the other hand, as no vestige of this story occurs in the Anglo-Saxon Chronicle, a sober and objective record compiled at the time, it is almost certainly a fabrication designed to discredit Harold, which it successfully did. Duke William was able to convince Pope Alexander II that his cause was just and to obtain from him a battle flag, a golden cross on a silver ground with an azure border.

By the summer of 1066 the proposed attack on England had taken on the character of a holy war. While the transports were being built on the river Dives, warriors assembled not from the duke's lands only, but from Maine, Brittany, Picardy, Poitou, Burgundy, Anjou and even southern Italy. In many cases they were mercenaries. In September, when the Duke was ready to sail, the wind blew steadily from the north. To shorten the sea crossing the whole fleet moved to the mouth of the Somme to await a change in the weather. Harold, who had assembled his men in Sussex, had sent them home to gather in the harvest when he heard that the north wind which had protected him from William had enabled his other rival, Harold Hardrada, King of Norway, to reach the Humber with a fleet of 300 ships and to defeat the local forces sent against him.

The King of England moved swiftly from London to York, and surprised a large part of the Norwegian forces at Stamford Bridge. In the hot weather they had left their mail shirts in camp, and almost all, including Harold Hardrada, perished. Prince Olaf was captured, but allowed to return home; only thirty ships were needed to carry the survivors. A change of wind three days later enabled Duke William's fleet to cross to Pevensey. As soon as the news reached King Harold he and his bodyguard moved south, hoping to surprise the Normans as they had done the Norwegians. They should have let the Normans face the winter in the open. Instead, the English, weary from their march, had to muster against the advancing Normans early on 14 October. Forming a

Falaise Castle, Normandy, where William the Conqueror was born in 1027

shield wall, they resisted every charge until, with Harold and two of his brothers dead, a rout began. By one bold stroke Duke William had won the kingdom, and received the Confessor's crown in Westminster Abbey on Christmas Day.

The land-hungry Normans who sailed for England in 1066 and subsequently did not number more than 15,000, but their military skill and domineering harshness gave them complete mastery. The English had built a system of local government unequalled for efficiency anywhere in Europe. An assembly of chief men met regularly in every county and shire for the assessment and collection of taxes. The Normans with a fierce show of arms called each assembly together and waited for it to vote the taxes they required. To their astonishment, caskets of coin, minted at over sixty mints all under royal control, arrived at the treasury in Winchester. The most powerful duke in Europe had become the richest king. When William died twenty years later, England and large parts of Wales were divided among a mere 180 great landowners, and of these only six were Englishmen; the rest were the king's companions in arms or their relatives. Out of sixteen bishops, each with large dioceses, only one was English. Native builders, using the massive Romanesque style adopted before the conquest by the great abbey at Westminster, were reconstructing in stone almost every cathedral and monastery church. Although William on his deathbed arranged to separate the kingdom from the duchy, leaving Normandy to his vain and foolish eldest son Robert who pawned it and joined the first crusade, and England to Rufus, the close ties between the two countries were never broken. England had, in a social and cultural sense, become permanently attached to western Europe, where in the next century powerful monarchies based on feudal hierarchies like that established by William the Conqueror began to emerge.

CHAPTER FOUR

The Twelfth Century

Feudalism and Monarchy

The Viking invasions of the tenth and eleventh centuries had shown that no region could be protected unless its inhabitants had available a sufficient force of men trained to fight on horseback with lance and spear at short notice. Rather than wait for some distant king or duke to come to their aid, villagers and townspeople preferred to trust the lord of some nearby castle. In return for building him a fortress, supplying the garrison with food and performing a number of other services, such as the upkeep of roads and bridges, they could in times of danger ask to take refuge in his castle yard. This intricate network of duties and obligations is known by the general name of feudalism. King and vassal, lord and peasant were bound together by unwritten contracts, voluntarily accepted by the majority as reasonable and necessary. In the twelfth century these customary arrange-ments were still further developed in the documents, charters and deeds of gift by which kings, dukes and nobles, when they gave land to vassals or the Church, specified the exact number of men-at-arms required or the sums of money that would be accepted in lieu of men. The vast lands which the Church acquired in this process provided the resources necessary for Christianising semi-pagan populations but drew bishops and abbots into numerous private and semi-private wars as well as major conflicts initiated by kings and emperors.

The image of a pyramid is sometimes used to describe society at this time, the monarch being at its apex, 'the people' at its base and the nobility and clergy, tier on tier, between them. The same simile might be used to represent the nation state of the twentieth century, where the apex is a small committee of powerful men called 'the cabinet' or 'government'; the place of the nobility is filled by banks, commercial corporations and insurance companies; and the functions once performed by the clergy are carried out by the civil service. The payments received by the nobility in services, money and kind are now paralleled by those made to state insurance funds. On the other hand, of all the structures known to architects the pyramid is not only the simplest to build but also the most stable and least useful when completed, and in none of these respect is it a good image of either medieval or modern society. Feudalism was not only highly complicated, but strictly practical and precise in its arrangements. For the majority of men at the base of the pyramid life may have been a hard monotonous round of labour as ploughman or

Christ bestowing a king's crown on Roger, the Norman ruler of Sicily in the first half of the 12th century; a mosaic by Byzantine craftsmen in the church of the Martorana, Palermo. The Latin form of his name, Rogerios, is written in Greek letters. Under his rule, which he extended to include southern Italy, peace reigned between Latin and Greek Christians, Moors and Jews

The interior of the church of the Martorana, Palermo, founded by Roger's Greek admiral, George of Antioch. The architecture is partly Norman and partly Arab

shepherd, weaver or fisherman; but only in the most isolated parts of Europe was it possible for the population to remain unaware or unaffected by change and progress. By the end of the century feudal society, which drew its vitality from local and family loyalties, had been profoundly modified by three fresh developments—the continued expansion of the papacy; the growth of self-governing towns; and the attempts of the German emperors to create a new middle kingdom covering the Netherlands, western Germany, eastern France and Italy.

Monasticism and the Crusades

The outstanding success of the comparatively obscure nobles who joined the first crusade became in the memory of the kings and queens of western Europe an alluring mirage. When, in 1147, news arrived that the Turks were on the move against the kingdom of Jerusalem, the pope's summons to a crusade was received with enthusiasm. In the previous fifty years the religious life of Europe had undergone a complex transformation. From the Burgundian monastery at Cîteaux and its English abbot, Stephen Harding, had come a call for renewed devotion to the ideas of St Benedict (480-543), who founded the mother house of the Benedictine order at Monte Cassino in the Apennines in 520. Cîteaux and its daughter houses of the Cistercian order distinguished themselves from existing monasteries by insisting upon an extremely ascetic life, welcoming physical hardship of all kinds as an imitation of the life of Christ as they understood it from careful study of the Gospels.

Among the early novices attracted to Cîteaux was the young son of a Burgundian nobleman named Bernard. He was not naturally self-assertive, and hestitated to contradict the strong arguments of his family against monasticism, but, after some years of inner struggle, he found words to convince them of its desirability, and presented himself at the gates of the monastery with two uncles, two cousins and four of his five brothers. They were put to severe tests and eventually in 1115 the abbot sent Bernard

Le Moulin Mystique, *a 12th century carving in the monastery church at Vézelay*

to Clairvaux near Troyes to establish a new house. Bernard made it the foremost monastery in Europe and by his eloquence and energy, expressed in a torrent of books, letters and speeches over the next thirty-five years, he became the most influential man in Europe, his advice sought by kings and emperors as though he were an oracle. His personal saintliness and humility prevented universal admiration from spoiling the quality of his mind and spirit. In judgement he was by no means infallible, nor was his charity universal, but in selfless devotion to Christ he never wavered. When asked, for example, to judge between pope and anti-pope, he inquired only which man had the more goodness and strength of character. He tried always to penetrate hearts rather than explain words, and this led to his most unhappy act, a condemnation of a brilliant teacher of the rising new university of Paris, Peter Abelard (1079-1142). Abelard, with that excessive fondness for abstract argument to which university lecturers are so prone, had published quotations from early Christian writings under the title *Sic et Non* (*Yes and No*), setting out apparently incompatible statements on important points of doctrine and asking his students to find an inner harmony between them. Bernard's practical and conservative mind rejected such methods as an encouragement to heresy, as indeed they might have been among people unused to academic teaching methods.

Vézelay, Burgundy, where on 31 March 1146 Bernard of Clairvaux preached a crusade in the presence of Louis VII, King of France, and his queen. The king and many nobles among those present took the cross. The highest building in the town is the monastery tower

The return of a crusader. This 12th century sculpture from Belval in the Vosges shows the loving welcome of a wife for her husband who had been reported missing after a battle. Now he has returned, his clothes in rags

About the need for a crusade Bernard was in no doubt. To hear him preach the King and Queen of France and a great company of nobles assembled at Vézelay. There was perhaps some magic in the spring air as lords and ladies made their way through the fresh green of the deserted forests to that hill-top monastery where, as Bernard spoke, they could look out over the steep hillside to mountains receding ridge by ridge into the misty east. All present promised to prepare at once for the journey to the Levant. In Germany Bernard, though speaking in a foreign tongue, was equally successful and King Conrad III (1138-1152) also set out with an army eager to save the Holy Land, only to find on arrival that the Christian governments preferred to conciliate rather than fight the Turks. Mismanagement, quarrels and jealousies ruined everything, and when the remnant of once great armies returned home. Bernard remarked that their mutual hatred was 'an abyss so deep that I must call him blessed who is not scandalized thereby.'

The spirit of the crusaders had begun to rely on a new force, national pride. Two orders of soldier-monks had been formed to recruit men to serve in Syria and Palestine—the Knights of St John (Hospitallers) and the Knights of the Temple (Templars). Each order received such numerous grants of land in every country of western Europe and proceeded to erect such elaborate buildings for their administration that they soon aroused the covetousness of their neighbours. Paradoxically, because the orders were organised on a continental scale, language difficulties made it convenient for French, German, Spanish and English knights to live in separate houses and fight in separate units and so the crusades, initially expressions of European unity, developed the national spirit of the countries who took part in them.

In 1187 the Templars suffered a military disaster in Palestine. On this occasion the Master of the Temple, the head of their order, was present, and it was suspected that the defeat had been the result of collusion between the Moslems and Raymond, regent of the kingdom of Jerusalem, the Master's personal enemy. Soon afterwards the Moslems, united after a long period of dissension, trapped a large force of Christian knights on a rocky hill near the Sea of Galilee, where their horses were useless, and the knights fighting in armour under a burning sun, were annihilated. The news of this catastrophe led to a third crusade. Three monarchs answered the summons, the German Emperor, Frederick Barbarossa, Philip II of France and Richard I of England. Each travelled by different routes and their first major success was the capture of the seaport of Acre. The siege took so long that the besiegers themselves were nearly defeated by a relief force. The danger was averted by Richard I, who after a sea journey during which he turned aside to conquer Cyprus, arrived when the other crusaders were about to abandon the siege. An excellent general, he soon took the town, but, unable to achieve anything further, concluded a three-year truce with Saladin allowing pilgrims free access to Jerusalem. Philip II had already returned home. The aged Emperor had never reached the Holy Land, having lost his life in crossing one of the rivers of Asia Minor. Richard, on his way home through the Alps, was captured by the Duke of Austria, who had been on the crusade and left it because of some insult from Richard. The Duke handed his captive over to the new Emperor, Henry VI, who threatened to sell Richard to his worst enemy, the King of France. After a period of bargaining Richard paid a huge ransom, 150,000 marks of silver, which the English taxgatherers collected without difficulty. In 1199 Richard was mortally wounded while besieging the castle of one of his French vassals.

The Rise of the French Monarchy

At the beginning of the twelfth century France, Germany and Italy were only geographical expressions, describing territories whose boundaries were often impossible to define. The languages spoken by their inhabitants were recognisably similar to modern French, German, and Italian, but showed so many local dialectical differences that a German from the south would find difficulty in understanding one from the north; a Neapolitan would regard a Venetian as a foreigner; and a vassal of the Count of Provence would be almost unintelligble to a Parisian. In the south of France a whole region was called Languedoc because in the tongue (*langue*) of its people *oui* (yes) was pronounced *oc*.

Fortunately French, German and Italian flourished as spoken languages for centuries before they were adopted by literary men, who, with their passion for grammatical forms and precise definitions, tend to inhibit the vigorous growth of a living tongue. Nor was Latin at this time 'dead'—it was in constant use as a lingua franca for clergy, lawyers, diplomatists and scholars throughout Europe. At the universities of Paris and Bologna the study of the Emperor Justinian's *Digest* of Roman law was revived and its adaptation for contemporary purposes gave new life to its ancient virtues of brevity and precision.

The kingdom of France, compared with the vast territories where French was spoken, consisted of a comparatively small area lying between Paris, its capital on the Seine, and Orleans on the Loire. Even the lower part of the Seine lay outside the king's control, for in 1106 the dukedom of Normandy was rejoined to the kingdom of England following the battle of Tenchebrai, where William the Conqueror's eldest son Robert, who had inherited the duchy, was defeated and captured by his brother Henry, who, after the mysterious death of William II in the hunting field, had seized the English crown.

Two years after Tenchebrai Louis VI inherited the French kingdom and reigned for twenty-nine years. It was not until his last years that disease made him so enormously fat that he could not ride; for most of his life he travelled ceaselessly, exercising his rights as feudal overlord not only in lands inherited from the founder of his dynasty, Hugh Capet, King of the Franks from 987 to 996, but also in the dukedoms and counties where the heads of noble families had previously ruled as virtually independent princes. If anywhere in the king's dominions an abbot or bishop died, Louis relied on his friends to inform him and rode out at once to be present at the election of a successor, hoping to ensure by his presence that the choice fell on an efficient and loyal ally. If he were to miss two consecutive elections, he would forfeit the right to be consulted on subsequent occasions, since 'twice made a custom'. It was also necessary to protect those who had been duly elected. The Bishop of Clermont, for example, was twice expelled by the Count of Auvergne, and in 1122, Louis went with his feudal levies to restore him and punish the count.

In 1124 Louis reaped the reward of sixteen years' hard work. The German Emperor, Henry V, entered eastern France at the head of an army. He had married Matilda, daughter of the King of England, and with her father's aid, hoped to extend his control over the Netherlands where cloth-weaving towns provided a valuable market both for English wool and for German goods shipped down the Rhine. To meet this threat Louis called out the whole feudal might of France. From the north and west came the Counts of Flanders and Brittany, from the south the Dukes of Burgundy and Aquitaine, each with his own army. The emperor's forces, hearing of this unprecedented response, lost their appetite for battle and melted away. There was no fighting and Henry V returned to Germany, where he died the following year.

With the intention of uniting northern with southern France Louis arranged for his son, the future Louis VII, to marry Eleanor, the fifteen-year old heiress to the great duchy of Aquitaine, and on his death in 1137 the pair became King and Queen of France. In 1147 they went on crusade together, but by 1152 had become so much estranged that

Louis had the marriage annulled on grounds of consanguinity. Within two months Eleanor had married Henry of Anjou, a man eleven years younger than herself who two years later became Henry II of England. Henry was, like Louis VI, a man of immense energy and intellectual power under whom the administration of justice and the collection of revenue were organised with unprecedented efficiency throughout his dominions. These, combined with those of Eleanor, stretched from the southern border of Scotland to the Pyrenees and, if they had remained united, might have linked England permanently with western France. Eleanor, however, reputed the most beautiful woman in Europe, was no more faithful to her second husband than to her first. She stirred up her sons Richard and John to rebel against their father and as a punishment Henry kept her in confinement from 1173 until his death in 1189. She was then sixty-seven and, being released by Richard, was given power to act for him during his absence on crusade. When John succeeded Richard in 1199, Eleanor gave him vigorous aid in fighting for his rights in Anjou. She died in 1204, aged eighty-two.

Not a little of the French monarchy's strength came from the longevity of her kings. Louis VII reigned for forty-three years, much more than the average life span of his day, and his only son by his second marriage, Philip II, whose ability earned the name of Augustus, reigned for an equal period (1180-1223). His birth caused great rejoicings in Paris, the news coming at night and the people pouring into the streets with torches. A student, Gerald of Wales, saw two old hags dancing and, on asking them the reason for their joy, was told that an heir to the kingdom had been born who would be a man of great might and cause dishonour, defeat and shame to the English king. Gerald, who later became a famous chronicler, may have seen the beginnings of French nationalism. Certainly the main aim of Philip's policy was the expulsion of the English from France, an object he pursued all his life, claiming that the English kings should pay him homage for their French lands, but relying upon hatred of England to inspire his troops when a resort to arms was necessary.

The Career of the Emperor Frederick Barbarossa

The German-speaking peoples had no more sense of political unity in 1100 than those who spoke French, but by 1200 the prospect of an enduring German kingdom seemed by no means impossible, provided that the feudal princes could be subordinated to one ruler. The title assumed by Charlemagne in 800 had remained in theory elective, though the emperors of the eleventh century had all been chosen from the family of the dukes of Saxony. Henry IV (1056-1106), the emperor who submitted to Pope Gregory VII, was succeeded by the last of the Saxon dukes, Henry V, who died childless in 1125. This gave the princes an opportunity to choose a neutral candidate, Frederick, the twenty-five year old grandson of Henry V's sister Agnes, who had made two important marriages, the first to Frederick's grandfather, the Duke of Swabia, and the second to Leopold of Babenberg, Margrave of Austria, The Margrave's son by her, Conrad III, reigned as King of Germany (1138-1152) but was never crowned emperor. Frederick was elected as his successor by the princes of Germany assembled at Frankfurt-am-Main. From there he took ship down the Rhine and, after landing at Sinzig, rode to Aachen,

The Emperor Frederick Barbarossa and his sons, from an illuminated MS

Charlemagne's capital, where he was crowned king. His gracious manners, tall figure, handsome features and red-gold beard (*barbarossa*) made a very favourable impression.

On the day after his coronation Frederick proposed a military expedition to Italy, his aim being an empire astride the Alps in which he, as the supreme monarch, should dispense justice among the kings, princes and city republics of Christendom. He found that the nobility of Germany regarded his schemes as risky and expensive, and the condition of Italy gave them every justification. The pope was virtually a prisoner of the Roman mob, which, stirred up by an orator of great power, Arnold of Brescia, was demanding the confiscation of the estates and palaces of the higher clergy. In the south both the mainland and Sicily had been ruled for over twenty years by a Norman king, Roger II, whose court at Palermo had attracted scholars and artists from far and wide. With ruthless skill he had forced Arabs, Jews, and Christians of both the Roman and the Greek allegiance to live together peacably, and so had built up one of the wealthiest states in Europe. In the centre and north the rivalries of towns, each a jealous guardian of its liberties and trading priviliges, kept the country in a turmoil—Bologna fighting Modena, Mantua with Verona, Brescia with Cremona, and Milan, the most powerful of all, against every neighbour.

After two years of argument and delay Frederick entered Italy by the Brenner pass in 1154. In that year a new pope was elected, Hadrian IV, by birth Nicholas Breakspear, an Englishman of humble origin who by his skill as a diplomatist won what no other man of his race achieved, the triple crown. Being a foreigner he was even more unpopular with the Roman mob than his predecessor, and so was willing to seek Frederick's aid. Their meeting near Viterbo symbolised for the spectators the lack of confidence between them. Frederick refused to dismount and lead the pope's horse through the crowds, a traditional courtesy which might have been interpreted as a sign that, like his predecessors, he regarded himself as the pope's vassal. Hadrian, suspicious of Frederick's motives, refused him the customary kiss of peace. After some discussion they were reconciled and entered Rome, where they found the hostility of the people made it necessary to hold the coronation in semi-secrecy on a Saturday morning. When the Romans found that they had been cheated, they began invading the part of the city where Hadrian was staying. Frederick was banqueting in camp outside the walls, but immediately ordered his men to stop the riot, which they did by massacring some 3,000 people. Arnold of Brescia was captured and executed. Frederick was bitterly aware that he must return to Germany, but did not abandon his ambition to be master of Italy.

In 1159 he was engaged in an inter-city war in Lombardy when news came that Hadrian IV was dead. At the ensuing election of a new pope, Frederick's representatives voted for Victor III and the opposition for Alexander IV. To decide which pope had been rightfully elected, Frederick called together a Council of the Church at Pavia. It was not well attended. Pope Alexander and his supporters refused to appear on the ground that not even the emperor was entitled to sit in judgement on papal elections, and so Frederick declared for Victor. Alexander then excommunicated the emperor and not only stirred up opposition against him and Victor all over Christendom, but encouraged Milan, the most formidable walled city in the north, to continue its resistance. This was not the first time that the city had opposed the emperor. Bernard of Clairvaux and three Cistercian abbots pleaded in vain with Frederick to be merciful, for in Germany he was the special protector of their order. After a siege of nearly two years the Milanese, to avoid death by starvation, surrendered. Frederick expelled every inhabitant, and forced them to live in four separate camps while the entire town with all its workshops, houses, churches and fortifications was razed to the ground. Rainald, Archbishop of Cologne and Frederick's chief minister, carried off the bones of the Three Wise Men, Milan's most sacred relics, and enshrined them in his own cathedral. Contumaciousness in a feudal vassal was something Frederick could understand, but in a body of shop-keepers and tradesmen it appeared destructive of what he regarded as the natural order. His sense of history was highly selective. It suited his policy to revive the glories of the Roman empire, but the argument of the Milanese that their city had enjoyed uninter-rupted command over river, road and plain since before the days of Julius Caesar counted for nothing.

The other Lombard cities gave the emperor's officials the taxes and obedience that they demanded, and waited for an opportunity to combine against him. This occurred in 1167 after Frederick had fought yet another unsuccessful campaign in central Italy, where his army was decimated by malaria and Rainald was among the dead. The survivors, led by the emperor, escaped across the Mont Cenis pass, and the Lombard cities, forgetting their quarrels, formed a league and began rebuilding Milan. When the emperor returned, the Milanese met him in a pitched battle at Legnano on 29 May 1176. As a rallying point for their infantry they took into the fight a huge caroccio, or waggon, from which rose a cross and a flag embroidered with the picture of St Ambrose. The hedge of spears round these emblems resisted the German cavalry, and the emperor was unhorsed. In the ensuing panic the Germans were scattered by Lombard cavalry and lost all their loot. Frederick remained in hiding for some days. When he emerged he made peace with Alexander IV and in July 1177 went to meet him in Venice. When he prostrated himself at Alexander's feet in the porch of St Mark's, both men were in tears. Alexander raised the emperor to his feet and gave him the kiss of peace, after which they entered the cathedral together.

On returning to Germany Frederick showed that his desire for peace in Italy, however sincere, meant no change of heart. Among the German princes Henry the Lion, Duke of Saxony, had refused to join Frederick in Lombardy; he had successfully suppressed Slav piracy in the Baltic and encouraged Germans to set up trading stations in Prussia and Russia; in 1160 he had deprived the Count of Holstein of the newly founded town of Lübeck; and in Bavaria he had built a bridge over the swift-flowing Isar and established Munich as a fortress town to guard it. Such achievements did not prevent condemnation by the imperial courts that Frederick called to sit in judgement on him. He was deprived of all his dominions, except those he had inherited from his family, and sent into exile. He took refuge with Henry II of England, whose daughter he had married.

During the 1180s Frederick was again active in Italy, seeking to gain by diplomacy what he had failed to win by force. In 1186 he crowned his son Henry King of Italy and married him to Constance, the elderly heiress to the crown of Sicily, at Milan. Against the revived danger of German domination the papacy could do little, since in these years there was a swift succession of short-lived pontiffs, four in ten years. The last of these, Clement III, persuaded Frederick to go on the crusade from which he never returned. Perhaps his restless spirit was disturbed by the thought that his Holy Roman Empire had brought death to so many and he meant, as other crusaders before him, to atone for past cruelties. His policies in peace and war, by seeking to subordinate the lesser powers of Italy and Germany, had greatly increased those centrifugal tendencies so much deplored by historian of the nineteenth and twentieth centuries, who took it for granted that no sensible German or Italian would wish to live except under a single government with authority over all his compatriots. In fact the multitude of small, virtually independent, states in which Germans and Italians sought refuge from foreign interference attained the highest possible variety of achievement in politics, commerce, art and science.

Centuries afterwards a legend grew up that Frederick Barbarossa was not dead, but sleeping in a cave in the Kyffhauser mountain, which rises sharply from the Thuringian plain near the banks of the river Unstrut. After the reunification of Germany by Prussia in 1871 an enormous monument was erected on the peak, showing William, King of Prussia, and first Emperor of the Second Reich, on horseback as if about to leap into the sky. Below him a huge image of the sleeping Frederick was carved into the rock face of a cavern. Such are the fantasies engendered by modern purveyors of perverted patriotism.

CHAPTER FIVE

The Thirteenth Century

Pope Innocent III and Francis of Assisi

Few small events have had more momentous consequences than the visit of Francis of Assisi to Rome in 1210. He was the son of a cloth merchant, twenty-eight years old, who wished Pope Innocent III to sanction a new religious order for which he had won twelve recruits. Innocent, who as a young man had studied in Bologna and Paris, was related to several of the most noble Roman families and had been elected almost unanimously at the age of thirty-eight. After twelve years in office he had made his power felt all over Christendom. Like many intellectuals he avoided mixing with men outside his own walk of life, preferring to devote all possible hours to desk work, developing the bureaucratic influence which the papacy already had over every branch of ecclesiastical life. Many volumes of his letters and official pronouncements have survived, for he corresponded ceaselessly on matters great and small, now writing to some distant bishop on a minor legal problem, then turning to the tangled quarrels of two rival emperors in Germany, or of Philip II of France with his Danish wife, and to the long, violent opposition of King John of England to the papal choice of an Archbishop of Canterbury. Most unwisely he seldom met the protagonists in such affairs, preferring to judge everything from words on paper, and failing to realise that few kings or princes could survive without deceiving their enemies or breaking promises made under duress. To him matters of heredity, manners, physical prowess and natural aptitude meant little. Everything must be subordinated to his lofty conception of an office which could not without cowardice ignore that vast field of temporal affairs where moral values were endangered by the unruly desires of sinful men. It was, he believed, his responsibility first patiently to weigh the likely consequences of this policy or that, and, having decided on a course of action, to pursue it to the end, no matter how much suffering might result.

Francis was received by Cardinal Hugolini, to whom he told his story. At the age of twenty he had been captured fighting for Assisi against Perugia, both hill-top towns in the mountains of north-central Italy, and confined for a year. On returning home he had been ill and deeply disturbed in spirit. A voice heard in a trance told him to rebuild a ruined chapel dedicated to St Pietro Damiani, an eleventh century reformer. He obeyed this command, left home and lived as a hermit begging for alms. On a visit to Rome he changed clothes with a beggar and together with other mendicants sat at the porch of St Peter's. In a small church in Assisi, the Portiuncula, he again heard a voice commanding him in the words of Matthew's Gospel: 'Preach, saying the Kingdom of Heaven is at hand . . . Get you no gold or silver, no brass in your purses, nor scrip for your journey . . . for the workman is worthy of his meat.' This was to be the rule of life for himself and his disciples. Could he have the verbal approval of the pope?

The cardinal was aware that on all sides the Church was being criticised for its misuse of money, lands and possessions, but few critics showed the Christ-like humility of this man or the desire to obey implicitly. Nervously he asked his guest to address the other cardinals. Instead, Francis, full of joy, danced a jig and carried all before him. His brotherhood was approved, and began to multiply rapidly. Some authentic details about his personality and methods, mixed with a great quantity of legend, were preserved. One witness says that he did not have the manner of a preacher, but relied on conversation and a kind of play-acting. He suffered much ill-health, yet travelled ceaselessly. In 1219 he visited the crusaders at Damietta in Egypt, and from there gained an audience with their enemy, the Sultan of Egypt, who, half convinced by his arguments, gave him permission to visit the holy places, which owing to sickness he was unable to do.

Innocent III had died in 1216 and serious troubles had developed among the brethren or friars, as they came to be known. Many of them wished to adopt a more elaborate rule; to establish proper headquarters in the various towns to which the order had spread; and to recruit students. Francis considered the strength of his order was the ability of its preachers to speak to the poor in their own idiom. He was suspicious of academic education and the barriers it erected between the educated and the ignorant. Having stepped out of his own wealthy merchant class and mixed freely both with princes and beggars, he, like all men of genius, was not conscious that it was the quality of his mind and spirit, not his deeds, that made him welcome everywhere. He was persuaded to allow the Franciscans to modify their rule, and, aware that his gifts were not those of an administrator, resigned the office of Superior.

The death of Francis in 1226 at the early age of forty-four caused an outburst of sympathy and admiration all over Europe, not only for the brothers but for the sister order founded by Clare. Hugolini, now Pope Gregory IX, not only canonised them both but started to build a magnificent church in the centre of Assisi. In one of the frescoes painted on its walls Giotto (1266-1336) shows Clare and her companions coming out from San Damiano all in tears to kiss the body of Francis, as it is carried to the grave. With an artist's liberty he has made the chapel a rich church built of precious marbles On this a nineteenth century biographer, Paul Sabatier, remarked: 'Happily the real San Damiano is still there, nestling under some olive-trees like a lark under the heather; it still has its ill-made walls of irregular stones, like those which bound the neighbouring fields. Which is the more beautiful, the ideal temple of the artist's fancy, or the poor chapel of reality? No heart will be in doubt.'

The Tartar Invasion of Russia

In 1200 the Russians inhabited an area stretching from eastern Hungary to the Urals, the southern limit of their lands being the edge of the forest and the beginning of the steppe. The Great Princes of Kiev had not for half a century exercised any far-reaching authority along the great trade route from the Baltic to the Black Sea, and the Russians were ruled by a number of warring princes whose territories were liable to attack in the west from Swedes and Prussians and in the east from nomadic tribesmen.

An event in north China led to the last and worst of these invasions from Asia—the capture of Peking by the Mongols, or Tartars, as the Russians called them, meaning the subjects of Jengis Khan. The Great Khan, whose capital, Karakorum, lay 500 miles north-east of Peking, had united various and mutually hostile tribes in Mongolia, who earned their livelihood as pastoralists on the great plains, and recruited from among them a huge army of mounted archers. In 1215 they not only captured the capital of the Chinese empire, but, perhaps to their own astonishment, found its wealthy, civilised but supine peoples would out of terror obey them in everything.

Six years after this victory Jengis Khan sent an army eastwards to reconnoitre for an invasion of Russia. They defeated the forces sent against them in the south and returned. Before any further attack could be mounted, Jengis Khan died and in the confusion that followed his vast empire split into four parts, Mongolia, which became linked to China, where the khan's descendants were known as the Yuan dynasty; Turkestan; Persia; and the lands of the Golden Horde, which lay between Lake Balkhash and the mouth of the Volga.

The invasion of Russia began in 1237. Batu, the leader of the Golden Horde, advanced as soon as frost and snow had made the ground easy for travel, the intense cold having no terrors for these men from the Asian plateau. They chose for their attack the forest area on the middle Volga, where the Russians least expected them. Moving swiftly from town to town the Tartars burnt every house and killed or enslaved the inhabitants. After penetrating as far as Moscow, where the survivors afterwards reported finding 24,000 corpses, they attempted to take the most important place in the north, Novgorod, but the spring thaw of 1238 came in time to save it, turning the trackways—they could not be called roads—into rivers of mud and the rivers into torrents filled with broken ice. Batu retreated to the steppe to enjoy the summer and count his loot, then descended next winter on Rostov-on-Don, terrorising the countryside as before and, marching westwards by way of Kiev into the Danube valley, did vast damage in Hungary, Bohemia and Moravia.

The Russian princes, to avoid further massacres, met the leaders of the Golden Horde, acknowledged them as overlords and agreed to pay tribute. In 1252 the Prince of Vladimir refused to make the customary visit to the khan in his capital at Saray near the mouth of the Volga. As a punishment his lands were devastated once again.

This vassaldom had its most lasting effect upon the poorest people in Russia, the peasants. In one sense they were never conquered; with incredible patience they surmounted every hardship, labouring to satisfy not only their own landowners but to provide the goods required as tribute by the Tartars, but they learned to regard all foreigners with suspicion and fear. With ample reason they eyed every stranger in their villages as either a potential tax collector or a spy preparing some fresh invasion. For centuries after they had won their freedom from the Mongols this mentality persisted and still colours the outlook even of highly placed government officials.

Gregory IX and the Dominican Order

Among those massacred by the Tartars in 1239 were ninety friars of the Dominican order who were working in Hungary. This remarkable brotherhood had only been in existence for twenty-three years and yet its missions had reached almost every country in Europe. Its founder, Dominic, who was born in Caleruega in Spain about 1172, became a monk and with his bishop had gone to Languedoc to preach to the Cathari heretics. He travelled from place to place barefoot and clothed only in a rough garment, for he wished to convert people who were in love with poverty. The Cathari (Pure Ones) sought after holiness by attempting to dispense entirely with the material side of life; the most extreme among them even despised marriage because it perpetuated life on earth, and refused to eat flesh, eggs or cheese. This cult found many followers in Italy as well as southern France. Its madness seemed so dangerous that Innocent III decided that in France it must be suppressed by force. The Albigensian crusade, as it was called, was initiated at Lyons in 1209. It attracted adventurers of all kinds eager to plunder one of the richest provinces of France. Terrible atrocities were committed, and it was probably the sight of these that led Dominic to divert his small band of preachers to Paris and Bologna, seeking adherents among the students at the two most famous universities in Europe.

When he arrived in Rome to seek the pope's approval for his brotherhood, he was received by the same cardinal who had befriended Francis of Assisi. Innocent III was not convinced that he should give this new order of preachers official approval, but in 1216 his successor, Honorius III, did so. When Dominic died five years later, his followers had already established sixty houses, distributed through France, England, Spain, Germany and Italy. Yet their founder's character remains obscure. His first biographer, Jordan of Saxony, seems deliberately to have omitted personal details of the kind that made Francis so famous. Jordan became head of the order and imparted to its international network of 'chapters', or committees, an efficiency that was universally admired. Perhaps Dominic's power lay in his self-effacement.

Hugolini, after he became pope, canonised Dominic, as he had done Francis and encouraged both orders to take on many new responsibilities. While not neglecting their original work of caring for the poor, they entered the world of learning with such zeal that they were soon renowned throughout Europe for their new and original thinking. Thomas Aquinas (1227-1274), the son of a noble family in southern Italy, after being educated as a boy at Monte Cassino and Frederick II's *studium* in Naples, was trained by Dominicans in Paris and Cologne, where he became a pupil of Albertus Magnus, a German Dominican famous for his great learning. Thomas in his vast work, *Summa Theologiae*, distinguishes between knowledge derived from the Bible and Church doctrine, which he describes as truth by revelation, and truth based on reason, in which he included the learning of ancient Greek and Roman writers, among whom he especially admired Aristotle. His range of interests was immense; on the most debated question of his day, when kings and emperors were beginning to claim divine right for actions of distinctly doubtful morality, he boldly confirmed Aristotle's view that mixed constitutions were best, with elements of monarchy, aristocracy and democracy combined. The object of government should, he said, be the common good; if laws were made for the private good of the ruler, they were unjust and perverse. So powerful an intellect was a valuable ally to a Church hotly criticised, and Thomas's influence was enduring, his work being chosen during the Counter-Reformation as the basis of training in Catholic seminaries, where it is still studied with enthusiasm.

Louis IX and the Development of Gothic Architecture

News reached Paris in 1238 that one of the most precious relics found by the Crusaders, the Crown of Thorns worn by Christ at his crucifixion, was in Constantinople and had been pledged to a Venetian merchant in settlement of a debt. King Louis IX of France at once sent out a knight and a party of friars to buy it and bring it home. When on their way back the friars reached Troyes, Louis and his brother, Robert of Artois, set out to meet them, and, walking barefoot through the streets carrying the Crown, they placed it in the cathedral of Sens to await transport by river to Paris. In the next few years the king also obtained the True Cross and its superscription, the Holy Lance and Sponge and fragments of stone from the Holy Sepulchre. The Sainte-Chapelle was then planned as a reliquary in stone, a work of art worthy of these sacred treasures. For architect, Louis chose Pierre de Montreuil. His design was quite small, the floor space inside being only 33 metres by 10.7 metres but very tall, over 42 metres. This height, with the delicate spire above, makes the chapel one of the chief glories of the new Gothic architecture which was then beginning to replace Romanesque. The weight of the steep roof is supported by beautifully proportioned buttresses, leaving the walls as little more than screens to hold in position the tall, spacious windows for which artists painted on glass over a thousand pictures illustrating Bible stories and the lives of the saints. A large proportion of these have survived, and the interior, which suffered gross damage from the revolutionaries of 1792, has been beautifully restored.

While the Sainte-Chapelle was under construction the cathedral of Paris, Notre Dame, was being rebuilt in the new style, the first design, on which work began at the end of the eleventh century, being modified to let in more light. Its interior is still dark compared with later buildings in the same manner, but the splendour of the west front with its intricate sculpture, and the vastness of the interior, capable of holding thousands of worshippers on feast days, were an inspiration to devout people all over northern France.

The stonemasons of Notre Dame, who discovered how to build a structure so lofty on an island in the middle of a river, astonished all beholders. The King of England, Henry III, who was a friend of Louis, visited Paris and afterwards, in his devotion to St Edward the Confessor, began pulling down the east end of the Romanesque abbey church at Westminster in order to raise a coronation church in the new style. At Chartres, to the east of Paris, where the Romanesque cathedral was almost entirely destroyed by

Chartres cathedral, a view from the south-east

fire in 1194, the citizens had no hesitation in starting to rebuild to a plan so magnificent that by any normal calculation it was entirely beyond their means. Again the inspiration came from a relic, the tunic worn by the Virgin Mary at the birth of Christ, which had been housed in the crypt of the old cathedral and rescued during the fire by a priest. This attracted pilgrims from all over Europe and the citizens of Chartres worked so fast that the design by 'the Master of Chartres' (his name was not recorded) was completed between 1200 and 1220, apart from the transepts, which were finished by 1260. The splendid north porch with its elaborate sculptures is called 'royal' because it was the gift of Philip Augustus, Louis IX and his mother Blanche of Castile. The windows, taller and wider than in any previous church, still display the painted glass placed in them by the artists of the thirteenth century and, since the church is set on the pinnacle of a solitary hill rising from the rolling wheat lands of Beauce, they catch the light and shade of sun and cloud, and cast within all those transient colours that in Shelley's phrase 'stain the white radiance of eternity'.

At Amiens the stories from scripture illustrated in the sculpture of the western porches inspired the English writer John Ruskin to write *The Bible of Amiens*, a work translated into French by Marcel Proust. Other builders in northern France soon caught the passion for size and height and at Beauvais, where they intended the cathedral to be taller and more splendid than all its sister churches, only the choir and transepts were ever completed.

Outside France the Gothic style was adopted for new cathedrals and churches in

73

(above) '*My days are swifter than a weaver's shuttle*' (*Job 7, 6*). *A weaver at work, 13th century stained glass in Chartres cathedral*

(left) *Amiens cathedral, begun in 1220 and completed in 1269. In the middle ages Amiens, on the south bank of the Somme, was a rich wool manufacturing town*

(lower left) *Beauvais cathedral choir, begun in 1227. The builders were determined to make it the highest and most spacious building of the age. The vaulting of the east end, 47m high, twice collapsed before completion. The building of a nave proved to be beyond the resources of the region*

Cologne, Strasbourg, Burgos and many other places. In Cologne the building planned was so vast that it was not completed until the nineteenth century. At Strasbourg the masons strove to make twin spires that should be the tallest in Europe, but only one proved possible. In Burgos King Ferdinand III (1217-1252) gave his architects a wonderful site on the steep slope below the castle hill. The design owed much to France and one of the architects was probably a Frenchman, but the exuberant Spanish masons decorated the exterior with carving even more intricate than that of the earlier cathedrals of the north.

The source of the enthusiasm filling both king and peasant and driving people of every class to build so magnificently at a time when the friars were winning widespread acclaim for their devotion to a life of poverty is not immediately obvious. Yet it sprang from their preaching; since few could read or write, and manuscripts were too costly for any but the rich, they first retold the gospels, including Christ's parables and miracles, and did so with a new simplicity allied to the old rhetorical skill handed down by the monastery schools. This Biblical material became familiar to all, and when occasionally a traveller returning from the east was able to describe what he had heard and seen at the Holy Places, popular imagination, raised to feverish intensity, was prepared to accept that such objects as the Crown of Thorns could still exist. Few were able to grasp what effect natural decay and the chances and changes of twelve hundred years must have had on textiles or wood, and so the ready salesmanship of Levantine merchants had little difficulty in providing, at small cost to themselves, alleged relics in ample quantities. Louis IX, a crusader whose open, sunny nature, noble generosity and love of justice prevented him from deceiving even his enemies, was only one of countless men and women to be duped in this way. On the other hand it is plain that faith in a religion firmly based on historical events should not be derided because the unscrupulous took advantage of it. In spite of a certain misplaced credulity the people of the thirteenth century laid as solid a foundation for modern science as they did for their own lovely temples.

The Emperor Frederick II and the Downfall of the Hohenstaufen

Frederick II, a grandson of Frederick Barbarossa, was an orphan at the age of four, his father, the Hohenstaufen Emperor Henry VI, having died in 1197 and his mother, the Empress Constance a year later. He was brought up in Palermo, the capital of the Norman kings of Sicily to whom he was related. A long dispute between Frederick's uncle, Philip of Swabia, and Otto of Brunswick, each of whom claimed to have been duly elected emperor was not ended until Frederick, at the age of nineteen, was crowned in Mainz. He was a youth whose intellectual powers astonished all his contemporaries, a linguist able to speak at least six languages, including Arabic; intensely interested in religion without being in the least devout; a learned writer on the noble art of falconry; and entirely lacking in common sense, the most valuable of all political gifts. In the manner of his Moslem subjects he kept a harem and later sought to advance his illegitimate sons equally with those born in wedlock. His first aim was to strengthen his hold on Sicily and southern Italy. He transferred the Arabs from Sicily to the mainland, where, being given freedom to practise their religion, they were consistently loyal and, to the disgust of his enemies, supplied him with excellent archers.

In matters of little consequence he was an actor who loved to dazzle and amuse his audience, travelling from place to place accompanied by camels, elephants and pet monkeys and delighting in the society of scholars from all over Europe and the Levant. On the other hand in important points of policy he showed an inflexible will to persist where previous emperors had failed, namely in subordinating Italy and Germany to one government. To win over the German princes he gave away powers which he could not exercise, and so increased their independence, but all his hopes of mastery in central and northern Italy were wrecked by the remorseless opposition of Gregory IX, who showed in his dealings with the young emperor a hot-tempered vindictiveness which contrasted strangely with his loving kindness to the friars. Frederick before his accession had vowed to go on crusade, but put off doing so, and for this the pope excommunicated him. When eventually he did arrive in Egypt (1228), he argued so forcibly with the Sultan that the Moslems handed over the Holy Places and Jerusalem on the sole condition that they should not be molested there. This proviso so offended the other crusaders, and especially the fanatical Templars and Hospitallers, that Frederick, bitterly disappointed, returned home.

His quarrel with the papacy continued, for Gregory, who seemed almost immortal, did not die until 1241, and, after the short reign of Pope Celestine, Innocent IV proved an enemy at least as formidable as Gregory, outliving the emperor, who died in 1250, and so damaging the Hohenstaufen that they never recovered. He believed that, if this 'brood of vipers', as he called them, succeeded in establishing themselves as the supreme authority throughout the empire and the Italian kingdom, the popes would lose not only their lands and wealth but their independence. Innocent, like Gregory, fulminated against Frederick's pretensions and split every town in Italy into two factions, one supporting the papacy, known as Guelf, and the other, fighting for the Hohenstaufen, called Ghibelline. The war of pamphlets between the two sides became a major scandal.

Half a century later Alighieri Dante (1265-1321), who had been a pamphleteer for the imperial cause, in composing *La Divina Commedia*, placed Frederick in *Inferno*, giving him a literary immortality that he scarcely deserved, for the atrocities he committed were not unusual in Italian warfare. Perhaps Frederick would have escaped such condemnation if he had learned, in dealing with a race of irrepressible talkers, to keep a still tongue. Some of his remarks, uttered under extreme provocation, were interpreted and repeated as outrageous blasphemies. The contrast between the worst and the best in human nature, demonstrated so vividly in the thirteenth century is nowhere better exemplified than in another part of Dante's epic, where with marvellous insight he writes of *L'amor che muove il sole e l'altre stelle* (The love that moves the sun and the other stars).

The Sicilian Vespers

On Easter Monday, 1282, a French soldier in Palermo insulted a young married woman on her way to vespers at the church of Santo Spirito. He was a member of a hated army that Charles of Anjou, at the pope's command, had brought to Palermo sixteen years earlier to deprive Frederick II's illegitimate son Manfred of the throne of Sicily. In this Charles succeeded, but French tax collectors made themselves detested and this chance encounter led to a riot and a massacre in which over 3,000 French perished. For the next twenty years the Sicilians fought for their independence, holding out against all the forces sent to subdue them. They called to their aid the King of Aragon, James II, who made himself popular by his just rule, granting a constitution and a parliament to the islanders. So began an alliance between Spain and Sicily which gave no offence to the Italians and provided a much stronger defence against invasion than the Germans could ever do.

The Hanseatic League

No commerce can be successfully conducted without mutual confidence between buyer and seller and the strict observance of the rule that when a man gives his word it will be honoured without reference to a written bond. Discretion also demands a certain degree of secrecy, and for this reason the early history of that society of merchants and city corporations called the Hanseatic League is not easily unravelled. Its founding members did not at the time wish their operations to be too well known, since they were creating a trade empire of a new sort and might arouse the jealousy of governments. Consequently even in the Middle Ages the meaning of the word Hansa was disputed. The first open declaration of its existence came in 1230, when the townsmen of Hamburg informed those of Lübeck that they were granting their merchants equal rights. In 1241 they concluded a formal treaty agreeing to police the roads across the isthmus along which goods were carried to avoid the long and difficult voyage through the

Walls of Visby, the Hansa town on the Baltic island of Gotland

Sound between Denmark, Norway and Sweden. Many fishing fleets working in these waters sent their catches to Lübeck for salting and distribution inland. Hamburg, like a number of other places, was a 'double town', the oldest part having grown up round the cathedral, while in 1188 the Count of Holstein had established a merchant town nearby. The two parts amalgamated in 1215. Brunswick, the largest town in Lower Saxony, had several sections, the ducal castle on the left bank of the river and the old merchant town on the right, each with later 'suburbs'.

The League soon after its foundation benefited from two successes in the east. Albert, Archbishop of Bremen, created a new military order, the Brethren of the Sword, to subdue the warlike pagans of Lithuania. in 1202 he founded Riga, settled German traders there and introduced the code of law in force at the Scandinavian trading station at Visby in the island of Gotland. Germans and Scandinavians were making Visby a place of great importance, which later had a ring wall 4 kilometres long enclosing the merchants' houses and their eighteen churches.

The second advance occurred when Hermann von Salza, Grand Master of the Teutonic Order, a brotherhood of Crusaders, undertook, with the authority of the pope and emperor, the conquest of East Prussia, a pagan land lying between the rivers Vistula and Pregel. He succeeded in only five years, and consolidated his gains by building castles and fortified towns, laid out with great precision, their streets being on a grid pattern. In 1237 Hermann absorbed the Brethren of the Sword into his order and all was going well when the knights, attempting to colonise still further to the east, encountered an army under the Russian Prince Alexander of Novgorod. Trapped on the frozen Lake Peipus the Germans suffered heavy loss. Two years earlier the same prince had repulsed an attempted Swedish invasion across the river Neva, for which he was given the name Nevsky and later canonised.

The merchants of the Hanseatic League supported both the Archbishop of Bremen and the Teutonic Knights, supplying them with ships and food, but they did not allow military reverses to interrupt their trade. They had been established in Novgorod for ten years, and found that the Russians, though possessing a monopoly of the fur trade with the forest dwellers of the north, were not interested in travelling abroad themselves, gladly selling to the Hansa and letting them take the pelts to the west. The Tartars, hearing of this valuable commerce, forced Prince Alexander to pay them tribute.

Westwards the League was equally successful. The King of England granted the Hansa a trading station on the Thames close to London Bridge. This was called the Steelyard and to govern it the Germans appointed an alderman who arranged that they should help to mount guard at Bishopsgate. In Bruges, a port where men of all nations went on business, two streets were named after those from Lübeck and Hamburg. Here the Countess of Flanders bestowed special privileges similar to those enjoyed in London. In 1280, however, the Flemish began to whittle these away and the League decided to employ a new device to protect themselves. They transferred their organisation to Aardenburg. The loss to Bruges was so considerable that after two years of negotiating the Flemish arranged for the Hansa to return on favourable terms. At about the same time the Norwegians also began to curb the activities of the League in Bergen, and

Marienburg, now Malbrok, the principal fortress of the grand masters of the Order of Teutonic Knights, 70km south of Gdansk. The river Nogat, a branch of the Vistula, protects the walls on the west

as a counter-move a blockade was started which prevented German grain, flour and beer from reaching Norway. This operation induced the Norwegians to agree in 1294 to a treaty which allowed the Hansa to trade freely as far north as Bergen, but no further.

To settle a dispute in this way without recourse to fighting the Hansa called not for personal but civic courage based on the habit of obedience to higher authority, a national trait often noted since. The people of Bremen, who would have suffered most from loss of Norwegian trade, refused to join in the blockade, and in 1275 were expelled from the League. Clearly such associations depend not only on obedience but on self-sacrifice, and the success of the Hansa in spite of the defection of Bremen made a deep impression throughout Europe.

The Reconquest of Spain and Portugal

The boundary between the Christian and Moslem princedoms in Portugal and Spain in 1220 ran along the Tagus in the west, across the central mountains north of Granada, and then north to the frontier of Aragon. Valencia was still in Moslem hands, but by the end of the century all this was changed. Divisions and quarrels among the Moors gave the Christians an opportunity to expand. From Castile Ferdinand III (1217-1252) advanced to Cordova, which he captured in 1236, and then to Seville and Cadiz, which were his by 1248. The Moorish kings of Granada and Murcia became his vassals. In the same period James I of Aragon attacked the Moorish pirates in the Balearic islands, which he colonised with Catalans, and in 1238 captured Valencia.

The Moslem peasants in these reconquered territories were not expelled, but lived in peace and prosperity under their new masters. The Moorish and Jewish culture of

79

Interior of the Alcazar, Seville, a palace erected in the 14th century for the Christian King of Castile, Pedro the Cruel, by Moorish craftsmen from Granada. Here the marriage of the Emperor Charles V was celebrated

the south was respected by Ferdinand's son, Alfonso X (1252-1284), called the 'Learned', who employed lawyers to compose a comprehensive summary of Spanish Law. Underlying this was an assumption that the king's power should be absolute and this made the monarchy unpopular with the unruly nobility of Spain, yet kingship eventually proved to be the best means of holding together a country where provincial customs and geographical divisions delayed every attempt to achieve national unity.

The kingdom of Portugal at this time was extended to the south of the Tagus as far as the Algarve coastline. Dinis, who ascended the throne in 1279, took steps to improve agriculture and fisheries, planting forests in Leiria to hold back the coastal sand dunes, and appointing a Genoese admiral to teach his subjects better methods of shipbuilding. At Coimbra he established a university, and, being himself a poet, gave the Portuguese dialect the status of a national language. In 1289 a concordat was concluded with the Church; its existing privileges were confirmed, provided that no new estates were added to its already vast holdings. Contemporaries noted how much Dinis differed from other monarchs and awarded him the uniquely honourable title of 'the Husbandman'.

CHAPTER SIX

The Fourteenth Century

The Beginning of the Hundred Years' War

The French monarchy had become so strong in the thirteenth century that it seemed intolerable to Charles IV, who came to the throne in 1322, that the English should hold the great duchy of Aquitaine in the south-west, including the rich wine-growing district round Bordeaux. Knowing his brother-in-law, Edward II of England, to be incompetent, he invaded Aquitaine and occupied the duchy with the exception of a small coastal strip. To make peace Edward sent his beautiful wife Isabella to Paris, but she deserted him and, having scandalised the French by becoming the mistress of Roger Mortimer, Earl of March, she moved with her young son, the future Edward III, to the court of the Count of Flanders and betrothed him to the count's daughter Philippa. On returning to England, she deposed her husband and had him murdered. In 1330 her son assumed power.

Two years before Charles IV had died leaving daughters and a widow who gave birth to another daughter after his death. The French therefore made Charles' cousin, Philip, Count of Valois, King with the title Philip VI, on the ground that no woman could succeed, a rule that in the circumstances suited his courtiers and was given a fabulous antiquity under the name of Salic law. The choice was not a good one, since Philip was a weak man whose head was full of the currently fashionable ideas about knightly chivalry and these were not conducive to winning wars. Yet with about 12,000,000 subjects, well-disposed relatives ruling in Naples and Hungary, and a French pope installed at Avignon, he appeared to be in a strong position to resist the English.

In 1340 the English won their first victory off the coast of Flanders. A large French fleet was trapped at Sluys in waters where it could not manoeuvre and its fighting men were shot down by English longbowmen. The longbow, a much more deadly weapon than the short bow used at the battle of Hastings (1066), had been recently developed in the Welsh and Scottish wars. It took some years for an archer to gain proficiency and a high rate of fire, but the arrows could pierce armour and inflict large wounds. The French relied on Genoese crossbowmen who needed no great skill, but had a much slower rate of fire. In 1345 the English recovered their lost lands in Aquitaine and the next year Edward III, having landed in Normandy, marched north towards Calais and successfully crossed the Somme in advance of Philip's pursuing army. At Crécy,

A crossbow. The bowstring, unlike that of a longbow, had many strands permanently in position and so was not easily protected from rain; it was winched into the firing position with the ratchet seen on the right

fighting in a prepared position, the English archers destroyed the French knights who charged recklessly on horseback. Those who escaped arrows fell before the spears of English men-at-arms who had dismounted to fight.

Edward then began a siege of Calais, which, blockaded from land and sea for nearly a year, was starved into surrender. The English weakness, one that eventually lost them the war, had been revealed. They had no artillery capable of breaching walls, but Philip was too cowardly to besiege the besiegers, and Calais became an English port for the next 300 years.

To the destruction of war was added that of disease. Bubonic plague, a fever carried by black rats and transmitted to human beings by Asiatic fleas living in their fur, reached the Crimea from Asia and infected ship rats on board Genoese galleys brought it to the Mediterranean. The first epidemic was in Provence, where the warm climate favoured the breeding of the fleas. Further outbreaks, spreading sporadically through western Europe, including Britain, caused great alarm by their sudden onset and horrifying symptoms. The poor, living in wooden huts with thatched roofs, ideal breeding grounds for black rats, suffered much more than the rich in stone houses and castles. Nobody suspected the rats and it was assumed that plague, like other fevers, spread through human contact. Townspeople wealthy enough to leave their businesses for a time could avoid infection, and the coming of winter cold, which destroyed the fleas, caused the epidemic to die out as quickly as it had come. Plague probably killed one-twentieth of the population, though the death roll was put at a much higher figure by contemporaries. When the rat population had recovered, fresh outbreaks occurred, but none were so serious as that of 1348, known as the Great Pestilence and later as the Black Death.

The state of war between England and France continued after the death of Philip and the accession of his son, John II, who shared his father's faults. Edward III's eldest son Edward, known as the Black Prince, made a raid northwards from Gascony and was trapped by John with a much larger force at Poitiers. This time the French dismounted to attack the prepared position the English had chosen, and suffered from their archers an even more severe defeat than at Crécy. King John was taken prisoner and lived in honourable confinement in England for most of the remaining eight years of his reign.

At both Crécy and Poitiers the English should have been forced by starvation to move from their positions and attacked as they retreated. The French could have won without fighting, and this lesson was learnt by a Breton general, Bertrand du Guesclin. After four years of harassment the English sued for peace, and at Brétigny near Chartres it was agreed that John's ransom should be the enormous sum of 3,000,000 gold crowns. He was released in exchange for the Duke of Anjou, who was to be held till the ransom was paid. When the duke escaped, John, with a chivalrous regard for his family honour, insisted on returning to captivity, where he remained until his death in 1360. The English retained Aquitaine in full sovereignty and their soldiers, instead of going home, formed 'free companies' that roamed over the countryside looting. In the north du Guesclin hunted them down, but in the south they threatened the pope in Avignon and spilled over into Italy.

John's successor, Charles V, was rightly called 'the Wise', and it was unfortunate for France that he died young. When the war was renewed in 1369 he encouraged the un-chivalrous but effective methods of du Guesclin, and in six years the English held nothing but Calais and the coast of Gascony. In 1380 Charles was succeeded by Charles VI, who was subject to recurrent periods of mental illness, but remained on the throne for forty-two years. For both contestants the war had been an unending tragedy. The fighting men on either side had no appreciation of the true source of wealth—ingenuity and hard work—they thought it enough to accumulate land and possessions, forgetting that the French peasants, seeing their crops so frequently pillaged and their houses burnt, stopped cultivating the fields and imitated their enemies by taking to armed robbery.

Denmark and the Hanseatic League
The Hanseatic League reached its greatest prosperity during the fourteenth century, but, before it could do so, had to face the opposition of Waldemar IV, King of Denmark,

The Schifferhaus, Lübeck, meeting place of the guild of mariners

who in 1360, the twentieth year of his reign, suddenly attacked and burnt the Hansa town of Visby. The other towns in the League considered this an act of war that could only be answered by a display of force.

Embassies from the League obtained promises of support from the King of Sweden, the Duke of Schleswig and the Count of Holstein. The Hansa towns on the Zuiderzee refused to join in a commercial blockade, but, as the League had readmitted Bremen two years before, the merchants were hopeful that they could humble Waldemar. A fleet of fifty-two ships under the command of the Bürgermeister of Lübeck set sail for Copenhagen. On the way he landed some of his troops for a minor shore operation, and when the Danes attacked the fleet they captured twelve large ships and put the rest to flight.

By 1367 Waldemar had added to the number of his enemies by harassing not only Hansa ships from the Zuiderzee but also Prussian vessels from towns not belonging to the League. A great diet, or conference, at Cologne which included non-Hansa towns, agreed to a war tax payable on all goods entering or leaving member ports or towns. A fleet destroyed all the installations in Copenhagen harbour, and demolished the town. With Swedish help the Danes were also driven out of southern Sweden, and in 1370 they sued for peace. Negotiations were held at Stralsund; the Germans did not demand any new privileges, but insisted that four ports from which Waldemar had attacked trade through the Sound should be handed over for fifteen years. Waldemar also agreed that on his death his successor should not be elected without Hansa assent, and so, five years later, the Danes accepted the regency of Olaf of Norway, a minor whose mother Margaret acted as regent. In return the League received confirmation of all the rights enjoyed in Norwegian ports by foreign traders before the attack on Visby. This sensible settlement, which was in strong contrast to the inability of the Kings of England and France to make a lasting peace, shows the strength that the League had acquired with comparatively little aid from kings and princes.

The Rise of Poland and Lithuania

By the beginning of the fourteenth century German power and influence, symbolised by the adoption of 'the customs of Magdeburg' in many Polish towns, appeared to have forestalled the emergence of a Polish national state. Danzig at the mouth of the Vistula was a prosperous port, but in effect a German one. In spite of this a Polish prince named Vladislav the Dwarf obtained approval from Pope John XXII for the revival of the monarchy and in 1320 was crowned in the cathedral at Cracow. To gain allies he married his son Casimir to a Lithuanian princess and his daughter to Charles Robert, the Frenchman who ruled in Hungary.

Casimir, on succeeding his father, who died at the age of seventy-three, made peace with the Teutonic Knights, with whom Vladislav had frequent wars, and, to assist the restoration of order, began the work of writing down the customs of the various Polish provinces, harmonising them with royal decrees, and issuing them as one comprehensive statute. To provide lawyers and judges trained in the methods of Paris and Bologna he founded a university in the royal city of Cracow. When his long reign (1333-1370) ended, people said of Casimir: 'He found Poland of wood and left it of stone'. The chief reason for this economic success was his decision to give Jews the protection of royal courts of justice. One of the horrible by-products of crusading enthusiasm in western Europe had been the sudden flaring of anti-Semitic feeling; a quarrel in the street, a chance word even, would provoke a riot and sometimes a massacre. Fear induced large numbers of Jews to migrate; Poland attracted them because it was a comparatively empty land where the government actually welcomed them as newcomers. They moved as complete communities and lived a life of their own within the towns where they settled. Judaism with its daily observances and strict food laws influenced their lives from the cradle to the grave. They were a prolific race, but marriage between Jews and non-Jews was stongly discouraged, if not prohibited, by the rabbis. Gifted boys of humble origin were not, as among the Christians, encouraged to be celibates. Speaking Yiddish and writing Hebrew, they never learnt Polish or Ukrainian except for business. In a century when other Catholic countries drove out these free, hard-working and law-abiding people, Poland grew prosperous by their labour.

At the same time as the Poles were expanding southwards the Lithuanians, breaking out of their homelands on the lower courses of the Dvina and Niemen, advanced up the valleys of those rivers into western Russia, where resistance was weak, since the Russian princes were vassals of the Tartars. For dealings with western Europe the pagan rulers of this new empire used Latin, giving themselves the title *Magnus Ducatus* (Grand Duke) *Lituaniae et Russiae*. Their own language had not yet been written down like the Russian spoken by their subjects. Soon Kiev had been recaptured from the Mongols and the fertile 'black earth' lands overrun down to the Black Sea coast between the mouths of the Dnieper and the Dniester. In past geological ages this soil had been formed from decaying grass killed by periodic droughts, which alone set limits to its productivity. Irrigation was impossible as the rivers rose in comparatively low hills and flowed slowly along deep trench-like beds.

The Grand Duke Orgerd (1341-1377) repeatedly attacked the Russians along the road from Smolensk to the east and was twice repelled from Moscow. In the south the furthest limit of Lithuanian power was reached under Grand Duke Witold (1388-1430). He forced his cousin Duke Jagiello, who had married the heiress to the Polish kingdom, to be content with the title King of Poland, and the two countries had henceforward one dynasty though the reigning sovereign was not always the same. The Poles were the more aggressive partners in this empire, acquiring estates in the newly-won lands and persuading both pagan and Orthodox Lithuanians to adopt Roman Catholicism and make it the religion of the state.

The Conquests of the Ottoman Turks in Europe

One of the consequences of the Tartar invasion of Russia was the migration southwards of scattered Turkish tribes into Asia Minor. In the fourteenth century these semi-nomads found leaders capable of uniting them and began a career of conquest that sapped the strength of Christian Europe for over 400 years. They took the name of their first great leader, Osman, and became known as the Ottoman Turks. To fight them the Byzantine emperor, who claimed authority over most of the coast of Asia Minor, called in a small army of mercenaries from Catalonia; they succeeded in defeating the Turks, only to find the emperor could not pay them. They therefore marched into Macedonia and, after ravaging the country, settled in Thessaly.

The durability of the Ottoman Empire was soon ensured by the more sophisticated methods of a new Sultan, Orkhan by name. He allowed Christians in conquered territories to practice their religion and was content with less revenue from them than the emperors had exacted with the result that they showed no inclination to rebel and even provided the Turks with a new regiment known as the Janissaries, who became famous for their personal loyalty to the sultans. In 1353 the Turks crossed the Hellespont, seized Gallipoli, gained command of the passage to the Black Sea, and made Adrianople (Edirne) their capital. Under Sultan Murat I (1359-1389) they defeated the Serbs and all Macedonia except Salonika came under their rule. At the same time the Tsar of Bulgaria acknowledged Murat as his overlord.

In 1389 Murat launched a great campaign for the conquest of Serbia. The armies of the two powers met at Kossovo in the mountains south-west of Nish. In the middle of the fighting a Serbian posing as an informer reached Murat's presence and killed him. In spite of their loss the Turks, whose archers were strongly entrenched, won the battle and captured the Serbian leader, who was at once executed by the new sultan.

The empire that Murat had acquired, could not, he knew, remain a great power unless new and ruthless methods of government were devised. The mixture of races that it contained was dangerously explosive at all times. Murat therefore introduced a new 'tax'. Where among his subjects Christian boys of exceptional physical strength and intellectual capacity were noticed, they were collected as 'revenue' and taken away to the Turkish capital. There they were brought up in a military academy as strict Moslems, given a strenuous education in swordsmanship and cavalry fighting, and trained as administrators. Parents of such talented sons were fortunate if they ever saw them again; if they survived and grew to manhood, they were not posted to their homeland. Fear of such tax collectors kept whole populations in a quiet subservience that masked much bitter hatred. The ruling Turkish minority was kept in idle luxury, and the prosperity of the conquered lands slowly declined. The Turks, being nomads by instinct, were suspicious of townspeople and saw no point in promoting the welfare of cities.

The Russian Church and the Princes of Moscow

The 'Tartar Yoke' had the effect of encouraging the mutually hostile princes of Russia to cooperate, for their Mongol masters insisted on holding periodically a population census as a basis for the assessment of tribute, which was in effect a head tax. The first impulse towards unity was given by the Orthodox Church. The Metropolitan Peter, a Russian by birth, made Moscow his headquarters in 1305, and under a later Metropolitan, Alexis (1353-1378), the religious enthusiasm of the time found an outlet in monasticism. Hermits set up innumerable small cells along the forest trackways and, as their reputation for sanctity grew, they would be visited for advice, comfort and healing. At death their tombs would become places of pilgrimage and sometimes the site of a great monastery with stone buildings and encircling walls. The cell of St Sergius of Radonezh, who died in 1392, was in a wood between Moscow and Pereslav, and there the Troitsa (Trinity) monastery was founded and became one of the greatest of the new houses. Monasteries of a type more usual in the west were set up near towns and both kinds became the possessors of vast estates.

In the south the advance of the Ottoman Turks into the Balkans caused many Serbian and Greek refugees to seek asylum in Russia. In 1390 a Serb named Cyprian became Metropolitan in Moscow. Under Serbian influence religious literature began using the stately forms of Church Slavonic; and two ikon painters, Theophan the Greek and a monk of Troitsa, Andrey Rublev, raised what had been a traditional and impersonal form of art to new heights.

The first attempt to break loose from the Tartar yoke came in 1380. Prince Dimitri defeated the Tartars at Kulikov near the source of the Don, for which he earned the name Donskoy, but this did not set Russia free. The Tartars returned two years later and captured Moscow, now a large and flourishing town; according to one estimate they slew 35,000 and took 25,000 prisoners. After this disaster the Great Prince had to pay the Tartars tribute again.

The Suppression of the Templars

One of the results of establishing orders of knights vowed to defend the Holy Places was the creation in Europe of preceptories where recruits and money could be collected for the wars against the Turks and old or wounded knights might live when no longer fit for active service. The Order of the Poor Knights of Christ of the Temple of Solomon, known as the Templars, had acquired, besides property in land and castles, vast sums

Knights Templars arrested and imprisoned by order of King Philip IV of France in 1307

of money and set up a highly profitable banking business. Their houses, being well-built of stone and occupied by soldiers, served in an unsafe world not only as banks but as repositories for valuables and jewels. The Temple in Paris was such a treasure house, and the King of France, Philip IV, called the Fair (1285-1314), who often borrowed money from the Templars, once took refuge there when a mob, enraged by his debasement of the coinage, attempted to lynch him.

When Acre, the last post in the Holy Land, fell to the Turks in 1291, the Templars transferred their headquarters to Cyprus, then a kingdom ruled by Frenchmen. The Hospitallers, with papal permission, seized Rhodes, and built a huge castle to command the harbour. Plans for recovering the Holy Land began to be discussed in Europe. Pope Clement V, a Frenchman living in France, whose election had been secured by bribes offered through Philip IV's agents, asked the heads of the two orders to meet him. The aged Grand Master of the Templars, who had fought against the Turks for thirty years, landed in Marseilles accompanied by sixty knights and bringing 150,000 gold ducats. They were staying at the Temple in Paris when Philip's soldiers broke in and arrested them. This was part of a royal plot; at the same time some thousands of other Templars and their adherents were arrested all over France and faced with trumped-up charges of idolatry, sodomy and other crimes. To extract confessions, torture was used. The Grand Master, to escape from Philip, admitted to spitting at a crucifix. All hoped that the pope would save them, but he for some reason believed their confessions and ordered the arrest of the Templars in all other European countries. The Grand Master and many officers of the order in France were burnt alive, protesting their innocence as they died. The pope directed that the Templars' property should be transferred to the Hospitallers. The king, who benefited financially far less than he hoped, had demonstrated his absolute power, humiliated the papacy in the most shocking manner and introduced a new and terrible instrument of 'justice', torture.

No serious charge was proved against the English Templars, but they were suppressed. In Spain and Germany they were declared innocent, but deprived of their property. In Italy and Cyprus, where torture was used, they were found guilty.

The Avignon Popes

In the middle of his quarrel with the Templars Clement V moved the diplomatic and legal services of the papacy from Rome to Avignon in order that the popes should be free from the pressure of the Roman mob and the ambitions of noble Roman families. He supposed that the Kings of France would protect him against his Italian enemies and be, as in the past, champions of Christendom against the Moslems.

A later Avignon pope, an austere Cistercian, Benedict XII (1334-1342), worked hard to reform the orders of monks and friars and to remove abuses. From friars in distant countries he received letters asking for help, which he readily gave. Friar Jordanus, a Dominican writing from the vicinity of Bombay in 1323, described the martyrdom of four of his brethren. Friar Pascal, a Spanish Franciscan, in a letter dated 1338, said that his preaching had taken him all through Persia and northwards to the region of Lake Balkash. These lands, later reconquered by the Russians, had been recently taken over by the Mongols of the Golden Horde whose priests, called shamans, handed down powers of magic and healing from father to son. They combined the offices of witch doctor and psychopompos, claiming to be able to separate soul from body and conduct the spirits of the dead to the next world. Such frightful superstitions did not terrify the friars, but when Timur the Lame, known as Tamerlane (1369-1405), a fanatical Moslem, devastated the remnants of the Mongol empire, the links with Europe that the friars had made were all broken.

Clement VI (1342-1352) was a wealthy man in his own right and completed the fortress-palace on the banks of the Rhone, but his patronage of artists, writers and musicians emptied the treasury. The disadvantages of Avignon compared with Rome were all too apparent, and Gregory XI, elected in 1370, determined to return to Italy. Perhaps he received the greatest encouragement to do so from Catherine of Siena (1347-1380), a Dominican tertiary whose teaching, expressed in simple language, touched many hearts. In 1378 what the Italian poet Petrarch unfairly called the 'Babylonian Captivity' in Avignon ended. Gregory returned, but died the same year. The cardinals, divided and quarrelsome, proceeded to elect two popes, one to please the French and remain at Avignon, the other to be in Rome. This scandal, called the Great Schism, lasted until 1415 and still further damaged the reputation of the papacy, since each pope attempted to collect in revenue as much as one had previously done.

The last of the crusades left for the east in 1396; the best soldiers in it were French and Burgundian knights, but once they entered the sultan's dominions they plundered his Christian subjects. They met the Turks at Nicopolis near the confluence of the Aluta and the Danube; the knights charged but were shot down by the Janissaries on their flanks. The Emperor Sigismund escaped with difficulty. The heir to the Duke of Burgundy and many other noblemen were captured and held till a heavy ransom was paid; their men were massacred. For the papacy it was an end to all hopes of uniting the west for the defence of Christendom.

The Swiss Confederation

The wars of the Hohenstaufen emperors in Italy had given the Alpine passes a new importance. Travellers from Germany leaving the shores of Lake Lucerne had to enter the gorge of the river Reuss and follow it southwards to the head of St Gotthard pass. Here hard-working, semi-independent Swiss peasants belonged to three cantons: Schwyz to the north, from which Switzerland took its name; Uri to the south; and Unter-walden to the west. The German lords who, like the Habsburgs, claimed the Swiss as their vassals, could not safely send their men into the valleys as tax collectors; it was better to rely on collective payments fixed by charter. When in 1315 the Habsburg Duke Leopold I invaded the cantons, hoping to end their independence, his horsemen took a road between the mountains and the shore of Lake Ageri. At Morgarten they were ambushed by the Swiss, who pushed rocks down on to the terrified horses and then used their halberds on the riders.

After this disaster both the duke and the emperor made peace with the mountaineers. The Swiss, to strengthen their confederation, secured the aid of the towns of Lucerne and Zurich. In 1352 Glarus, Zug and Berne, which had won its freedom in 1339, also joined and so opened up the road to the west by way of Interlaken and the Aar valley. Conditions on Swiss roads were improved by the acceptance of a regulation forbidding highway robbery and private war.

Hostilities with the Habsburgs were renewed in 1385, and in the next year Duke Leopold III was defeated at Sempach. His knights dismounted, but could not resist the long Swiss halberds. These heavy weapons, half spear and half axe, were to win Swiss soldiers a European reputation. Mercenaries became for centuries the chief export of the country and at home the confederation was able to protect itself against its powerful neighbours.

Giotto and his Patrons

It is sometimes said that in Italy the art of painting began to flourish when it ceased to be dependent on the patronage of the Church. This is a misuse of the word 'Church', restricting it to mean 'the clergy' as distinct from the laity, whereas it should include both. Ever since the sixth century, kings, bishops and nobles had built and endowed

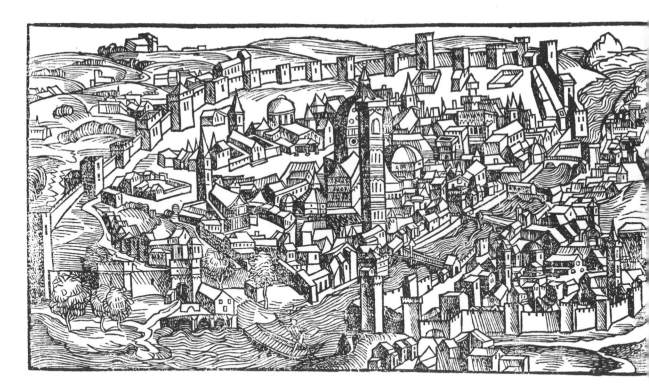

Florence as a walled town in the 15th century, from a woodcut illustration in an early printed book

churches and abbeys and contributed towards their adornment. They have never ceased to do so, but in the fourteenth century the custom of commissioning chapels,

The prophet Haggai, a sculpture by Giovanni Pisano (1250–1314)

religious pictures and other works of art was taken up by the middle class in the towns, whose devotion to the Church was no less than that of earlier benefactors. Yet historians often note with scorn that Giotto's patrons were 'hard-headed bankers' or, for good measure, 'moneylenders' and imply that for his genius to have flowered in the service of such masters is peculiar. Such comments are misconceived. There is no reason to suppose Giotto found them less cultured or more hard-headed than the nobility. Genius is always unpredictable, but it cannot prosper without affection and encouragement. The unheard melodies of painting need an audience, and there is no reason to suppose that Enrico Scrovegni, who commissioned Giotto to adorn the walls of the Arena chapel in Padua, was deaf to them because he was a banker.

Giotto, a man of forty when he began this work, was born near Florence about 1265. No other information about his early life and education has survived, but his work shows that he may have set out to emulate in paint the new achievements in sculpture of Giovanni Pisano (1250–1328). The Arena was a small, plain building and Giotto painted directly on the walls, dividing his space horizontally and depicting scenes from the life of the Virgin and of Christ arranged in 'frames' and linked one with another by dramatic continuations of line and movement. In addition the actors in his drama were depicted as real creatures of flesh and blood, expressing with their eyes and gestures how moved they were by love and hate, joy and sorrow, pity and terror. The walls of churches had for many centuries been covered with paintings and mosaics, but Giotto's originality lay in the unprecedented realism and sympathy of his figures. The innovation was so startling that it was nearly a century before painters began to advance along the path that he had pioneered.

The contribution of the Scrovegni family cannot have been without influence on this achievement. Padua was an exchange and mart for ideas as well as goods, situated only a day's journey from Venice on the main road to Milan and the other towns of Lombardy. Every June pilgrims flooded in to worship at the church containing St Anthony's shrine, for which, a hundred years later, Donatello bronzes were commissioned, and so it was probably with affection that Giotto included in his design a portrait of Scrovegni presenting a model of his chapel to three angels.

At this time the development of European trade was too rapid and new methods too complicated for the clergy to comprehend. They had an old rule against lending money at interest, which was called committing the sin of usury, but for the most part ignored until borrowers failed to repay debts and complained. It was seldom then pointed out that no man is obliged to borrow money; he is free to do without it, but, if he agrees to terms of repayment, he should keep his word. Ethically it was no more wrong to charge interest on a loan than to expect rent for a house, but such arguments were not acceptable. It was easier to blame the rich and call them usurers.

The banking families of Florence who next employed Giotto, the Bardi and Peruzzi, were, like those of Padua, men of wide horizons with friends and connections all over Europe. They had for many years financed and organised the export of English wool, and when Edward III began his war with France they lent him money to raise an army, a debt he failed to repay. For them to honour the memory of Francis of Assisi was not hypocrisy. They were free men, proud of their country, and, wishing to commemorate one of its greatest sons, they commissioned Giotto to paint scenes from his life on the walls of the church of Santa Croce. Francis had taught that to speak to the poor about Christ without living a life of poverty was ineffective. His compatriots understood this; not all could become friars, and the merchant princes of Florence who helped to make their city pre-eminent in art deserve, not the sneers, but the gratitude of posterity.

CHAPTER SEVEN

The Fifteenth Century

The Fall of Constantinople

Sultan Beyazit I, who took over the leadership of the Ottoman Turks at Kossovo, laid siege to Constantinople in 1400, threatening to massacre the inhabitants if they refused to surrender. The mighty walls built on the landward side by the Emperor Theodosius the Great nearly eleven hundred years before were repaired and strengthened under the direction of a French knight, and the Turks were defied. Then news came of a Mongol-Turkish invasion of Anatolia. This had been ordered by Tamerlane, who had recently made a devastating raid on India. Beyazit had to leave Constantinople and march to the east. The armies of the two most powerful Moslem rulers met at Ankara in 1402; the Mongols were completely victorious, capturing Beyazit and allowing him to die in captivity. Three years later the death of Tamerlane caused the Mongols to withdraw and Beyazit's sons went to war over their inheritance. It was not until 1453 that the Turks were ready to besiege Constantinople again. In the meantime the sultans had been involved in much fighting in Europe with the Venetians, Serbians, Hungarians and Albanians. George Castriota, an Albanian whom the Turks had taken in boyhood from his home and trained as a soldier, having proved himself under the name Skanderbeg an excellent general in their service, changed sides. Reverting to the Christian faith he won for his countrymen a period of independence. This ended when he died in 1468.

The ablest of the sultans, Mahomet II, came to power as a young man in 1451 and reigned for thirty years. Something of the hardness of his character is revealed in the portrait attributed to Giovanni Bellini. The capture of Constantinople was his first objective. It was defended by about 8,000 of whom a third were Venetians and Genoese. The walls began to crumble under fire from the heaviest cannon yet manufactured. Reinforcements from the west only once broke the chain that the Turks cast across the entrance to the Golden Horn. On 29 May 1453, after desperate fighting, the Janissaries delivered the final assault. The last emperor, Constantine XI, was killed in action. After massacre and pillage many of the churches, including the magnificent domed cathedral of St Sophia, built in the sixth century by the Emperor Justinian, were turned into mosques, their glittering mosaics obscured by enormous lettering and their airy spaciousness ruined by dangling lamps required by readers of the Koran seated on the

94

Sultan Mahomet II, who captured Constantinople in 1453. A portrait attributed to Giovanni Bellini

floor. The Orthodox Church quickly made its peace with the sultan, the patriarch undertaking to collect tribute from the Christian population. Venice retained forts and castles on the coast and among the islands, including Crete, and in 1489 acquired

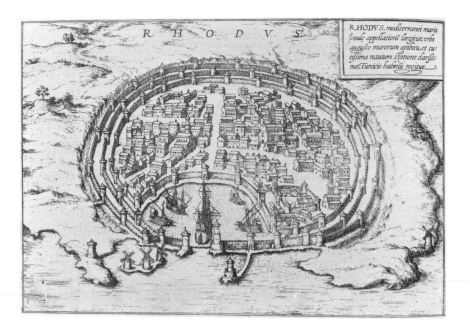

Rhodes and its harbour, from which the forces of Mahomet II were repulsed by the Knights Hospitallers in 1480. The palace of the grand master of the order is on the right. One of the seven wonders of the ancient world, the Colossus of Rhodes, once spanned the harbour entrance

Cyprus, but, with the lower Danube in Turkish hands, a Moslem conquest of central Europe seemed by no means impossible. A dull sterility settled on the lands over which the sultans ruled. Mahomet II was a learned man with artistic tastes, a patron of poets, who loved to cultivate the tulip, once a wild flower from the highlands of Asia, now to be grown in Europe for the first time, but none of these virtues could compensate for the nomadic habits of his people, who allowed their herds to denude the land of trees and grass by overcropping once fertile hills and valleys.

The End of the Hundred Years' War
With the accession of Henry V of England Anglo-French rivalry flared up again. For France the renewal of the English claim to the French crown came at a moment of division and weakness. The immensely wealthy duchy of Burgundy, which included the Flemish clothing towns, had been inherited in 1409 by the crusader John the Bold. He had been ransomed from the sultan, and was determined to extend his dominions. His first step was to have his chief rival among the nobles of France, the Duke of Orleans, murdered as he went down a Paris street. This he tried to justify on the ground that the

dead man had oppressed the people with taxes to pay for his extravagant pleasures. In the civil disturbances that followed the Paris mob was on the Burgundian side.

In 1415 Henry V invaded Normandy and laid siege to Harfleur. Lack of good artillery delayed him and sickness began to cause more English casualties than the enemy. Not until Harfleur had fallen and Henry's depleted army had marched inland, did the French join battle. They had assembled a huge force, but, forgetting the strategy of du Guesclin, they attacked the prepared position of the enemy at Agincourt. Going forward on foot over slippery, rain-soaked ground against fierce archery fire, they were either killed or exhausted before reaching the enemy lines. Among the slain was the Constable of France, seven princes, more than 1,500 knights and possibly 4,000 men-at-arms. The young Duke of Orleans was among the prisoners held to ransom, and spent most of his life a captive in England.

The Dauphin escaped from the battle and set up his government at Bourges, leaving France north of the Loire open to the English armies. In 1419 the Duke of Burgundy was murdered during an altercation with the dauphin's representatives. His successor Duke Philip the Good, had possession of the King and Queen of France and of their daughter Catherine and, to be revenged on the dauphin, made peace with the English at Troyes, arranging for Henry V to marry Catherine. On the death of Charles VI Henry was to be crowned King of France.

The treaty proved abortive, for both Charles VI and Henry V died two years later; the Dauphin Charles refused to honour its terms; and the war continued. For a time under Henry V's brother, the Duke of Bedford, the English held northern France, but the national pride of ordinary Frenchmen was steadily rising. Away to the east, in Lorraine, a peasant girl named Joan of Arc heard voices and saw visions commanding her to lead the army of France against the enemy. At seventeen she set out with a few friends across hostile country to seek an audience with the Dauphin. It took her two months to persuade him and the court to allow her to attempt the relief of Orleans. She succeeded, and went on to rout the English at Patay. The way was open for Charles to go to Rheims for his coronation.

From this moment Joan began to falter. Her voices told her that she would be captured. Taken prisoner by the Burgundians, she was sold to the English for 10,000 crowns, tried before an ecclesiastical court on a charge of witchcraft, convicted and burnt alive, meeting death with calm resignation. Twenty years later her mother, with extraordinary courage and persistence, succeeded in persuading the king to order a re-trial. Evidence was taken down from numerous men and women of all ranks who had known Joan personally; the records of the first trial were re-examined; and Joan was declared innocent. No story in medieval history is better authenticated than hers. She had predicted that the English would be driven from all their possessions in France, and this was achieved. The Burgundians changed sides and with the French had by 1453 expelled the English everywhere, except from Calais.

Heresey in Bohemia
One result of the Great Schism (1378-1417) was a slackening of discipline among the

97

diocesan clergy and the religious orders all over Europe. Saints like Bridget in Sweden and Catherine of Siena, no less than heretics like John Wyclif, an Oxford don, denounced in writings copied and circulated in foreign countries the shortcomings of the higher clergy.

When, following the marriage of Princess Anne of Bohemia to Richard II of England in 1382, Wyclif's writings reached Prague, criticism of the Church there, already vigorous, increased inter-racial feeling, because most of the clergy were German and the laity Czech. Two laymen had founded a chapel called Bethlehem where hymn-singing and sermons in Czech attracted enthusiastic interest among all classes. A university-trained theologian named John Huss, appointed preacher at the chapel, asserted the authority of the Bible as against that of the Church. With it, he indicated, laymen could find salvation for themselves without a priesthood, while a corrupt Church might lead men away from religion; priests, for example, had, in his view, no scriptual authority for reserving to themselves the consecrated wine at communion and giving the laity only the consecrated bread. As Huss came increasingly under the influence of Wyclif, the Archbishop of Prague in alarm excommunicated him and laid the city under an interdict. The Emperor Sigismund, anxious to make his peace with the Church, treacherously invited Huss to attend the Council of Constance in 1415. Huss accepted safe conduct and when examined asserted that he could not accept the council's ruling on his teaching unless it could be justified on scriptural grounds. To cast doubt upon the authority of a general council of the Church was heresy. Huss and his friend Jerome, who had come from Prague to defend him, were condemned and burnt at the stake. Civil war followed in Bohemia; doctrinal disagreements proliferated; and a number of half-mad sectarians fought among themselves.

Ivan III, Tsar of All Russia

When Ivan III became Grand Duke of Muscovy in 1462, he had no wish to be on good terms with his western neighbours. Russia had been invaded almost as often by them as by the people of the steppes. In the north he coveted the wealthy town of Novgorod and the wide territories over which it ruled, and attacking it in 1471 he compelled its citizens to recognise him as their ruler. The bell with which they had summoned town meetings was taken away and hung in a Moscow belfry. Novgorod lands were distributed among Russian boyars, or nobles, who became absolute masters of their new estates and through an assembly, or *duma*, had great influence on the grand duke, who consulted them on all important matters. Lower in rank than the boyars were the gentry, who were granted land on condition that they served, when required, as horsemen in Ivan's army. His infantry were conscripts from the towns, strengthened by his own bodyguard.

Though his army was efficient Ivan preferred diplomacy to war. To weaken the grand duchy of Lithuania he persuaded the Tartars of the Crimea to attack Kiev, then in the Lithuanian empire, but when he stopped paying tribute to the Golden Horde, the Khan attempted an invasion. Finding the Russian army too strong, he retreated and was later killed in battle during a civil war among the Tartars. Russia was at last free. Envoys

The Kremlin, Moscow. The height of the walls, built to keep out the Tartars, may be judged from the itinerant traders' stalls in the foreground

from the Emperor Frederick III offered Ivan a king's crown but he proudly declared: 'Our appointment comes from God, as did that of our ancestors, and we beg God to grant us and our children to abide for ever in the same state, namely as sovereigns of our own land; and as formerly we did not desire to be appointed by any one, so now we do not'. As guardian of the Orthodox Church he regarded himself as thé successor of the emperors whose rule in Constantinople had come to an end, adopting their two-headed eagle as his state emblem together with the title Tsar, another form of the word *Caesar*, meaning emperor. For the Russian peasantry a new tyranny had replaced the old.

The Expansion of France

The kingdom of France had long been at the mercy of 'over-mighty subjects' when Louis XI came to the throne in 1461. He devoted his reign to three objects; the destruction of the great duchy of Burgundy; the elimination of English influence on the continent; and the abolition of that independence still enjoyed by Brittany, Provence and other parts of what is now France. He pursued all these aims simultaneously, making progress in one direction contribute to success in another. His methods were devious and his treacheries numerous.

The Duke of Burgundy, Philip the Good, had long lived in splendour. Louis was parsimonious. Philip made his court the resort of writers, musicians and painters. Jan van Eyck entered his service in 1425, and was paid 100 livres a year; acting as both ambassador and artist he went to Portugal in order to arrange a marriage with Princess Isabel. Few of the many portraits made by him have survived, but his picture of an

Italian merchant, Arnolfini, and his wife, who resided in the duke's capital city Bruges, is a masterpiece of European renown. The duke also spent lavishly on tapestries and illuminated manuscripts, accumulating a library of 900 volumes. Louis bent his energies to finding new sources of revenue, carrying out many experiments in state-financed enterprise, only some of which were profitable.

The long struggle in England between the Lancastrian and Yorkist branches of the royal family, known as the Wars of the Roses, had not ended when Duke Philip died in 1467 and was succeeded by his son Charles. Both father and son favoured the Yorkists, and so Louis took the Lancastrian side. lending the Lancastrian Queen, Margaret of Anjou, money for an invasion of England in 1471. His loan was ill-placed, for she was defeated and her son murdered. This blunder Louis remedied when the young Yorkist king Edward IV invaded France in 1475, expecting to receive support from Burgundy which never came. The French persuaded him to leave the country by paying a bribe of 75,000 crowns and promising 10,000 crowns a year thereafter.

The following year Duke Charles was tempted to attack the Swiss, whose confederation now consisted of thirteen cantons. They had made raids into Burgundy, but Charles found their foot-soldiers, supported by money from Louis XI, the best infantry in Europe. He was forced to retire after losing two pitched battles and a year later, fighting to defend Lorraine, was defeated and killed at Nancy. As heiress he left his nineteen-year-old daughter Mary. To diminish her inheritance by force was too great a temptation for a man of such evil character as the French king. He at once annexed the old duchy of Burgundy in east-central France, and also Picardy and Artois. To gain the rest he proposed that the Duchess Mary should marry his seven-year-old son Charles. After such treatment she not unnaturally chose to marry a potential enemy of France, Maximilian, son and later successor of the Emperor Frederick III, the head of the Habsburg family. Their grandson Charles became, on his father's death, Emperor of Germany, lord of the Netherlands, and King of Spain with all her overseas possessions, including Mexico and Peru. Louis by his small-minded attack on a weak neighbour had deprived his country of an opportunity to become by alliance the chief power not only in Europe but also in the New World.

By 1483, when Louis died and his thirteen-year-old son Charles succeeded him, France also included Provence and for the first time the great port of Marseilles, and French galleys were ready for an attack on Italy. After long preparations Charles VIII led an army of 30,000 French and German mercenaries over the Alps, entering Milan at the invitation of its Sforza duke; Florence at the request of Savonarola; and Rome at the bidding of the pope. Then, having captured Naples, he realised the consequences of his adventure. Italy, it was said, had been 'conquered with chalk', the chalk used to mark the doors of houses requisitioned as billets for his troops. Billeted troops seldom behave well, and this roused such anger that an Italian league was quickly formed to take revenge. This Charles defeated at Fornovo near Parma, and so extricated his army, which reached France laden with loot, but with little other gain. The plunder was remembered; the league was forgotten. In the next century the wealth of Italy seemed to the French kings more desirable than the harvest of ocean trade.

Portugal, Spain and the Ocean Route to India

In Portugal and Spain there was the same crusading enthusiasm as in other parts of Europe, but it was directed against the Moslem states of Granada and Algiers. Prince Henry, third son of Juan I of Portugal, organised a crusade that in 1415 captured the town of Ceuta, opposite Gibraltar, from the Sultan of Algiers. This victory brought him fame throughout Europe, but he turned his back on a military career in order to study the sea, building a palace-observatory on the cliffs at Sagres on Cape St Vincent and making

Lagos harbour, southern Portugal, from which the ships of prince Henry the Navigator set out in the 15th century

the nearby port of Lagos the base for a long series of maritime expeditions in search of an ocean route to India. The bolder of his captains took advantage of the prevailing north-east winds (later to be called the trade winds) to sail far out of sight of land. A thousand kilometres away they found the Madeiras, and there the Portuguese planted a colony, cut timber and began to grow sugar cane, a plant that had earlier reached the Mediterranean from Asia.

Prince Henry's ships, called caravels, were better designed for the Atlantic than any previously used, and in 1445 those sailing south along the African coast reached Cape Verde, so named because the tops of the palm trees gave that desolate shore a false appearance of greenness. Before Prince Henry died in 1460, the Guinea coast had been discovered. People had scoffed at him, calling him 'the Navigator' and adding 'He never sails'. Twenty-seven years later his vision and persistence were rewarded. Bartolomeo Diaz, a relative of the captain who discovered Cape Verde, rounded the Cape of Good Hope. He had added nearly 2,000 kilometres to the coastline previously explored and knew the way to India, but he was not chosen to lead the first expedition.

In the years following the return of Diaz the courts of Spain, Portugal, England and France all listened to a new proposal for reaching India. A Genoese, Christopher Columbus, who had studied the ideas of Italian geographers, proposed an expedition to the west, but all rejected it. Only a priest and a lady-in-waiting to Queen Isabella of Castile were convinced, and they persuaded her to give Columbus money for three small ships. These set out in 1492 and after five weeks' sailing, during which the crew nearly mutinied, a landfall was made in the Bahamas. Columbus brought back nothing but a handful of gold and a few captive 'Indians' who spoke an unintelligible language,

Interior of the court of the lions in the 14th century palace of the sultans of Granada, the last of whom was expelled in 1492, the year in which Columbus reached the West Indies. This palace was inside a citadel set on a rocky hill and called al-hambra in Arabic meaning 'the red', being built of red stone

but the Castilians persisted, sending him on three further expeditions. Independently, other seamen, some of whom had sailed on his first voyage, discovered the principal islands of the Caribbean and travelled along many miles of the American coast. Columbus himself never realised that he had found a new continent; for him it yielded no wealth, and he died a disgraced and humiliated man.

In Portugal the Spanish discovery of 'the Indies' spurred on the expedition of which Vasco da Gama had been given command; sailing in 1497 he reached Mombasa on the east coast of Africa and then, waiting for the monsoon, took the route of the Arab spice traders to the Malabar coast of India. His men were amazed by the stately palaces, ornate temples and bejewelled princes of Calicut. Returning after twenty-six months' absence, they and their captain were received with honour by the king. He, excitedly describing the voyage to his father-in-law, King Ferdinand of Aragon, signed himself: 'Lord of the Conquest, Navigation and Commerce of Ethiopia, Arabia, Persia and India'. Vasco da Gama, after several further visits to India, died a rich man, loaded with honours, and was buried in the chapel at Belem built by Prince Henry for the use of his mariners.

The Italian Renaissance

The flowering of Italian literature, painting, sculpture and architecture that occurred in the fifteenth century so amazed the Italians that they referred to it as a renaissance or rebirth, meaning a renewal of the glorious Italy of Roman times. The Florentine architect Leon Battista Alberti wrote: 'What can be the reason that just at this time all Italy should be fired with the kind of emulation to put on quite a new face? How many towns, which when we were children were built of nothing but wood, are now lately started up all of marble?'

Historians cannot answer this question. When so many men of genius appear together at one time as contemporaries and friendly rivals, it is necessary to remember that 'the final step of reason is to recognise that there is an infinity which surpasses it' (Pascal). In Florence the young architect of the cathedral of Santa Maria del Fiore, Brunelleschi; Ghiberti, the sculptor of the bronze doors of the bapistery; Masaccio, affectionately nicknamed Tomasaccio (clumsy Tom) by his fellow citizens, who painted the Brancacci chapel frescoes; and Donatello, who astonished the town with a nude bronze figure of David, were all at work there in the first half of the century. During the second half Michelangelo carved his David; Botticelli painted the Birth of Venus; and Leonardo da Vinci opened his studio to thronging crowds eager to see the cartoon of Madonna with St Anne.

Town life in Italy had reached a height of affluence unknown elsewhere in Europe and could provide the education and leisure that the appreciation of art required. In Florence there were excellent schools, and the standard of literacy among men very high. 'A high standard of education' wrote Vittorino de Feltre at the time, 'is only to be reached by one who has seen many things and read much. Poet, orator, historian and the rest, all must be studied. One's learning then becomes full, ready, varied and elegant, available for action and for discourse.' Nor was schooling directed merely to self-advancement; as Vittorino also wrote: 'Not everyone is called to be a lawyer, physician, or philosopher, to live in the public eye, nor has everyone outstanding gifts, but all of us are created for the life of social duty, all of us are responsible for the personal influence which goes out from us.'

The self-confidence of the age prevented admiration for the literature and art of Greece and Rome from becoming retrospective and uncreative, as it did later. The Italians believed that their great men had not only absorbed what the ancients had to teach but gone on to excel them. Brunelleschi, when the workmen on the dome of his cathedral feared that, without centring, its weight might prove insupportable, went to Hadrian's Pantheon in Rome to study its vast cupola and, reassured, returned to Florence to finish his own masterpiece.

Scholars of the day usually referred to ancient literature as *literae humaniores*, implying that it was the product of a more humane, that is, more civilised, world than their own, and hence the word humanist has in the past been applied to Renaissance art. Today those calling themselves humanists are deeply divided from those who acknowledge the truths of Christianity. No such division was dreamt of by the men of the fifteenth century, who never doubted that their masterpieces added to rather than subtracted from human understanding of religion.

The Florentines attributed their triumphs to the republican forms of government under which they lived, contrasting their civic freedom with the military dictatorship enforced by the condottieri of the Visconti or Sforza families who ruled Milan. In Florence money not arms was the instrument of peace, for the substance as distinct from the shadow of power lay with the Medici, a banking family whose operations extended to almost every major town in Europe. Cosimo de'Medici, who was forty when he became head of the bank in 1429, perfected a method of controlling the affairs of the city through subordinates while remaining a private citizen. Without scruple he taxed his opponents more heavily than his friends. His weakly son died five years after his father, and at the age of twenty-one Cosimo's grandson Lorenzo, called the Magnificent, continued as a private citizen to wield an influence equal to that of Cosimo. Like his grandfather he had to deal with conspiracy. In 1478 a rival family of bankers, the Pazzi, hired men to murder him and his brother Guiliano. They stabbed Guiliano to death while he was praying in church, but Lorenzo, having escaped, was protected by the Florentines, among whom he remained both popular and powerful until his death in 1492.

The Renaissance, though it showed its early splendour in Florence, is rightly called Italian, for not only did Florentines go out to fulfil commissions in Milan, Mantua, Padua and other towns, but gifted artists from other parts of the country came to Florence to study. The master painters of Siena and Urbino won fame throughout Italy, while in the next century Rome and Venice fostered artists whose work, though different in character from that of earlier generations, was no less original.

The Invention of Printing

The first book printed with movable type, a massive Bible, was by Johann Gutenberg of Mainz and appeared about 1453. The type face was modelled on the best scrivener's hand of the day. It was an immense undertaking for the text contains more than 3,500,000 letters, each set by hand. The outline of each letter, being complicated by 'gothic' decoration, gave this and other early books a dark and heavy appearance. Gutenberg

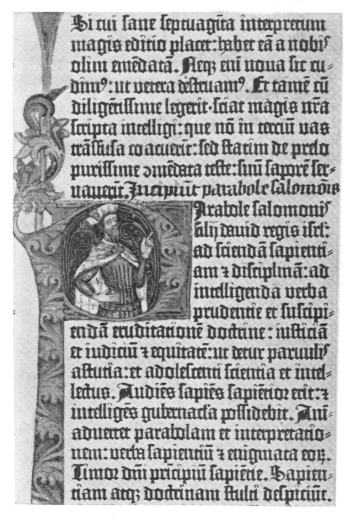

A page from Proverbs *in the Bible of Johann Gutenberg, the first book printed with movable type, published at Mainz about 1455. The illuminated initial P, with the head of Solomon inset, was done by hand, the artist being Heinrich Cremer*

soon had a number of rivals. They issued small editions, from 200 to 1,000 copies, of books for which they knew there would be a ready sale. Ninety-four editions of the Bible in Latin and thirty of parts of scripture in vernacular languages had appeared by 1500. In spite of many difficulties, not least the suspicion with which the new invention was treated by governments, German craftsmen had soon set up presses abroad or

105

trained others to do so. Their influence on the progress of both Renaissance and Reformation was therefore immense. The prices of books was high, but not prohibitive. coming within the reach of artisans and small traders. If the methods of manufacturing paper from rags had not been so slow and cumbersome, publications of all sorts would have been still less expensive.

The possibility of printing instead of copying manuscripts sent scholars on a thorough search of old libraries for 'lost' masterpieces of ancient Greek and Roman literature. One of the first scholar-printers, Aldus Manutius, who began work in Venice about 1494, devised a clear 'roman' type that was later adopted or imitated in other countries, driving out the early 'black letter'. His books still rank among the most beautiful ever published.

CHAPTER EIGHT

The Sixteenth Century

Progress with Gunpowder

Gunpowder, a material no less revolutionary than printed matter, transformed warfare in this century. For infantrymen a new weapon, the arquebus, was introduced. In comparison with the hand-gun of the 1400s, which required two men to handle it, the arquebus could be fired by one man, provided that the muzzle rested either on the prop he carried or on the edge of a trench or wall. The powder in the flash pan had to be touched with the glowing end of a length of wick, called match, and a trigger mechanism, the matchlock, held this ready in position while the weapon was aimed. One night when English sailors were raiding the Spanish treasure route through the Panama jungle, they mistook the fireflies for the burning ends of enemy match and feared they were about to be fired on. A sudden storm of rain could therefore decide the course of a battle if soldiers failed to keep their match and powder dry.

For officers a horse-pistol came into use. This had a much more intricate and expensive trigger mechanism called a wheel-lock, and could be fired with one hand. Light artillery capable of being manoeuvred in battle was not introduced till the seventeenth century, but for siege warfare heavy guns were manufactured on a rapidly increasing scale. Military engineers, aided by mathematicians, constructed fortresses with low silhouettes and wide gun platforms to protect towns and harbours.

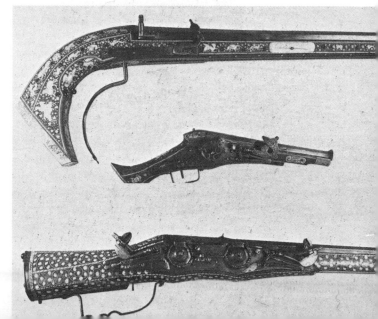

Three 16th century small arms: (a) a French matchlock arquebus of about 1560. The walnut-wood stock is inlaid with stag-horn showing Heracles fighting the Nemean Lion. The butt is designed to be held against the chest, not the shoulder; (b) a wheel-lock pistol made in Nüremberg about 1575; (c) a double-wheel-lock arquebus, dated 1581. It is slightly shorter than the match-lock, being 1.14m long. Two cartridges were loaded at a time and there are two toothed catches for holding the match, not one, as in the other two weapons. A cavity in the butt held three cartridges

The Spanish owed the superiority of their infantry during the century to the genius of Gonzalo de Cordoba, who commanded in Italy. He was the first to increase the proportion of arquebusiers to pikemen and to 'brigade' his men so that they could protect each other in battle. New and complicated drill had to be learnt because the arquebusiers, after firing, took some minutes to reload and during this time the pikemen were ordered forward to protect them. In this way volley firing was achieved and its effectiveness against masses of infantry encumbered with armour was demonstrated at Biocca in 1522 and against the French cavalry at Pavia in 1525.

The Affairs of Italy

As Leonardo da Vinci predicted, the political divisions of Italy and the ceaseless quarrelling of her cities resulted in invasion and subjugation. National pride did not build up resistance in time to prevent the country becoming the scene of war between the French, Germans and Spanish and their allies. The youthful Francis I who succeeded to the throne of France in 1515, at once led an army across the Alps and recovered Lombardy, which his uncle Louis XII had lost. In the same year the Habsburg Charles of Austria, soon to be his rival, became at fifteen ruler of Burgundy, including the Netherlands, and in 1516 inherited from one of his grandfathers the crown of Aragon with Sicily and Naples, as well as the regency of Castile with its American conquests. In 1519 Charles' other grandfather, the aged Emperor Maximilian, also died, leaving him heir to Austria, the Tyrol with its valuable mines, the south-eastern Alps, and the original Habsburg family lands on the upper Rhine between Switzerland and the old duchy of Burgundy. A new emperor then had to be elected. The seven electors—the Count Palatine of the Rhine, the Elector of Saxony, the Margrave of Bradenburg, the King of Bohemia, and the Archbishops of Cologne, Trier and Mainz—were torn between two candidates, Francis and Charles. They disliked Habsburg power and feared a French king with his heavy-handed methods of taxation. The Elector Frederick of Saxony refused to be an alternative candidate, and Charles, after distributing 850,000 florins in bribes, won. He spent his reign in debt to the imperial bankers, the Fuggers of Augsburg, who took the Tyrol silver mines as security. As 'King of the Romans', one of the traditional titles of the emperors, he could now claim to rule Italy for the popes; driven on by his devotion to the imperial dream and tirelessly engaged in the business of government, he prepared to expel the French.

In 1525 Charles' forces in Lombardy defeated and captured Francis at Pavia. When the news was brought to the emperor in Madrid, he forbade celebrations as 'the victory was gained by the blood of Christian men'. Italy now seemed to be in his power, but the finances of the empire were so ill-organised and its debts so vast that he had very little money even for personal expenses and to pay the army was impossible. In 1527, 40,000 of his men, starving and in rags, marched on Rome. Their commander was killed in the assault; his men, out of control, pillaged the city for ten days. Francis, who on his release broke every promise made to Charles during his captivity, sent an army and fleet to lay siege to Naples, but when they were on the point of success, disease decimated their forces and the Genoese sailor of fortune, Andrea Doria, who captained their forces in the harbour, changed sides. His galleys, campaigning for the imperialists, won command of the western Mediterranean.

Wisely Charles chose this moment to make peace; as a concession to Francis he withdrew his claim to the old duchy of Burgundy. Francis renounced his Italian ambitions and agreed to marry Charles' sister Eleanor. To conciliate Pope Clement VII, who belonged to the Medici family, imperialist forces laid siege to Florence, where Michelangelo was among those who took part in an heroic defence. The city fell through the treachery of a condottiere from Perugia and was handed over to Alessandro de Medici, the bastard son of a half-negro slave woman. The pope then went to Bologna where he bestowed on Charles the iron crown of Lombardy and the golden crown of the empire. The emperor, not content with these triumphs, then struck against the Turks and their piratical allies in north Africa. At the head of a splendid fleet he captured Tunis. To protect the straits he gave Malta to the Knights Hospitallers, who had been driven from Rhodes by the Turkish fleet of Sultan Suleiman the Magnificent, and there they built a formidable fortress which in 1565 withstood the Turkish army and navy for five months, finally forcing the enemy to retire. In its care for the people of southern Italy Charles' policy contrasts sharply with that of the French, who did not scruple either in the sixteenth or the seventeenth centuries to ally themselves with the Turks if by so doing they could harm the Spaniards. Yet Charles and his son Philip held both French and Turks in check. At the sea battle of Lepanto (1571) a combined fleet of Spanish and Venetian galleys destroyed the Turkish navy. As so often before and after this century, the safety of Italy hung upon a Mediterranean balance of power.

Reformation and Counter-Reformation

By 1500 the discontent caused by abuses in the Church was far more widespread than in 1400, when Huss and Wyclif had found comparatively little response to their teachings outside their own countries. Yet it was the Church that had educated and trained the most powerful of its sixteenth-century critics. At Deventer in the Netherlands the

A Calvinist cartoon showing the Bible in the balance outweighing the whole power of the Catholic Church

Brethren of the Common Life had established an excellent school, one of whose pupils, Erasmus of Rotterdam (1466-1536), became a leading authority on the text of the Bible and, with his satires on the clergy and their methods of raising money, won European renown. His books, written in a pure and simple Latin, were immensely popular, but unlike other reformers he considered that the international and corporate character of the Church should be preserved at all costs.

In Germany popular resentment at the extravagance of the higher clergy was converted into a revolution in religious thought and practice mainly through the fiery, often coarse eloquence of Martin Luther (1483-1546), a miner's son from Eisleben in Saxony. His father sent him to the University of Erfurt to read law and was furious when he studied theology instead. In 1505, at the age of twenty-three, he became an Austin Friar and three years later a lecturer at the new University of Wittenberg, where his meditations on the epistles of Paul led him to a profound mystical experience, an overwhelming sense of his own faults, and then a joyful conviction that he had received pardon direct from God. On a visit to Rome in 1510 he was repelled by the ostentation of the papal court. Seven years afterwards ,when sellers of papal indulgences came to Wittenberg he put up on the church door ninety-five theses, or arguments, condemning the sales. This was a customary procedure for inviting academic argument, and he was by no means the first to criticise indulgences, which were popularly believed to grant remission of sins. On this occasion half the proceeds were going to the Fuggers of Augsburg, from whom Albert of Hohenzollern, the Archbishop of Mainz, had borrowed 24,000 gilders. The papacy looked to the sales as a method of financing the new church of St Peter at Rome, where Pope Julius had demolished Constantine's old church and was rebuilding on the same site. Indulgences concerned forgiveness and were therefore particularly offensive to Luther, who held, on the basis of his own experience, that, pardon for sins came *sola fide* (by faith alone). From this it followed that, if men could, by studying the Bible, find salvation for themselves, the mediation of the Church and the priesthood, bringing God and the sinner face to face, was unnecessary. Once launched on the path of denial, Luther rapidly widened the front on which he attacked the institutions of Catholicism. Soon he would accept only three out of the seven sacraments, baptism, holy communion and penance, and later penance too was denied.

Between his attack on indulgences in 1517 and his excommunication by Leo X in 1521 he published a treatise in Latin, *The Babylonish Captivity of the Church*, attacking the papacy, and two great works in German advocating the complete transformation of the Church as hitherto known: an *Address to the Christian Nobility of the German Nation*, and *The Liberty of a Christian Man*. On these the Lutheran churches of Europe subsequently based themselves; there could be no compromise; Lutherans were revolutionaries, not reformers. Their leader, since he preached 'the priesthood of all believers', was not interested in Church organisation. The choice of ministers and the evolution of a new liturgy was left to secular rulers.

The bull of excommunication Luther ceremoniously and publicly burnt at Wittenberg. He had already concluded that Leo X, a mild and scholarly pope, and a patron of Raphael, was the Antichrist predicted in the Apocalypse. In 1521 the young Emperor Charles V, anxious to reinforce the authority of the Church, summoned Luther to appear at Worms before a council or diet of the empire. Luther faced his examiners, though some feared he might be executed, and asked to be judged on the authority of scripture. Inevitably he was condemned, but left the diet under the protection of the Elector of Saxony, and living in seclusion produced an inspired translation of the Bible in German.

The princes of Germany were quick to realise that by supporting Luther they could weaken Charles and increase their own independence. Soon the possibility of taking over Church property proved an additional attraction. In 1525 Albrecht of Hohenzollern, Grand Master of the Teutonic Knights, dissolved the order, secularised its lands and became the first German Duke of Prussia. On the other hand when in the same year the peasants of the Rhineland rose in rebellion, killing, burning and looting, they were cruelly suppressed with Luther's approval. Neither he nor his adherents had any wish to change the social order. When an extreme Protestant sect, the Anabaptists, set up a polygamous community in Munster and were starved into surrender, Luther showed no pity for them. He wished the princes who had adopted his views to be absolute masters in their own dominions, and when the diet met at Speyer in 1529, six Lutheran princes and fourteen cities signed a Protestation, affirming their right to answer to God alone for what concerned their salvation. From this the name Protestant was given to the Reformed Churches everywhere.

Sweden established Lutheranism as early as 1528 but, alone among the Protestant Churches on the continent, retained bishops who had been consecrated by a Catholic bishop. Denmark adopted the new faith in 1537; Norway and Iceland followed her example later. Among Charles V's subjects in the Netherlands and particularly in the cosmopolitan town of Antwerp, which had become the largest trading city in Europe, Lutheranism attracted early and widespread attention, but was swiftly and cruelly persecuted. In France, suppression was also immediate and severe. Francis I was quick to encourage Lutherans abroad but not at home.

In Switzerland theological controversy was as violent as in Germany. A musician and classical scholar, Zwingli of Zurich, born in 1484, a year after Luther, attacked indulgences in 1519. Five years later he was for abolishing Mass and 'restoring the Lord's Supper', a subject on which he and Luther conferred at Marburg but failed to agree. Against those cantons that refused to accept his reforms he organised war, and in 1531 was killed in battle together with twenty-two pastors. From 1541 the self-governing town of Geneva began to replace Germany as the most influential centre of Protestantism.

Geneva, the New Jerusalem of the Calvinists

A French scholar, John Calvin (1509-1564) was invited by the confused and divided reformers to go there and restore good government. Under his rule Geneva became for reformers a 'New Jerusalem', an asylum for the persecuted and an admired university for scholars. Refugee printers hastened to issue translations of the scriptures in vernacular tongues and a mass of theological literature.

Calvin was a lawyer's son from Noyon and had read law and theology at the Sorbonne, where students to whose idle ways he objected called him 'The Accusative Case'. At twenty-seven he became famous through the publication of his *Institutes of the Christian Religion*. These had the appearance, not wholly justified, of a clear-cut body of doctrine; baptism and holy communion were the only sacraments accepted; and the *Institutes* have remained the basis of Protestant teaching. The pattern of organisation adopted by Calvinists was everywhere the same, and became known as Presbyterianism. They had three kinds of official, ministers, elders (or presbyters) and deacons. Each community formed a consistory, above which came the colloquy, and above that the synod. In some countries this form of Protestantism spread quickly among all ranks of society, and its methods preserved converts from any feeling of isolation. Where Calvinists found it impossible to take over the existing government, they aimed at creating a state within a state. Like the Lutherans, they held that salvation came by faith alone, and so toleration was out of the question. Since they condemned veneration of the Virgin Mary and the saints, their followers encouraged the removal or destruction of images in churches, chapels and shrines; in consequence these, together with bejewelled reliquaries, priceless vestments, illuminated missals and a thousand other ancient treasures, perished.

The papacy, whose shortcomings had in part provoked the Reformation, was also the chief instrument of the Counter-Reformation. In 1545 Pope Paul III called together a general council in Trent, a town at the southern end of the Brenner pass. Many, including the emperor, hoped that the delegates would make concessions to the Lutherans, but the pope was determined that they should not. Protestant doctrines were specifically repudiated and the Church strengthened by the clear definition of traditional doctrine. This unexpected development has often been bitterly criticised by historians, but in the circumstances of the sixteenth century, when Catholics were as much confused as Protestants, clarity and firmness were the first essentials. The decisions of the Council of Trent were not revised until the second Vatican Council met in the 1960s, but the men of 1545 should not be blamed for the ultra-conservatism of subsequent generations.

Two new religious societies assisted the pope and council, the Oratorians and the Society of Jesus. The first Oratorians were Italian clergy who bound themselves to austere living and works of charity. Six of them were made cardinals by Paul III. The founder of the Society of Jesus was Ignatius Loyola, the eleventh child of a Basque nobleman, born in 1491. In 1521 he was badly wounded in the leg while campaigning in Navarre. The realisation after months of pain that he would be permanently lame and unable to fight sorely tried his ardent and romantic nature. During convalescence he was given lives of Christ and the saints to read and conceived the idea of becoming a missionary in the east. As soon as he could travel he went to the monastery of Montserrat near Barcelona and then retired to a cave near Manresa. There, like Luther, he had a series of mystical experiences, but they were of a very different kind, and in order that others might share them he composed his *Spiritual Exercises*, which became a training manual for his followers. He then begged his way to Jerusalem and on his return, when he was thirty-three, decided to become a university student in preparation for his mission. At the University of Paris, where he was a contemporary of John Calvin, he came to the conclusion that his work must be to combat heresy in Europe. In 1534 he and six fellow students, only one of them a priest, formed the nucleus of the Society of Jesus, pledging themselves to poverty, chastity and obedience at the Benedictine convent in Montmartre. After some difficulty they obtained a bull from Paul III in 1540 giving official recognition to the Society, whose members vowed to obey the pope and the general of their order absolutely. They were exempt from the orders of any other ecclesiastical authority, an exemption that sometimes made them unpopular, but their influence was quickly felt, especially in teaching, for which long training and study of the latest astronomical and geographical knowledge specially fitted them. Excellent schools and colleges were set up in all Catholic countries, and the Gregorian University founded in Rome. One of the Society's first six members, Francis Xavier, also a Basque,

Rome: the college of the Society of Jesus. Its foundation stone was laid by Pope Gregory XIII in 1582, when the Jesuits were already world-famous for their devotion to learning and education

went as a missionary to India and Japan, others to America, everywhere teaching colonists better standards of behaviour and converting pagans. The excesses of the Protestant reformers had already produced a natural reaction, but the revival of Catholicism in the second half of the century derived very largely from the example and devotion of the Oratorians and the Jesuits.

The Habsburgs and Hungary

The Habsburgs, one of the noble families of Germany to whom the feudal system had brought wealth and power, never lost the medieval mentality that went with feudalism.

They regarded the nascent nations of Europe as tenants on family estates that could be disposed of by marriage and inheritance, and their pride and arrogance grew with the increase of their possessions.

Charles V's grandfather, the Emperor Maximilian, much occupied towards the end of his life with planning royal marriages for his grandchildren, wished to ensure that the kingdom of Hungary should be part of their inheritance. His ambassadors obtained a promise from Vladislav, King of Hungary, that either Charles or Ferdinand should, when they grew up, marry Vladislav's daughter Anna. The plan was opposed by many Magyar nobles who wished Zapolya, Prince of Transylvania, to become their king, but when Maximilian heard that Vladislav's wife was pregnant he proposed a double wedding. If the unborn child were a boy, he should marry the baby Habsburg princess Mary. A boy, Louis, was born, though prematurely, and his mother died in giving him birth. In 1515 a magnificent double wedding was celebrated in Vienna. As a proxy husband for Anna the aged Maximilian knelt at the altar beside her while the child Mary married the boy Louis. Later Anna was again married by proxy to the boy prince Ferdinand. The anti-Habsburg party in Hungary tried in vain to get the marriages annulled.

When Louis was twenty, he received a demand for tribute from Sultan Suleiman the Magnificent, which he refused. The Magyar nobles, much preoccupied with the advantages to be gained by becoming Protestants, either Calvinist or Lutheran, made no preparations for invasion. In 1526, when the Turkish army, numbering perhaps 50,000, moved on Budapest, Louis rode out to meet them at Mohacz with only 18,000 men. Almost all of them were killed, and Louis, in attempting to escape, was thrown from his horse and drowned. Of his short, sad life it was said: 'Born too soon, married too soon, king too soon, and dead too soon'.

After Mohacz the Turks withdrew to Constantinople, taking with them a large part of the Hungarian population for sale in Turkish slave markets. Three years later they returned and encamped outside Vienna. Preparations were made for a siege, but had to be abandoned at the approach of winter. To weaken Hungary, Suleiman played off one Magyar party against another, and forced their leaders to pay tribute. Ferdinand, who claimed Louis' kingdom, was defeated and he too had to pay tribute for that part of Western Hungary that he retained. For the Turks, even though their empire stretched eastwards to Basra, Vienna, the Habsburg capital, remained the prize that lured successive sultans to the west.

Philip II and the Netherlands

The Netherlands had emerged from the middle ages a conglomeration of estates, often differing sharply in language and customs even within a small area, some belonging to great lords, others to old and decrepit abbeys, some to bishops, others to dukes. The lakes and waterways that divided them, the ever-present threat of sea and river floods and the hard life of their sailors made the population a strange mixture of quiet home-lovers who hated change of any kind and hard-drinking gamblers who mixed trade with piracy. To the administrative mind the whole region from Arras in the south to

Rotterdam harbour

Friesland in the north was without any political cohesion. Its systems of taxation were a scandal of inefficiency, giving exemption to the rich and oppressing the poor.

To Philip II of Spain, who became overlord of the Netherlands in 1556, no people could have been less sympathetic. He was an arch-bureaucrat with an intellectual's love of tidiness and uniformity in government, and as a human being he had to bear a wholly disproportionate share of family sorrow and distress. He was married four times: to Maria of Portugal, who died giving birth to Don Carlos, a dwarf and a homicidal lunatic; to Mary I of England, who died childless in 1558; to Elizabeth of Valois, who bore him two dearly-loved daughters, but to his great grief died young in 1568; and to Anne of Austria, the mother of Philip, his only surviving son, who inherited the throne, but was not, his father said, worthy of it. Before the age of sixty Philip had laid to rest in the Escorial no less than seventeen members of his family. This palace-monastery was the administrative centre of the Spanish empire, built for him in the hills a day's journey from Madrid as a memorial to his father. The exterior had a classical, un-Spanish austerity, but the interior was richly adorned with fine marble, tapestries and masterpieces by Titian and other living artists. Philip at his desk had little time to enjoy its sixteen courtyards, eighty-eight fountains and fifteen cloisters, but from his bedroom he could hear the chapel services. From his father he had taken bad advice, to attend to everything himself; he distrusted even the ablest ministers. Government offices waited

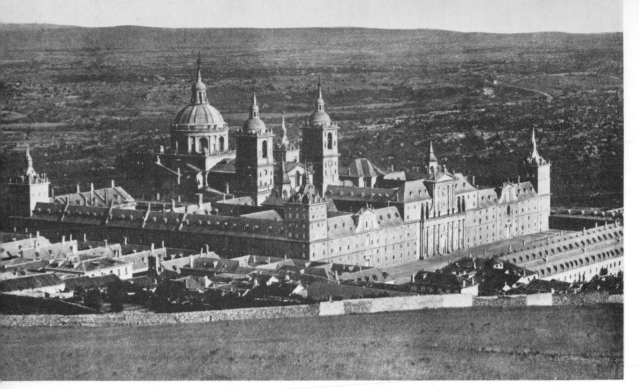

The Escorial, palace of Philip II of Spain, designed by Juan de Herrera, 'the Spanish Palladio'. Building began in 1563 and was completed in 1588. It contains the tombs of the kings of Spain

in despair for decisions, letters remained unanswered and his viceroys in America had a saying: 'If death came from Madrid, we would be immortal.'

Philip remembered too how his father had laboured to reach an accommodation with the Lutherans and, having failed, abdicated and retired to a monastery at the age of fifty-six. In 1555, the year before his father's retirement, the German princes had accepted at Augsburg the rule *cuius regio, eius religio* (each region must adopt the religion of its ruler). This meant that the emperor's authority within the empire was almost at an end, and Philip believed that Spain, Italy and the Netherlands would fall into anarchy if heretics were not mercilessly hunted down.

His dominions, though separated geographically, had strong economic ties, and trade was expanding rapidly. Far away in the Andes the royal mint at the great Potosi silver mine was pouring out bullion. At home in Castile immense flocks of sheep, whose masters spent the hot summer in the cool sierras and the cold winter in the plains, fed the weaving mills of Flanders, while fish from Holland was exchanged for corn from the Belgian plain. Philip's religious fanaticism ignored these links. By decrees against heresy he deliberately provoked opposition. To protest, great landowners travelled to Madrid; one of them, William of Orange, said: 'It is folly, when corn is dear'. Philip would grant no relief, and in 1566 came a great explosion of violence, 'the breaking of the images'. From Delft and Utrecht through Antwerp to Valenciennes churches were defaced and ransacked by mobs stirred up by Calvinist preachers. Philip's response

116

Ecclesiastical cope of red velvet embroidered in gold by Flemish craftswomen, probably presented by the Emperor Charles V to Burgos cathedral. It was vestments like these that were destroyed by Protestant mobs

was to send the Duke of Alva with a Spanish army to restore order. Two great nobles were arrested, held hostage and subsequently executed.

William of Orange took refuge outside the Netherlands. He had been a Lutheran in boyhood, but had become a Catholic and inherited large estates in the south of France, from which he took his name. Fortunately for the Orange faction Alva united all parties by imposing the Spanish system of taxes, which were, unlike those of Flanders, simple and unavoidable. There were many disorders, the worst being in Brill where some lawless sailors, 'the sea beggars', flying the Orange tricolour seized the port. Alva was recalled, but his successor, Requesen, carried on the war. In 1574 the Spanish, while besieging Leyden, were driven off when the Dutch cut the dykes and let in the sea. Two years later Requesen died, and his army, unpaid and mutinous, sacked Antwerp, murdering thousands of the inhabitants. Philip next sent out his half-brother Don John of Austria, who had some success but died after two years. A fourth commander, the Duke of Parma, at once accepted proposals for a truce from the provinces south of the Rhine mouth. Those to the north of it then formed a union, appealed to France and England for help, and made William of Orange their leader. In spite of several attempts on his life he took no precautions and an assassin, hired as a servant, shot him. The whole of the Netherlands mourned; Elizabeth I sent her favourite, the Earl of Leicester, with a small army, but he lost his way in the shifting sands of Dutch politics and returned home.

So far Philip had avoided open war with England; now he planned to send a fleet to the Netherlands to take on board part of Parma's army and invade England. After many delays and very scanty provisioning Philip's 'invincible Armada', heavily laden with soldiers, sailed in 1588. It passed through the Channel without serious loss, but off Calais took flight from English fireships before a rising storm which scattered the whole fleet. Only a third of the original number of ships and a fraction of their men reached home. Philip took the news of the disaster calmly. Parma continued his campaign, but the Dutch command had now been put in the hands of one good soldier, Maurice of Nassau, and when Philip died in 1598, the Spaniards gave up their efforts to advance to the north. Neither side believed that Dutch independence had been won for good, Spain still held the rich southern provinces, and the northerners remained armed, fearing for the future.

The French Wars of Religion

The term 'wars of religion' is used to describe the thirty-eight years of civil strife and massacre which France suffered between the death of Henry II in 1559 and Henry IV's promulgation of the Edict of Nantes in 1598. The contestants were divided between Catholic and Huguenot, but this did not mean that they adhered to the religious ideals of Catholicism or of Protestantism. One member of the leading Catholic family, that of Guise, was, for example, Archbishop of Rheims from the age of fourteen. In addition to the archbishopric he held the revenues of the bishoprics of Metz and Verdun and of numerous abbeys, and together these brought him an estimated annual income of 300,000 livres. Among the Protestants Admiral Coligny, a Montmorency, and for a brief while their leader, expressed no regret when he heard that the Duke of Guise had been murdered by a Huguenot, merely remarking that the duke had been 'an enemy of God and man'. The assassin was praised in Huguenot tracts as a brave tyrannicide.

The labels of religion were often no more than devices with which to cover a struggle for power between rival nobles, and this would have occurred had there been no religious dissension to aggravate it, for the royal family of Valois suffered during the period an altogether exceptional series of misfortunes. When Henry II was accidentally killed jousting in 1559, his eldest son, Francis II was only fifteen and a weakly boy who lived

Jousting scene by Albrecht Dürer (1471-1528), the German master of painting and engraving

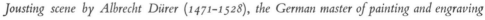

little more than a year. At fourteen he had been married to the daughter of Mary of Guise, who was two years his senior and had been Queen of Scots from infancy. The brother who succeeded him, Charles IX, a boy of ten, reigned for only fourteen years and also died childless; a third brother the childless Henry III, after an unhappy reign, was murdered at the age of thirty-eight by a Dominican friar. The mother of these three kings, Catherine de Medici, widowed at forty and, until her death twenty-nine years later, at the centre of every political storm, ardently protected what she conceived to be her children's interests. The French nobility considered her their social inferior, being merely the daughter of a Florentine banker. Though a foreigner, she outwitted all those at court and twice made herself in effect regent, first for Francis and secondly for Charles. A royal duke, Anthony of Bourbon, should have been appointed regent for Charles, but he was a weak man married to the Queen of Navarre, who had manoeuvred him into the Huguenot camp. His brother Louis, Prince of Condé, also a Huguenot, was an exceedingly dangerous man, restlessly ambitious, whose attempts to dispose of the Guise family by armed rebellion twice failed.

In 1561, in order to nullify the ambitions of the nobles, Catherine called together the leaders of the Catholic and Huguenot parties at Poissy, hoping that they might agree on some formula concerning the Eucharist that would enable them both to worship in the same church buildings, but too much blood had already flowed on both sides. Catherine, having tried in vain to appease the Huguenots, plotted with the Duke of Guise to murder their leader, Admiral Coligny. The wedding of her daughter Margaret to Henry of Navarre in 1572 provided an opportunity. Most other Protestant leaders were also guests, since they hoped that Henry might one day be King of France. An assassin shot at Coligny from a window with an arquebus, slightly wounding him. Catherine, to conceal her complicity, obtained the king's consent for an immediate and general massacre of the Huguenots on the eve of St Bartholomew's Day. Coligny was among over 3,000 killed in Paris. Henry of Navarre and his brother escaped, but hundreds more were slaughtered by mobs in the provinces.

The ensuing war was long and cruel, neither side understanding the meaning of compromise or toleration; the conflict subsided only when both sides were exhausted. On the murder of Henry III in 1589, Henry of Navarre, an excellent soldier and a highly popular man, having emerged victorious, claimed the throne. He then asked to be absolved and accepted by the Catholic Church. This was granted, and in 1594 he was welcomed as Henry IV by the fanatically Catholic population of the capital. 'Paris', he said 'was worth a mass'. The Huguenots, who at one time in the struggle had set up a republic with authority over all France south of the Loire, were granted freedom of conscience and freedom of worship under an edict issued by Henry IV from Nantes in 1598. 'The length and scale of the war', wrote Henry, 'have so desolated the provinces that most of the land is deserted and uncultivated.' Such an economic disaster cannot be accounted for by those who accept the Marxist theory that Calvinism appealed to capitalists whose freedom to lend money at interest had been hampered by the Catholic Church. The French nation had been split vertically, not horizontally; people of every class were to be found in each party, and many changed sides either out of conviction or from fear. The truth is that one of the mainsprings of Protestantism was a spirit of criticism and censure directed, often legitimately, at the Catholic Church. Too frequently this aroused such passion and resentment that mob violence resulted. To every mob hooligans, delighting in destruction for its own sake, quickly become attached. From destroying property to taking life is a short step, and so rioting merges into civil war.

Copernicus, Kepler and Brahé

Renaissance scholars had rediscovered the second century astronomy of Ptolemy, according to which the earth was the centre of a finite universe consisting of a series of crystal spheres. To these translucent but impenetrable spheres the sun, moon and stars were believed fixed. The motion of heavenly bodies could be accurately calculated on these assumptions and the Ptolemaic system had been accepted for that reason, until Copernicus questioned it. He was a Polish merchant's son who had learnt astronomy at the Universities of Cracow and Bologna, and circulated among friends a short manuscript suggesting that the earth moved round the sun. Being a devout Catholic, he did not fear to print this for religious reasons but because his theory seemed against common sense and might be ridiculed. Two Protestant friends eventually persuaded him to publish his *De Revolutionibus Orbium Coelestium*, a large work dedicated to Pope Paul III. In this his arguments were partly philosophical, attributing the theory to Pythagoras, and partly mathematical.

Copernicus died in 1543, the same year that his book came out, and never knew its effect. Not much attention was aroused until Tycho Brahé, a Danish astronomer, working at his own observatory on the island of Hveen, reported in 1577 the appearance of a new comet which could not be regarded as fixed to a sphere. He was also able without a telescope to catalogue 777 fixed stars. Later his pupil, Johannes Kepler (1571-1630), the son of a German mercenary serving under the Duke of Alva in the Netherlands, formulated three laws governing the movement of the planets. These showed by mathematics that they moved in ellipses, not circles, round the sun and the revolution in thought required by these new discoveries began to alarm the world of learning. Protestant professors turned Kepler out of the University of Tübingen, but he found refuge with the Jesuits. To accept that the universe, so long believed finite, was in fact infinite and the earth only a small part of a vast solar system required a generosity of spirit not easy to find in universities.

Uraniborg, the observatory of the Danish astronomer Tycho Brahé on the island of Hveen. A 16th century drawing

CHAPTER NINE

The Seventeenth Century

The Thirty Years' War

Calvinism, spreading through Germany, Poland and Bohemia a generation later than Lutheranism, resulted in even more numerous transfers of Church property into private hands and the fear that Roman Catholics might, in the wake of the Counter-Reformation, claim it back. This was the main cause of the series of international conflicts known as the Thirty Years' War (1618-1648). The struggle, though undertaken in the name of religion, was fought between princes, nobles and soldiers seeking to enlarge their fortunes and estates. Titles to Lutheran property acquired during the first phase of the Reformation were acknowledged under the terms of the Peace of Augsburg (1555), but not the titles of Calvinists, of whom there had been very few at the time, though by 1600 they dominated the Rhine Palatinate and Bohemia. As the Counter-Reformation gained in strength the Protestants in the Rhineland were in danger on two fronts: from the Spaniards, who had crushed Protestantism in the southern Netherlands; and from Maximilian, Duke of Bavaria, a powerful Catholic prince under whom a Catholic League was formed in 1609.

Before the death of the Emperor Matthias in 1619, Ferdinand of Austria, a Habsburg and an ardent Catholic, had been recognised as heir to the kingdoms of Hungary and Bohemia. The Czech nobles, who were Calvinist, met Ferdinand's two Regents in May 1618, and asked for his election to be annulled. The meeting ended in uproar, the nobles throwing the Regents and their secretary out of a window of the palace in Prague seventy feet above the ground. Falling into a ditch, they escaped with their

Prague: the royal palace crowns the hill on the left

lives. To a man of Ferdinand's nature war was the only answer to such an insult and for this the Czechs were militarily and financially unprepared. The idea that men should fight for their own liberties was not considered. Victory lay with that side which could hire better mercenaries or call in more foreign aid than its opponents.

One of the first German princes to congratulate the Czech rebels was Frederick, the Calvinist Elector of the Rhine Palatinate, a young, handsome but incompetent ruler. He secretly allowed the Catholic ruler of Savoy to send to Bohemia a mercenary army under Ernst von Mansfeld, which by the end of 1618 had driven most of the imperialists out of Bohemia. These troops, in doing so, earned an evil reputation for their disgraceful treatment of friend and foe.

The Emperor Matthias died in March 1619 and six months later Ferdinand was elected in his place. Ten days earlier the Czechs in Prague had declared Frederick king. One of the elector's German friends cried out: 'Now we have the means of upsetting the world!' He did not understand what he was saying. Prague does indeed lie at the heart of Europe, almost exactly half-way between Madrid and Moscow, but for this new king the election of Ferdinand as emperor had fatally shifted the balance of power against him.

Next spring Frederick's forces melted away like the winter snow. A skirmish with the imperialists outside Prague was enough to put him and his family to flight. His beautiful and high-spirited wife, Elizabeth, a daughter of James I, the first monarch of England, Scotland and Ireland, spent a long exile with their children at the Hague, never abandoning hope of returning; but Ferdinand, as King of Bohemia, with Jesuits to aid him reorganise the schools of the country, gradually stamped out Calvinism. By 1623 Frederick had also been expelled from the Palatinate and his title of Elector transferred to his Catholic ally, Maximilian of Bavaria.

The Emperor was now determined to extirpate Protestantism from the whole of his dominions and, since this meant war, he commissioned Albert Wenceslas von Wallenstein to raise an army and be his commander-in-chief. This Czech soldier of fortune, once a Protestant, but now a Catholic, had acquired a large fortune and lived in princely style. He insisted on being given supreme powers and, having recruited men of many nations regardless of their creed, was by 1628 master of almost all north Germany. The emperor then took the foolish step of issuing an Edict of Restitution, requiring that all land taken from the Church since 1555 should be restored, including the Archbishoprics of Magdeburg and Bremen, the Bishoprics of Lübeck and Brandenburg and much other territory which had been in the hands of Calvinist administrators for fifty to eighty years. Wallenstein was known to disapprove of the edict. The Catholic princes were already jealous of his wealth and influence, and so too was Cardinal Richelieu, the head of the French government, who sent an envoy to foment their discontent. Soon they demanded that the emperor should dismiss Wallenstein.

The prospect of a Catholic power in the Baltic also appeared as a threat to the King of Sweden, Gustavus Adolphus, a Lutheran, and in 1630 he chose the moment when Wallenstein was about to fall to invade Germany. He was not welcomed by German Protestants, but had the support of Richelieu, who had agreed to give the Swedes a subsidy of 400,000 thalers if they provided 30,000 infantry and 6,000 cavalry. This

Stockholm: an 18th century artist's view of the royal palace from across the harbour

force included several regiments of Scots and differed in weapons and training from any army previously engaged. It wore a uniform quickly recognisable in the smoke of battle and so men on the same side avoided killing each other. It had light artillery for preliminary bombardment of enemy lines and its cavalrymen had been taught to charge with swords drawn after firing a volley with their pistols.

The Swedes first conquered Pomerania in order to make sure of their Baltic communications, and this preoccupation enabled the imperialists under Marshal Tilly to take Magdeburg, where they behaved with a ferocity equal to that of the Spaniards in Rome and Antwerp in the previous century. After this, fear drove the Protestants to ally themselves with Gustavus and contribute some 15,000 Saxon troops to his army. When he brought Tilly to battle at Breitenfeld in November 1631, he destroyed the imperialist army as a fighting force, inflicting terrible casualties and taking thousands of prisoners. His natural caution then led him to a fatal error. Instead of marching on Vienna, he drove the imperialists out of Bavaria, entering Munich with the Elector Palatine at his side. Wallenstein was recalled and with great skill wore down the Swedish strength in a war of movement. In November 1632, the two armies met at Lützen; the Swedes were victorious, but Gustavus was killed. A man of his high character and intellectual ability (he spoke six languages) was a terrible loss, and those who ruled for his infant daughter Christina had not the talent required to make peace. The war dragged

123

on; Wallenstein again fell into disfavour and was murdered by two Irishmen and two Scots who hoped to please the emperor. The Swedes were defeated at Nördlingen in 1634 and had to retire from south Germany.

A 17th century Dutch sword with hilt in cast and chased silver. The Dutch organised the only well-paid army in Europe and it never mutinied

Peace negotiations began as soon as Christina came of age; she was determined to stop the bloodshed, overruled her father's ministers, and after four years the Peace of Westphalia was signed. Sweden was granted Pomerania and Bremen; the lower Palatinate was restored to Frederick's son, Charles; Brandenburg-Prussia, which benefited most from the treaty, gained territory in the far west and centre of Germany; France obtained Metz and Verdun; and the United Provinces in the northern Netherlands were formally recognised as free and independent after their eighty years of war with Spain. The German Calvinists and Lutherans were confirmed in their possessions, and the old rule of *cuius regio, eius religio* reaffirmed. This left the majority of Germans under Catholic rulers. The devastations of war were quickly repaired, the population began to increase rapidly, universities flourished, and a happy and gifted people continued the peaceful colonisation of the Baltic coast.

The Affairs of Russia, Poland and the Jews

From 1600 until the accession of Michael, the first Tsar of the Romanov dynasty, in 1613, Russia was in anarchy with rival candidates fighting for the throne, and the Poles, taking advantage of her weakness, captured Smolensk and entered Moscow. At the same time the Swedes overran most of north-western Russia including Novgorod. Michael, in order to obtain peace, had to surrender Smolensk to the Poles and, though he recovered Novgorod, had to leave the Swedes in possession of the whole coast of the Finnish Gulf.

At the time when the Peace of Westphalia was signed in 1648, the Polish kingdom had reached its greatest extent, stretching from the Oder in the west to the headwaters of the Dnieper in the east and from the Gulf of Riga in the north to within a hundred miles of Odessa in the south, but size did not bring strength. The Polish nobles who had acquired estates in the Ukraine were Roman Catholics, but their tenants and serfs were Orthodox and devoted to their priests. Absentee Polish landlords often left the management of their land in the hands of Jews, whose superior education gave them considerable power. They even collected dues for baptism and burial according to Orthodox rites. Discontent grew steadily and runaway serfs were constantly crossing the southern border into the land of the Cossacks, a people also devoutly Orthodox, who owed a nominal allegiance to the Polish kings.

In Russia an intermittent class war was being waged between the peasants and their landlords. Revolts were frequent and cruelty was the chief weapon used against them. In 1648 this social unrest flowed over the Polish border, where a Cossack leader stirred up a fearful peasant rebellion against the Jews, massacring tens of thousands. A flood of refugees began moving westward into Germany and the Netherlands, settling in whatever accommodation was available. They did not for the most part wish to mix with their new neighbours, but delighted in the secluded life of their own section in each of the larger cities, unaware of the jealousy that their prosperity aroused. They had not found Jerusalem.

When order had been restored in Poland, the Jews who had remained were given back their privileges, but the kingdom grew steadily weaker. Russia recovered both Kiev and Smolensk under a truce, signed in 1667, which specifically encouraged trade 'except for the Jews'. This ban, supported by the Orthodox Church, was later confirmed, but Jewish traders unwisely ignored it, crossing the frontiers in the north and south to attend trade fairs and sometimes staying for a year or more.

The desire of the Orthodox Church to isolate Russia from the west, exemplified in the ban on Jewish immigration, did not affect Alexis, the second Tsar in the Romanov line, who in a reign of thirty-one years (1645-1676) introduced many novelties from the west. He married twice; by his first wife he had two surviving sons, Fedor II, who succeeded him and John, who was feeble-minded. By his second marriage to Natalia Naryshkin he had a boy, the future Tsar Peter, born in 1672, and two daughters. Peter was only ten when Fedor died and the Patriarch of Moscow presented him to a chance crowd on the Red Square who acclaimed him Tsar in place of John. His half-sister Sophia would not accept this, and with the help of treacherous palace guards made herself regent. In the disturbances Peter watched helplessly while the guards murdered Matveyev, one of his father's most cultivated advisers, a man devoted to his collection of tapestries, pictures and clocks from the west. It was a scene Peter never forgot. The regent Sophia, who had received a good education, chose as her chief counsellor Prince Basil Golitsyn, who spoke Latin and could read German and Greek, and was noted for his liberal ideas. Peter thus grew up at a court already deeply interested in the countries of western Europe where in manhood his studies made him the most thorough and ruthless westeriser of his day.

The Frontiers of France
There were only seven years in the seventeenth century free from war in Europe,

1610, 1669 to 1671 and 1680 to 1682, and the main disturber of the peace was France. Henry IV's chief minister, Sully, had made war possible by accumulating a reserve of some 30,000,000 francs in the vaults of the Bastille, and his master's object was the destruction of the house of Habsburg that ruled in Spain, the Netherlands, Lombardy and Naples. There was also Habsburg territory on France's eastern border. Henry was an excellent general and had organised an alliance intended to provoke a major war in which all participants, if victorious, would make extensive gains at Habsburg expense. The conflict was only averted because a fanatic stabbed him to death on 14 May 1610 as he was walking along a Paris street to visit Sully.

Henry's heir, Louis XIII, was nine, and much depended on the person selected as Regent. The Duc d'Epernon surrounded the palace and the meeting place of the Paris parlement with the troops under his command. The parlement, a corporation of lawyers who had the right to refuse registration for royal edicts of which they did not approve, listened while Epernon, tapping his scabbard, said that his sword would be drawn if members did not at once approve an edict appointing the Queen Mother, Marie de Medici, Regent. This strange flattery of the lawyers and the Paris mob obtained the title for Marie. Sully fled, and she spent his treasure on her Italian favourites and in buying support among the nobility. In 1614 Louis was declared of age and the States-General was called to one of its rare meetings; indeed it was not summoned again till the eve of the French Revolution. Its three houses, which met separately, consisted of 145 clergy, 132 nobles and 192 of the third estate, who were mostly lawyers and petty officials. None of the three houses had any legislative power, but they were asked to enumerate their grievances, and this led to long, wordy quarrels between the third estate and the other two houses. Nothing was achieved. Two years later the queen mother, with complete disregard for French feelings, arranged a double wedding; her daughter Elizabeth married the heir to the Spanish throne, the future Philip IV, and Louis married Philip's sister Anne, known as Anne of Austria.

The forward movement on the frontiers was not resumed until Cardinal Richelieu became head of the government in 1624. Though the nobility and the Huguenots were both unruly and sometimes treasonable in their attempts to obtain foreign aid, the cardinal did not hesitate, while crushing the political power of the Huguenots within France, to send financial and military aid to their co-religionists in Germany in their struggle with the Habsburg emperor. After the death of Gustavus Adolphus he steadily strengthened French-held positions in Alsace, which lay within the empire, and sent an army over the Alps which captured Turin, cutting the line of communications between Madrid and Vienna through the Spanish-held duchy of Milan.

On Richelieu's death in 1642, his place was taken by his pupil, Cardinal Mazarin, an Italian who continued to carry out his policies and reaped rich rewards from them both for France and for himself. He gave the command of an army on the Netherlands frontier to the fiery young Duc d'Enghien, later Prince of Condé, who met a strong Spanish force in the marshes near Rocroy in 1643. French firepower and mobility were far superior to that of the Spaniards, whose infantry were routed by repeated French charges. Another and even better commander, Turenne, during the closing stages of the Thirty Years' War twice invaded and ravaged the Catholic duchy of Bavaria, held by Maximilian, the emperor's chief ally. At the end of the war France received wide new territories on her eastern border giving access to Lorraine for future campaigns.

War with Spain continued after 1648, but for five years France was torn by fresh civil disturbances between various factions led by the nobility and fomented by the Paris parlement. All hated Cardinal Mazarin, but no leader could be found under whom to unite. The movement was well named the Fronde, meaning catapult, an ancient and clumsy weapon. Mazarin survived, and through royal favour was able to get rid of his chief enemies among the nobility. Condé went over to Spain but his advance on Paris was repulsed by Turenne. The young king seeing his inheritance in danger of disintegration determined to concentrate all power in his own hands.

When the troubles of the Fronde were over, the French, with the help of Oliver Cromwell, whose hatred of Spain made him willing to help a more ancient enemy, took Dunkirk. Here in later wars were stationed galleys to harry London-bound shipping. When the exhausted Spaniards at last made peace in 1659. France gained Artois and other territory on the Netherlands border, and Roussillon in the south. Louis XIV, who had been only five when he succeeded his father in 1643, was married to his cousin Maria Theresa, daughter of Philip IV. The Spanish, hoping to prevent Louis from later claiming for himself what might otherwise have been her inheritance, the crown of Spain, arranged a dowry of 500,000 crowns in exchange for an act of renunciation.

Louis was as fortunate in his finance minister as Henry IV with Sully. The post was filled by the son of a Rheims draper, Jean-Baptiste Colbert, whom he created Marquis of Seignelay, and only the king's insane desire for glory and conquest prevented Colbert

Gunner's linstock, or match-holder, 17th century French. Could be used as a spear if the enemy came to close quarters; the match was held in the teeth of the two beasts' heads

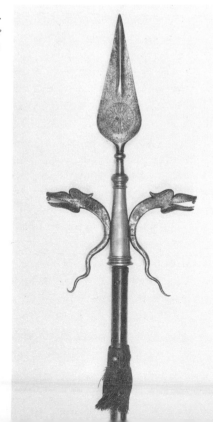

from making France the best managed state in Europe. Nor were Colbert's horizons limited. He understood the achievement of French explorers in America, where, following Champlain's example, they had discovered the route from the French settlements round Quebec over the great lakes into the Mississippi valley. Colbert, knowing that an overseas empire would need a navy, employed Vauban, the finest military engineer of the day, to build and fortify naval bases at Toulon, Rochefort, Brest, Havre and Dunkirk.

Le Grand Monarque was also well served by Louvois, his Minister of War, who reorganised the French forces and attached a company of trained engineers to every army. The unruly nobility of France, which had formerly disrupted discipline, was encouraged to seek commissions in corps d'élite and with them their reckless courage won many battles. Louis' motive in making war is mysterious; he ruled the most fertile land in Europe and could have been master of a large part of America; internal dissension had died away; Spain was in decline; and France after twenty years of peace could have bought her way to world power. As Louis said: 'Peace was established for as long as I myself should wish it'. With insatiable ambition and deceitful diplomacy he proceeded to extend the borders of France to both the east and the north. In 1672 he attacked the Dutch republic, and his army was repulsed only by the opening of the dykes. Through this campaign against an ancient ally he united all Dutchmen behind William of Orange, later William III of Britain.

Fifteen years later the French government revoked the Edict of Nantes and renewed the persecution of the Huguenots, who for fifty years had avoided any political action, and, when these thrifty, hard-working people began to seek refuge abroad, dragoons were given the cruel task of stopping them. To leave a kingdom reputed the most cultured in the world was legally possible only for those who could prove that they were baptised Catholics. Nonetheless thousands of Protestants did escape.

On all sides Louis was losing friends and making enemies, and when war came he was without a single ally. In 1688 William of Orange sailed with an invasion force from Amsterdam to Torbay. Without bloodshed King James II, the Catholic ally of Louis, was replaced at Westminster by his Protestant daughter Mary and her husband William, reigning jointly. After battles in Scotland and Ireland William brought their resources also into the war against Louis. Diplomacy, however, could not obtain concerted action in the field, and in 1698 the exhausted combatants agreed to the Peace of Ryswick, which imposed no great loss of territory on the French. When the century ended, the long-awaited death of Charles II of Spain, though imminent, had not occurred. It was taken for granted that his vast and scattered empire must be partitioned. To divide the spoils by diplomacy rather than war, even if Louis should by accident keep a promise, seemed almost beyond hope.

John Sobieski and the Relief of Vienna
The corrupt system by which the Polish kings were elected resulted in a succession of weak rulers who could not defend their dominions against encroachments from predatory neighbours. Russia, Prussia and Sweden each at various times attacked Poland.

'The Polish Horseman', painted by Rembrandt about 1657. This mounted archer rides like a man from the steppes with the 'forward seat' not used in the west till modern times

In the 1670s danger also came from the Turks, with whom Louis XIV had allied himself. The grand vizier of the Ottoman empire, finding the Cossacks ready once more to invade the Ukraine, joined forces with them. To meet this threat the Polish nobles set aside their domestic quarrels and appointed one of themselves, John Sobieski, a man of vast size and outstanding courage, as commander-in-chief. The Turks, whose policy it was to create terror among their enemies, soon learned to fear the skill and speed with which he organised his campaigns. To him the Emperor Leopold I sent for help when in 1683 a Turkish army of over 100,000 under the command of the grand vizier advanced on Vienna. The Turks moved slowly, committing calculated atrocities and driving a multitude of refugees in front of them.

The capital was defended by walls of tremendous strength, but, with a garrison of only 14,000, could not hope to stand a long siege. Leopold and his family departed for Passau, and the imperialist army waited some distance away for help to come. By August the Turks had encircled Vienna, but the grand vizier delayed an assault, hoping for a capitulation. This gave time for Sobieski, now a man of fifty-nine, to ride at the head of his cavalry to join the imperialists, over whom he took command. He advanced to the hills outside Vienna, lit beacon fires to encourage the defenders, and prepared for battle. His numbers were less than half those of the Turks, but he had won the most valuable asset in war, surprise. Moving swiftly down on to the plain, he was soon inside the vast Turkish camp, where his men created such confusion and panic that a general retreat began. The Turks, in flight through hostile territory, suffered terrible losses. Their commander escaped to Constantinople, where the Sultan had him beheaded for incompetence. Sobieski entered Vienna in triumph without waiting for Leopold, who, before meeting him, asked his advisers with what gesture of greeting an emperor should salute a mere king. 'With open arms, sir!' was the reply.

By 1699 the emperor had in alliance with the Poles recovered all Hungary, Transylvania and most of Croatia, while Poland had won back the Ukraine. Sobieski, who died in 1696, would not have been satisfied, for Europe ought not, he said, in dealing with the Turk, 'to conquer and curb the monster, but hurl him back into the deserts'.

Galileo and the Progress of Science

Astronomy, the oldest of the exact sciences, has as its basis mathematical calculation, but the students who thronged the lecture room of Galileo Galilei (1564-1642) in Padua

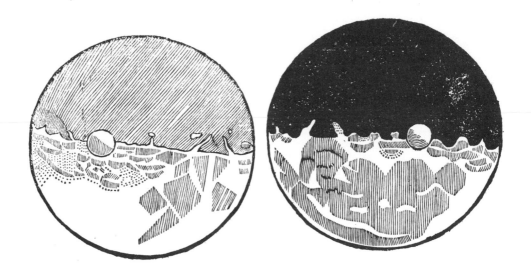

Galileo's drawings of the moon

during the first ten years of the century were in the same excited frame of mind as those who meet some eloquent explorer returned from a new country. Their teacher described how he had constructed a telescope for himself and become the first man to see the mountains of the moon, the four satellites of Jupiter and the phases of Venus and Mars. The Milky Way, he declared, was a cloud of very distant stars. When no traveller had a chronometer to help him ascertain the longitude of his position on a map, Galileo compiled tables from which, provided that the frequent eclipses of Jupiter's satellites could be observed, longitude could be accurately calculated. With biting sarcasm he denied the generally accepted observation of Aristotle that heavy bodies would fall in a vacuum more rapidly than light bodies and described experiments disproving it. With equal sarcasm he contradicted Kepler's view that the moon affected the tides, for, with the weakness that sometimes afflicts great men, Galileo was seldom generous to other workers in his own field.

As a boy at Pisa, his birthplace, he had observed the candelabrum in the cathedral and realised that whether it swung through a short or a long distance it took the same time for its swing, and forty years afterwards worked out the principles on which a pendulum clock was later constructed.

For most of his life Galileo enjoyed the protection and patronage of the Medici family, being mathematician to the Grand Duke of Tuscany, but in 1633 the Inquisition censured him for upholding the Copernican system, and obtained a recantation under threat of torture. It was the satire in his published work, where Aristotelians were represented as dunces, that had irritated the authorities. Galileo was furious. He was condemned to recite once a week for three years the seven penitential psalms; the imprisonment during pleasure, to which he was also sentenced, lasted no more than three days. After this no other man of science was made to recant his opinions. Freedom of discussion in scientific matters was new, and had not been easily won. For the rest of the century astronomy, aided by the mathematical philosophy of Descartes, a Frenchman working mainly in the Netherlands, where freedom was respected, and by the discoveries of Sir Isaac Newton, published in England in 1687, advanced further in a shorter space of time than at any previous period.

CHAPTER TEN

The Eighteenth Century

The Reign of Tsar Peter the Great

Everything that Tsar Peter did was connected, directly or indirectly, with his desire for victory in war, and only two out of the forty-three years of his reign were years of peace. His huge, muscular figure seemed to vibrate with energy and to be incapable of stillness. He hated Moscow and travelled ceaselessly, not only within Russia but also abroad, visiting Austria, Germany, Denmark, Holland, France and England. Everywhere he went his quick intelligence absorbed the mechanical details of iron smelting, ship-building, salt-mining and other industries that he intended to encourage in Russia, but he paid little attention to the feelings of others. If he was excited and boisterous, all about him must be so too; if angry, only his wife Catherine, once a servant girl in

The Old Admiralty, Leningrad. This building was the focal point of Peter the Great's plan for St Petersburg, which he intended as Russia's 'window on the world'

Marienburg, could calm him, for she shared all his interests, and could mediate between him and his counsellors.

In 1700 Peter joined Denmark, Prussia and Poland in attacking the kingdom of Sweden, whose ruler Charles XII, at eighteen, though lacking experience of war, had an instinctive love of soldiering and limitless physical strength, sharing all the hardships of his troops. In a short space he had defeated the Danes and then suddenly appeared before the Swedish fortress of Narva on the south coast of the Gulf of Finland to which Peter was laying siege. The huge untrained Russian army numbered 60,000 men, the Swedish only 8,000, but Charles attacked in the middle of a November snowstorm and put the Russians to flight. From Narva the victors marched on Warsaw, where they installed a new king. In the west the war of the Spanish succession had reached stalemate and the news of these victories prompted the French to ask for an alliance. To forestall them the Duke of Marlborough travelled to the Swedish headquarters and persuaded Charles as a Lutheran to remain neutral. Yet peace with honour did not attract him; Moscow became his goal; Mazeppa, an old Cossack friend of the tsar, promised to change sides and bring a great cavalry force to his aid. Peter, who refused at first to believe this treachery and killed the messengers who brought the news, found a better ally in a Russian winter so cold that man and beast were often frozen to death. Charles' army, which had not taken the Smolensk route, but made a southward détour to meet Mazeppa, was decimated by frost and disease. By June 1709, when he met Peter's retrained army and its new French guns, he was outnumbered by two to one, and utterly defeated. Twenty thousand Swedes surrendered. Charles, wounded in the foot, escaped to Turkey and for nine years carried on the war with the Sultan's help. He was killed in action against the Norwegians in 1718. The Swedish prisoners added to the number of foreigners whom Peter had imported to teach western crafts and manners. The officers whiled away their captivity giving instruction in music, painting, dancing and languages.

The Orthodox Church looked with disfavour on western ideas and customs. In the eyes of the priesthood even to shave off the beard was to commit blasphemy, since God, who made man in his own image, clearly intended him to be bearded. Peter would have none of this. For twenty years he put off appointing a new patriarch and subordinated the whole hierarchy to his personal rule. After his day to be clean shaven was the mark of a 'gentleman'. Shaving the head and wearing powdered wigs, as the fashion was in western Europe, caused even greater scandal. Yet educationally Peter's policy brought his country many advantages. With the help and advice of the German philosopher Leibniz he created an Academy of Science, and the study of foreign languages (he sent hundreds of Russians abroad to learn them) encouraged the development of native talent in literature, art and architecture. Peter's son Alexis, who was devoted to the Church, hoped for his father's death in order that Russia might revert to its old isolation, and in 1718 his father, believing him to have been involved in a treasonable plot, executed him.

The most notable achievement of Peter's last years was the building of a new capital, St Petersburg, on the marshes at the entrance to the river Neva. This had, until the defeat of Charles XII, been Swedish territory. Peter had also acquired Riga and Reval, but these did not satisfy him as ports, not being connected with the new system of canals and waterways which under his initiative stretched thousands of miles to the south and terminated in Astrakhan at the mouth of the Volga, where the goods of Persia and India entered the country. St Petersburg was built with extraordinary speed; streets, canals and public buildings were the work of foreign and Russian architects: Rossi, Thomont, Voronikhin and especially Zakharov, the designer of the Admiralty, headquarters of the navy on which the tsar had spent so much thought and care. By 1725 the city was comparable in magnificence with Paris, Vienna and London. Labour was cheap and plentiful; huge numbers of serfs were drafted in for pile-driving and canal digging and many lost their lives from frost, flood, hunger and disease. Most of the dwelling houses were of timber; only those of the royal family and nobility were of stone. In the mausoleum of St Peter and St Paul the great tsar was buried, having achieved what he so much desired, a window on the western world.

The War of the Spanish Succession

Although the diplomats of Europe had watched the declining health of the aged king of Spain, Charles II, the announcement following his death in 1700 that he had left a will bequeathing everything to a grandson of Louis XIV, Philip, caused great surprise

Louis XIV and his family. Behind the king stands the grand dauphin, who died in 1711; on his left is his eldest grandson, who died in 1712. The king lived until 1715. The child in leading strings held by his governess, the duchess of Ventadour, is the elder brother of the future Louis XV. The king was seldom portrayed in such an informal pose. He loved fruit and, as here, always had a basket to hand. The picture is by N. de Largillière

and relief. Spanish pride was salved because there had been much talk of partitioning the various parts of the kingdom. Charles had made one proviso: that Philip should renounce all claim to the crown of France. This at first allayed fears that nothing short of war would prevent Louis XIV from acquiring control of the Spanish Netherlands and Spanish-American trade. The emperor was disappointed that his younger son, the Archduke Charles, who had been named as King of Spain if Philip refused, seemed to have no chance of succession. Louis XIV accepted the will; the people of Madrid received their new king Philip V with joy; and peace could have been preserved if the French had not begun to behave with great arrogance, sending an army into the Spanish Netherlands and recognising the Jacobite claimant, James Edward Stuart, as King of England rather than William of Orange. The British and the Dutch Republic, headed by the Grand Pensionary Heinsius, took alarm and prepared to make war in alliance with the Emperor Leopold, the King of Prussia and the Grand Duke of Hesse.

The musket had replaced the arquebus and the infantry had to defend themselves from cavalry by fixing bayonets on their muskets. Volunteers and conscripts could not quickly learn the complicated drill needed to form front to a flank or answer in the din of battle to commands given by drum-beat or bugle-call. Regimental colours, borne aloft on a stout staff, provided a rallying point seen through the rolling smoke of gunpowder. Indiscipline was severely punished; armies went into action in close order and one well-directed volley from the enemy could cause panic among men not accustomed to obey every order on the instant.

Hostilities began in north Italy, where the imperialist commander, Prince Eugene, fresh from a great victory over the Turks, was so successful that the French general was recalled. In the Netherlands the Duke of Marlborough spent two years fighting for access to the valleys of the Meuse and Rhine. In 1704 he took an allied force of 52,000 of whom 9,000 were British, into the Rhineland. The secret of its destination had been well kept and Marlborough reached Bavaria, where Prince Eugene joined him with 18,000 men. The two at once became friends. After devastating the country they found further movement impossible without first defeating a French army encamped at Blenheim in a position near the Danube apparently protected by marshes. Early on 13 August the allies crossed the swamps in the morning mist and pierced the centre of the French line. Tens of thousands of prisoners were taken including the French commander. For the first time since the middle ages, the people of the continent found that the British again had an army with fighting qualities second to none.

Soon after Blenheim the Emperor Leopold died and was succeeded by his elder son Joseph. His younger son Charles was declared of age and sent to Lisbon. The Portuguese had recently joined the Grand Alliance and British troops marched from Lisbon to Madrid hoping to make Charles king, but they found the Spaniards loyal to Philip and they had to retreat. Later another fleet and army took Barcelona where the Catalans had many grievances against the Spaniards. The army succeeded in taking Madrid again, but could only hold it for a short time. In 1706, Prince Eugene, campaigning in north Italy, drove the French out, while Marlborough, to whom the cautious Dutch would not allow freedom of action, met the French at Ramillies, near Waterloo, and won another overwhelming victory, opening the road to Paris, but without Dutch consent he could not advance.

Louis XIV, with the invincible pride of an old man, would not consider making peace. In 1708 he sent an expedition to Scotland, hoping that his troops, aided by Jacobite rebels, could make James Edward king, but the commanders quarrelled and returned without even having landed. The following winter France suffered the same intense frost that had defeated Charles XII in Russia. The vines and orchards were destroyed and crops failed in many districts.

In 1711 the Emperor Joseph died of smallpox and the war became pointless; Charles, having succeeded Joseph, could not reasonably claim to rule both in Austria and in Spain. On the other hand he obstinately refused to make peace. His allies began negotiations without him and forced Louis to agree that the crowns of France and Spain should never be united, and to recognise George, the Protestant Elector of Hanover, and not the Stuart pretender, as rightful heir to the United Kingdom. Two valuable naval bases, Gibraltar and Minorca, captured by the British during the war, were recognised as British possessions.

While the Utrecht peace negotiations were proceeding, the French drove the imperialists under Prince Eugene out of Alsace, including Strasbourg, which became French under a treaty signed at Rastadt in 1714. The Austrians were given control of the former Spanish Netherlands, Milan, Mantua, Sardinia, Tuscany and Naples. Ostensibly the combatants had fought to prevent either the Bourbon or the Habsburg family from dominating western Europe, but as the conflict spread from country to country it ceased to be a dynastic war and became a conflict in which whole peoples, conscious for the first time of their interests, determined in future to protect them.

Artists in Porcelain

Coffee, almost unknown in Europe before the middle of the seventeenth century, then became exceedingly popular. It was not served in porcelain, unless the pots and cups had been imported from the east. The right to be named the first and one of the most admired porcelain factories in Europe belongs to Meissen in Saxony. This was founded by Johann Friedrich Böttger, an alchemist, whom King Frederick I of Prussia expelled

Harlequin in Meissen porcelain

Moritzburg, near Dresden. A hunting lodge was begun here in 1542 for Maurice, the Lutheran Duke of Saxony, who for personal advantage fought for the Catholic Emperor Charles V. It was remodelled in Baroque style about 1725 and is now a museum

from Berlin for practising dangerous arts. The Elector of Saxony, Augustus the Strong, a friend of Peter the Great, then invited Böttger to set up a laboratory in Dresden and there, in his search for gold, he melted down all kinds of earths and minerals. A friend, seeing his kilns and furnaces, asked him to produce an imitation of Delft pottery, and so the craftsmen were brought from the Netherlands who later formed the nucleus of the staff at Meissen, a short distance down the Elbe from Dresden. In 1709, Böttger began to make porcelain from a white earth obtained at Aue and long known as a good powder for wigs. Augustus heard that his protégé was on the eve of success and moved his laboratory to the Albrecht castle in order that no competitors should discover a trade secret of such high potential value. First experiments produced a reddish brown porcelain so hard that it could be sculptured and polished. Chinese pieces were copied at first, but the desire to compete with German silversmiths in the manufacture of coffee-pots, cups and candlesticks led to the adoption of their style. By 1713 a white porcelain was achieved, but the factory secrets had, in spite of all precautions, been sold by one of its workpeople and were known in Vienna by 1718.

In 1720 a miniature painter, Johann Höroldt, became manager at Meissen and he showed the workers how to decorate their products with brilliantly coloured pictures of that fairyland which Europeans then believed the Chinese and Japanese inhabited. Later he began imitating themes from Watteau, showing gardens, hunting scenes, sea-ports and rivers. In addition to coffee and tea sets the factory began to produce magnificent dinner services of a hundred pieces or more for use at banquets, and for these the court sculptor Johann Kaendler was employed to work with Höroldt and by 1750 these two artists had brought Meissen to the peak of its fame. Kaendler also made innumerable figures and groups for table decoration, using as models such popular characters as shepherds and shepherdesses, dancers and musicians, fishermen and street pedlars. Here in miniature was the essence of the baroque and the rococo styles that were bringing to the palaces, churches and theatres of Germany such exuberant beauty and charm.

Books and Despots

Educated people in the eighteenth century were convinced that they lived in an enlightened age free at last from the shackles of the middle ages, and a host of authors were willing to flatter them by fostering the belief that the ills of the world were due to the follies of priests and politicians, military men and tax-collectors. One of the first authors to do so was Montesquieu, who, as the hereditary president of the parlement of Bordeaux, was able to lead the pleasant life of a traveller and writer, satirising his own country and praising Britain, where, he believed, the secret of political liberty had been discovered. In 1748, after twenty-five years collecting material, he published from the safe distance of Geneva *De l'Esprit des Lois*. Human affairs, his thesis ran, are not governed by blind chance but develop on principles that can be discovered and understood. Like a physician writing about his sick patients, he quoted a host of examples to prove that man by taking thought could control the world.

Two years later a group of French publishers with the help of two editors, Diderot and d'Alembert, and headed by the royal printer, began work on a multi-volume *encyclopédie*, for which the inspiration came partly from England and partly from the *Dictionnaire Historique et Politique*, a work of propaganda published by Pierre Bayle, a French exile in Rotterdam. Diderot was a cutler's son educated at a Jesuit college in Paris. D'Alembert, a famous mathematician, was the illegitimate son of a noblewoman. The *Encyclopédie*, under the mask of providing knowledge on such subjects as iron-making and gunpowder, propagated an exceedingly limited view of human nature. The contribution on the intellectual history of Europe by d'Alembert contains no reference to anything earlier than the Rennaissance. Obviously French absolutism precluded the royal printer from consciously publishing anything subversive, but, after two out of its seventeen folio volumes of text and eleven volumes of plates had appeared, the Jesuits attempted to have publication stopped by the Council of State. They were overruled by Madame de Pompadour who was their enemy, and the books, being both popular and profitable, continued from 1751 to 1765. Diderot, with great courage, proclaimed his object '*pour changer la façon commune de penser*' and in this he succeeded.

Voltaire, who was nineteen years older than Diderot, having been born in 1694, admired his work, declaring 'a canal-sluice, a picture of Poussin, a fine tragedy, a truth

Frederick II of Prussia with Voltaire in the Sans Souci palace at Potsdam, where he stayed from 1750 to 1753

established are all of them things a thousand times more precious than all the narratives of campaigns.' The son of a well-to-do Parisian lawyer, Voltaire had been educated by the Jesuits and his collected works at the end of a long life filled fifty volumes. His success in catching the attention of the most important despots of his time, Frederick II (the Great) of Prussia and the Tsarina of Russia, Catherine the Great, was due not to any warmth of sympathy or depth of understanding but to a superb prose style that enabled him to make even banal observations appear witty and profound. Few of the idle rich who formed the majority of his admirers paid any attention to the doctrines of Christianity or the experience of the saints and Voltaire, in common with most other leading writers of his day, was consumed with a most unphilosophical hatred of the Catholic Church. Authors and readers were under the illusion that human beings, given the right education and environment, could be induced to behave reasonably, an opinion so absurd that only a self-styled Age of Reason could have conceived it.

Jean-Jacques Rousseau, a native of Geneva, was a year older than Diderot and lived sixty-six years. Although he was at various times on friendly terms with Voltaire and the authors of the *Encylopédie*, he was too sensitive and melancholic to share their confidence in human progress. On the other hand where their books provoked only talk, his inspired deeds. He was not interested in history but described an ideal education and an ideal state in which the actions of government conformed with the general will of the governed. Yet he commented sadly: 'Were there a people of gods, their government would be democratic. So perfect a government is not for men.' His ideas, especially those in *Du Contrat Social*, prompted Napoleon Bonaparte at the age of twenty to write a dissertation on royalty which concluded: 'There are very few kings who have not deserved dethronement.' It was a sentiment he later preferred to forget, and when as First Consul he visited Rousseau's tomb, he declared: 'It would have been better for the repose of France if that man had never been born.'

Habsburg and Hohenzollern

The Peace of Utrecht provided some twenty-five years of comparative peace. In Paris the people danced with joy at the funeral of Louis XIV. His quest for glory had become a burden, and Philip of Orleans, the regent for Louis XV, a boy of four, responded to the new mood. The diplomats had obtained most of the objectives for which their countries had fought, and in 1713 in order to avoid another succession war, the Habsburg emperor Charles VI drew up what he called a Pragmatic Sanction, half treaty half will, bequeathing all the Habsburg inheritance to his eldest living daughter if he should have no male heir. For a daughter to succeed was against the Salic law, and so he asked the monarchs of Europe to agree to the Sanction. All did so, but without serious intention of keeping faith. When Charles died in 1740 his twenty-three year old daughter, Maria Theresa, soon faced a possible partition of the Austrian Habsburg lands similar to that proposed for the Spanish Habsburgs in 1700. She had no army, no reserves in her treasury and two months after her father's death, Frederick II, the twenty-eight year old Hohenzollern King of Prussia, disregarding the Sanction, marched into Austrian Silesia at the head of a well-trained army of 33,000. He had in reserve about 60,000 more excellent troops. There was nothing unusual in treating kingdoms as private estates to be divided and bequeathed without regard to the wishes of their inhabitants but Frederick's action was considered outrageous even by the standards of the time. Silesia was known to be rich in minerals, but exploitation of them had scarcely begun. None of the signatories of the Pragmatic Sanction were willing to help the Austrians expel the Prussians; on the contrary, they began planning to annex other parts of Habsburg territory for themselves. The French sent an army into Bohemia and captured Prague and the Bavarians menaced Vienna.

Fortunately for Austria, Maria Theresa had many assets; beauty and charm; great physical energy; a strong will; and a lively mind. She had escaped the doubtful benefits of a conventional education; could not spell and knew little history; cared nothing for court etiquette and ceremonial, but, like the majority of her subjects, loved dancing and music. Though pregnant for the fourth time she called the Hungarian Diet together and addressed it with such skill and eloquence that it voted her six regiments. The Prussians, whom she attacked in April, were too strong, but she drove the French out of Prague and the Bavarian army out of Munich. Her husband Francis, Duke of Lorraine, whom she loved dearly, was elected Emperor. The British came into the war on her side and their king, George II, being Elector of Hanover, led an army against the French and defeated them at Dettingen. It was an astonishing reversal of fortune for the Austrians, but it was not until 1748 that war-weariness brought peace. Silesia remained in Prussian hands.

A fresh conflict, known as the Seven Years' War (1756-1763), was in part the result of the Empress Maria Theresa's persistent desire to recover Silesia. In her search for allies she found the French willing to support her. Their affairs had been for many years in the hands of Cardinal Fleury, who was nearly ninety, and a new generation of counsellors, who had forgotten the true nature of war, had visions of making France once more the arbiter of Europe. They had not considered the power of the Prussian army, backed by heavy subsidies from Britain, nor the consequences of a British naval blockade of French ports with the ensuing loss of trade. Frederick II, who in this war earned the title 'Great' by his resistance to a ring of enemies, had about 4,000,000 subjects (the Empress Maria Theresa had three times as many, Louis XV five times), but an army of 150,000 well-trained men. Without regard to casualties he used them in such an unorthodox manner that opposing generals were unable to anticipate his movements. Armies were accustomed to marches and counter-marches and weeks elapsed before two opposing forces could be brought face to face in the close-order fighting for which parade-ground drill had prepared them. Two of Frederick's early victories over the French and Austrians were obtained by flank attacks delivered at the head of the enemy's columns while they were crossing his own line of march. Before they could form a fresh front Frederick had thrown them into confusion and panic.

In the first year of the war the Prussians occupied Saxony, but by 1759 they had a new enemy, the Tsarina Elizabeth, and against the Russian masses they fought a costly drawn battle. Only divisions and suspicions among Frederick's enemies delayed their further advance. Shortly afterwards in Hanover an Anglo-German force defeated the French at Minden, where the river Weser breaks through a line of hills. For a time the Austrians occupied Berlin, but they were unable to destroy the Prussian army, and when in 1761 the Tsarina Elizabeth died and Peter III, a great admirer of Frederick, succeeded her, the Russians made a separate peace with him. The British war leader, William Pitt, later Earl of Chatham, resigned and the new government in London refused to pay any further subsidy to Frederick, who, in a fury, then made his own peace with Maria Theresa. He kept Silesia and promised to vote for her son Joseph as the next emperor.

While these minor matters occupied the European powers the British gained diplomatic recognition of their conquest of French Canada and the French trading stations in India and still further concessions from Spain. Britain, a country with a population of about one-third that of France, seemed for the first time to be a world power of at least equal strength.

Taxation and Revolution
At the end of the Seven Years' War the thirteen British colonies of settlement on the

eastern seaboard of America had a population of about 3,000,000. Boston and Philadelphia had harbours rivalling in size the largest ports in Europe and among the settlers were many Germans, Dutch and Swedes who felt no loyalty to Britain. Each colony differed from its neighbours in constitution and law. For geographical reasons they had developed habits of self-government more democratic than those of the mother country. They objected to taxes imposed from Westminster and any restrictions being placed on their continued advance into Indian lands. Hostilities broke out in 1776 and a British army capitulated at Saratoga in 1777, making victory for the Americans certain. Twelve French warships and 4,000 men then sailed to their aid. At the same time the Spaniards attempted to retake Gibraltar; and the Scandinavian countries and the Netherlands resented the British naval blockade against France. It seemed that with so many enemies Britain must succumb, but after defeating the French fleet in the West Indies, a new government in Westminster agreed in 1783 to recognise the independence of the United States of America. Canada and Gibraltar remained British.

The French volunteers who returned from America, headed by the wealthy young Marquis de Lafayette, who had become the friend of George Washington, brought with them idyllic accounts of the new republic, overlooking the inflation of the currency which had made rebellion synonymous with ruin in many homes. To the general ferment of French politics a new and dangerous conception was now added, that in America democracy was no longer an ideal but an accomplished fact.

On the death of Louis XV in 1774 Parisians once more expressed not sorrow but joy, cheering the young king and his beautiful Habsburg wife, Marie Antoinette, and holding a great banquet when their first son was born. Neither of them were opposed to reform, provided that it did not interfere with their pleasures; the king had a passion for stag-hunting and the queen for *fêtes champêtres*. This frivolity was to lose them their early popularity. The nobles and higher clergy, who should have been the chief support of the monarchy, were the instruments of its downfall. They were virtually exempt from

French peasants

taxes, and every attempt to make the tax laws apply to them was opposed by the parlements in Paris, Bordeaux, Rennes and other provincial centres. These ancient corporations were swept away in the early days of the revolution, but not before they had done great harm.

In August 1788 the king ordered the States-General, which had not met since 1614, to assemble the following spring. During a winter of bitter cold, prices rose and unemployment increased. A complicated system of indirect election was devised. Nowhere in the world had 5,000,000 taxpayers (men over twenty-five) ever been offered the vote before, but there were few revolutionaries among the 600 deputies elected to the *Tiers État*, or commons, who assembled at Versailles. They were bourgeois of established reputation, the majority over forty years of age. The towns were strongly represented, over one in ten deputies coming from Paris. The house of nobles had 300 representatives, and so did that of the clergy, but the Church did not speak with one voice, the higher clergy being mostly of noble birth and the parish priests being of humble origin. After much delay the *Tiers Etat*, at an unauthorised meeting held in the royal tennis court, took the first step towards revolution, naming themselves the National Assembly and swearing not to disperse till they had given France a new constitution. Soon after they issued the Declaration of the Rights of Man.

The Paris mob, ignoring the slow talkative proceedings at Versailles, assembled on 14 July 1789 and stormed the Bastille. In the fighting nearly a hundred were killed; the governor, losing his nerve, surrendered, and was soon after murdered with six of

Paris as a walled city; the Bastille appears close to the wall at the top of the diagram; the cathedral of Notre Dame is on an island in the Seine

his staff. The gloomy old fortress was quickly demolished and the event celebrated with great enthusiasm. Within its walls the revolutionaries had found just seven prisoners, one of them an Englishman. The next exploit of the mob took place in October—a march of twenty kilometres to Versailles to demand bread. The commander of the National Guard, the Marquis de Lafayette, followed with 15,000 of his men many hours later. To them the royal family surrendered and, escorted by the mob were taken back to Paris.

The National Assembly next attacked the Church. About one in ten of the population were either priests or members of one of the religious orders. It was decreed that bishops and clergy should be elected and paid salaries; religious orders dissolved; and church property auctioned. The money bags that peasants, feigning poverty, had kept hidden were soon opened to buy land. From this time on millions who had never previously taken part in politics turned a blind eye to the crimes of the revolution in the same way that receivers of stolen goods keep silence on the movements of thieves. To the Church lands offered for sale were added the king's personal domain in the spring of 1790, and, two years later, the estates of the nobles who had fled the country. The big lots, especially in the towns, went to the bourgeoisie, the smaller lots, such as Church lands formerly held by parish priests, went mainly to peasants some of whom organised buying syndicates. Most of this 'national property' sold well; low prices made it a good investment. In many parts of the country mobs had already pillaged and burnt châteaux. The number of possessions that changed hands, legally and illegally, was immense.

By the spring of 1792 a new Legislative Assembly had replaced the National Assembly, and in it the early talk about the brotherhood of man and international peace ceased and the old aggressive France reappeared in a new missionary disguise. The countries along her frontiers must be 'liberated'. The army had lost a third of its officers by desertion, but the remainder were enthusiastic for war since liberated property abroad was a more certain prospect than pay at home. As one deputy said: 'Let the troops march as far away as they can; they will then be less likely to cut our throats.' The royal families in Vienna, Naples and Madrid became increasingly concerned for the safety of their relatives in Paris. When France declared war, Austrian and Prussian armies advanced slowly, capturing Verdun, and entering the Argonne forest. On 20 September they were repulsed by artillery fire from a strongly held position near Valmy, and then retreated. This skirmish is sometimes described as one of the decisive battles of the world, but no foreign military intervention could have undone the revolutionary changes of the previous three years.

On the very day of Valmy the National Convention, elected by 1,000,000 voters, met. It contained a number of artisans, but was mainly middle class. Like its predecessors, it could destroy, but not create. It at once declared the monarchy abolished and France a republic. Yet what Paris most needed was someone to deal with the municipal government and the mob. Early in the month a carefully prepared band of executioners had visited the Paris prisons and massacred 2,000 of the inmates, most of them common criminals. The love of bloodshed spread, and public executions by the guillotine took place in the presence of great crowds. In January 1793 Louis XVI was given a brief trial before the Convention and condemned to death by 361 votes to 360. In October the Queen too was executed. Their surviving son was kept in prison till he died in 1795

In the summer of 1793 a small minority of determined men seized power by the simple device of dominating one committee of the Convention, the *Comité de Salut Public*, and giving its orders the force of law. Directions for the conduct of the war on the frontiers, conveyed by a new invention, the semaphore telegraph which passed visual signals from hill top to hill top, could travel from Paris to the armies in fifteen minutes. The need for more army recruits was met by making military service compulsory and universal. This *levée en masse* was imposed by a decree for which two deputies, Danton and Carnot, were chiefly responsible: 'Every Frenchman is commandeered—(*en requisition permanente*)—for the needs of the armies. Young men will go to the front; married men will forge arms and carry food; women will make tents and clothing and work in hospitals; children will turn old linen into bandages; old men will be carried into the squares to rouse the courage of the combatants, and to teach hatred of kings and republican unity'.

Robespierre, a country lawyer, by eliminating his rivals in the Committee of Public Safety, made himself a dictator. For eleven months, from July 1793 to June 1794, when his enemies sent him to the scaffold, France submitted to the one-party government of the Jacobins, whose clubs had set up branches in most provincial towns. Everywhere they flew the red flag and wore the red cap of liberty. Lyons, a great silk manufacturing town where there was much unemployment caused directly by the revolution, suffered devastation for its opposition to the Paris government. The army which had captured it was next directed against two other 'disloyal' towns, Marseilles and Toulon. In La Vendée fighting between Jacobins and counter-revolutionaries led to the usual atrocities and reprisals of civil war, but by the end of 1793 the Jacobins were supreme almost everywhere. The invasion of the Netherlands and the Rhineland, aided by large sections of the Dutch, German and Swiss middle classes, attracted by revolutionary slogans and willing to overlook the barbarities being committed in Paris, enabled a ring of satellite republics to be established. In October 1795, when the joyous reaction against Robespierre and the terror had gone so far that the members of the government were in danger of being lynched by the mob, Bonaparte was in Paris and was called on to deal with the situation. He sent for artillery and did not hesitate to give the order to fire on the insurgents at point-blank range. As a reward he was given command of 'the army of Italy'. From that moment the history of the revolution became indissolubly linked with his ambition.

The Early Career of Napoleon Bonaparte

Napoleon Bonaparte was born in 1769 in Corsica, an island recently annexed to France, and grew up without any feeling of loyalty to the monarchy. His father died young and his mother disliked him, sending him away at the age of ten to a military academy in France where the teaching was far from good. It was as a young officer in an artillery regiment that his education began; his seniors were military reformers, and books on history and politics provided his quick intelligence with a vast amount of rather super-ficial knowledge.

The revolution suited him; talent, not birth and family connections, would be the passport to advancement. Promotion at the age of twenty-four to the rank of general was facilitated by friendship with Robespierre's brother and service at Toulon under a Corsican general. In the north Italian campaigns of 1796 and 1797 against the Austrians his bravery in action earned the personal loyalty of the troops. He was sure, having escaped Austrian fire, that he had been spared for some high destiny and began to write dispatches to the government in Paris not in the manner of a servant, but of its master to be.

On his return from Italy, he suddenly became engrossed in schemes for making France an oriental power, not understanding that without command of the sea the Egyptian expedition of 1798 was senseless. When the British navy had destroyed the French ships in the battle of the Nile, Bonaparte should have saved the army; instead, he deserted it. A venal press in Paris presented him as a Christian hero who had defeated the infidel Turk. In his absence the Russians, operating in north Italy under Suvarov, a sixty-eight year old general of genius, recovered most of what the French had won. Bonaparte, on returning from Egypt, was welcomed with enthusiasm as the Republic's most successful general. By intimidating the Senate he obtained supreme powers and the title of First Consul. Many throughout Europe imagined that he would be content to rule a France confined to her natural frontiers. Within months he was proving that not even the melting snow of the high Alps could deter his armies from fresh conquests.

The Partitions of Poland

The kingdom of Poland, which in the last half of the eighteenth century included millions of peasants who spoke Russian, Ruthenian and other languages, and also large Yiddish-speaking Jewish communities, was surrounded by three strong and aggressive states, Prussia, Austria and Russia. The monarchy was not hereditary but elective and any one of the nobles could veto the choice of a king made by the rest; hence periods of anarchy intervened between the death of one king and the election of the next. By 1772 Russia was ruled by the Tsarina Catherine the Great, by birth a princess of Würtem-berg, who extended her domains to the Black Sea and annexed the major part of eastern Poland where the 1,500,000 people were mostly Russian-speaking. To avoid incurring the jealousy of the Austrians, Catherine proposed that the Empress Maria Theresa should take an even larger portion of southern Poland. 'Lady Prayerful', as Catherine called her, protested that it was immoral, but did so. At the same time Frederick the Great of Prussia took the lower part of the Vistula valley, but not Danzig.

Twenty years later a second partition was carried through, but much less smoothly. French 'liberalism' had found ready adherents among the middle classes of the towns and the less wealthy of the nobles. The King of Poland, Stanislas Poniatowski, accepted a new constitution which made the crown hereditary, subjected the nobles to taxation and granted religious toleration. Catherine the Great had been antagonised by the revolution and feared the prospect of a strong Poland. In 1793 the Russian army, having occupied about twice the area taken in 1772, and overpowered all armed resistance, invited the Prussians and Austrians to join in the dismemberment of the country. The Prussians extended their earlier annexation southward to the border of upper Silesia which was already theirs. A year later the Poles rose in rebellion, led by Kosciuszko, a general who had fought the British in Washington's army, but the Russians were too strong. Kosciuszko took refuge abroad; and the Russians occupied Warsaw and Cracow. The Prussians seized Danzig and doubled the size of east Prussia. Two states in which anti-Semitic feeling was strong had acquired large Jewish minorities. The Polish state had ceased to exist, but the Polish nation flourished, its musicians and scientists becoming world famous.

CHAPTER ELEVEN

The Nineteenth Century

Nations in Arms: the Napoleonic Period

The biggest changes in land warfare in the nineteenth century were due not to the introduction of any new weapon but to the adoption of compulsory military service. This
gave governments larger armies than before and allowed politicians to risk higher
casualties, but made prolonged wars extremely dangerous to the stability of states.
Conscription brought with it the concept of 'the knock-out blow' and a dictated peace
in contrast to the negotiated peace of the previous century. Bonaparte was the first
to demonstrate this new technique of war and politics. It exactly suited the combination
of gambler and showman that made up his character. In 1800 he desired, as newly
appointed head of state, a spectacular success, and decided on the reconquest of north
Italy. In order to take the Austrians by surprise he led an army at speed over the Great
St Bernard pass, crossed the Po and engaged the enemy at Marengo. He had not stopped
to coordinate the movements of his forces and was compelled to retreat, and only

*Schönbrunn, the imperial Austrian palace on the outskirts of Vienna; a view of the emperor's
garden*

the timely arrival of Desaix's corps turned defeat into victory. Bonaparte was able to conclude a treaty without delay, obtaining Austrian recognition for the pro-French republics in the Netherlands, Switzerland and north Italy.

After a brief interval of peace, during which Napoleon reorganised the legal, educational and local government systems of France, the struggle with Britain and Austria was resumed. For the invasion of England an army of unprecedented size, 210,000 men, assembled at Boulogne. Some were veterans of earlier campaigns, but a large number were conscripts. Napoleon had now assumed the title of Emperor of the French, so challenging the claims of the Habsburg emperors. When the combined fleets of France and Spain failed to gain command of the Channel, he ordered 'the army of England' to march eastwards against Austria. Owing to the cowardice and inaction of one Austrian general a large army capitulated at Ulm and the French marched on into Moravia, where the main Austrian force was joined by the Russians under Kutusov. The allies, instead of accepting the Russian plan for strategic withdrawal, allowed themselves to be drawn into a great battle at Austerlitz on 2 December 1805. This was Napoleon's military masterpiece, as he frequently reminded his courtiers. The Russians withdrew and within three weeks of the battle the Austrians made a separate peace, concluded in the Habsburgs' summer palace, Schönbrunn near Vienna. In this magnificent building, already a century old, Napoleon sat at Maria Theresa's desk to sign orders. Even the most beloved of the Habsburg lands, the Tyrol, was signed away. Mainland Italy also came under the control of the French, but their losses at the battle of Trafalgar, which took place on 21 October 1805, the day after the Austrian capitulation at Ulm, had left the British navy in unchallenged command of European waters, a power they held for the next hundred years.

A year later the Prussians declared war, confident that their army was, as in the days of Frederick the Great, invincible. When it met the French at Jena in Saxony in October 1806, disaster resulted. Napoleon occupied Berlin and dictated there decrees forbidding all continental trade with Britain. At the same time he called up fresh troops for war with Russia in 1807. After two costly victories at Friedland and Eylau, he obtained a private conference with the Tsar Alexander I. They met on a raft in mid-river at Tilsit and Napoleon's charms won the tsar's consent to the trade embargo against the British and the creation of a Grand Duchy of Warsaw. Numerous humiliations were imposed upon the Prussians; their army was to be limited to the low figure of 42,000.

Up to this point the new style of warfare appeared to have succeeded; it had created an empire that stretched from the Pyrenees to the mouth of the Elbe, yet what the army had made only a victorious army could maintain; within seven years the whole structure was in ruins. Nationalism, the force that destroyed it, first showed its strength in Spain. Napoleon pretended that, to intercept British goods, it was necessary to invade Portugal. A French army entered Spain under this pretext and reached Lisbon. The King of Spain and his heir were summoned to meet the Emperor in France and forced to abdicate in favour of Joseph Bonaparte. Then came serious reverses; a British army turned the French out of Lisbon; and Spanish guerrillas forced a French army to capitulate at Baylen in Andulasia. A rising in Madrid was put down by the French with fearful bloodshed. Nowhere could French soldiers travel, unless in companies over twenty-five strong, without risk of ambush and murder. This resistance by provincial levies without central direction was a new and horrifying method of warfare, providing the only physical means of expelling the organised forces of an enemy equipped with superior weapons and supplies. The gorgeous uniforms of the imperial armies made their wearers a conspicuous target for opponents who might pass along the highway in beggars' rags. A British army, commanded by Sir Arthur Wellesley, later Duke of Wellington and based in Portugal, also campaigned against the French in Spain and after five years of hostilities drove them back into France.

News of Spanish resistance encouraged the Austrians. In the Tyrol the mountaineers had considerable success before yielding to ruthless 'pacification'. Not for a single year had the Napoleonic empire been at peace. In 1809 the treaty with Austria was broken and the French, though victorious, suffered such heavy casualties in the two principal battles of the campaign that Napoleon made peace. His childless marriage with Josephine

The Empress Josephine; a marble bust by Joseph Chinard dating from about 1808. Napoleon, her second husband, married her at a civil ceremony in 1796 and at a religious ceremony in 1804

had been annulled and now he married an Austrian princess, Marie Louise, who bore him a son, named in infancy King of Italy. The emperor's claim to the status of a legitimate monarch was never accepted. Marie Louise was happy to be an empress, but when Napoleon abdicated she deserted him.

The cessation of trade between Britain and the continent had caused much hardship in Germany. Prussian statesmen, hoping that a day of retribution might come, undertook the reorganisation of the schools and universities. Prussian serfs working on the land were set free. Sugar beet was cultivated to make good the loss of imported cane sugar. Potato-growing was encouraged. By transferring a third of the army to the reserve each year and training an equal number of new recruits, the letter, but not the spirit, of the treaty was observed.

It is doubtful whether Napoleon comprehended the meaning of nationalism. He was fond of attributing particular characteristics to each race in Europe, but his interest went no further; he judged all by their degree of loyalty to himself. He regarded the Russians as good soldiers, but did not inquire the source of their fortitude. It was enough that they had never been decisively defeated and were a threat to his empire. In 1812, after a dispute with the tsar, he assembled a force of 500,000 men, of whom about half were from allied states, and set out for Moscow. Summer thunderstorms turned the roads into quagmires. Horses, worn out with overwork, sickened and died, for the lush grass was unsuitable fodder. The Russians made a strategic retreat, and then in an attempt to save Moscow fought the battle of Borodino, following which Napoleon entered the capital. Soon after it was deliberately destroyed by fires secretly lit by the Russians. The emperor had met a foe with will-power equal to his own. He had only 95,000 men left, and, deceived by a mild autumn, delayed the order to withdraw. When the frost overtook the French, most of the remaining horses lacked the special shoes required on snow and ice. Only a fifth of those who had entered Moscow were able to reach Poland. Napoleon returned to Paris before the disaster was known, determined to raise fresh armies. Conscription provided nearly 200,000 young men. France, with a population of 42,000,000, was, as the emperor said, still the richest country in the world, but the youth of the nation, a precious part of that wealth, he sacrificed in order to prolong his career.

In 1813 he took this new army to Saxony and there the ring of his enemies, Russia, Prussia and Austria closed in. At Leipzig 'the battle of the nations' was so terrible a defeat for the French that a sane leader would have sued for peace, but Napoleon was no longer quite sane. Not until the allies had pursued him to the outskirts of Paris did they receive his abdication. Banishment to the island of Elba was decided on as a temporary measure, until some safer place could be found.

A great congress of soldiers and diplomats from all the belligerent nations assembled in Vienna. For the Austrian emperor and his chief adviser, Prince Metternich, it was, after twenty years of defeat, an exhilarating moment. Yet there was scarcely any plan for the future on which all four allies agreed. Hatred for Napoleon was the one force that had held them together, and, when he fell, the Tsar Alexander and his huge army soon came under suspicion. Louis XVIII, uncle of the dead heir of Louis XVI, a middle-aged and unheroic figure, was chosen as a constitutional monarch for France because no better candidate could be found. When in the spring of 1815 Napoleon escaped from Elba to the south of France, raised his last army and crossed the Belgian frontier, neither the Austrian nor the Russian armies were ready to meet him, but the British, Dutch and German forces under Wellington held the ridge at Waterloo until the Prussians under Blücher arrived to complete the rout of the French. Napoleon fled and later surrendered to the British. Louis XVIII, who had left Paris on the approach of Napoleon, returned there. The congress reassembled in Vienna and imposed on the French their unwanted king, an army of occupation numbering 900,000 and a vast war indemnity. The new militarism made such measures easy, but the diplomats who adopted them failed in their professed objective, the prevention of further revolution. The hundreds of thousands of widows and orphans, the scarred and crippled remnants of Napoleon's armies were ignored or forgotten, and his foolish captors allowed him six leisurely years at St Helena in which to create his own legend. In this he appeared to credulous readers in France as the misunderstood apostle of European peace.

Italy: Campanilismo and Liberty

A Londoner will sometimes describe himself as 'born within the sound of Bow bells'. In Italy a campanile rises above the roof tops in almost every town and village, and *campanilismo*, the passionate attachment to the place of one's birth, is more than a childhood memory of chimes that called to Mass; it is a local patriotism that treasures a particular way of life. None but the most powerful personalities could have triumphed over *campanilismo*.

The Napoleonic period (1800-1814), with its transient republics and kingdoms, rudely awakened Italians in every part of the peninsula and in the islands to the dangers, as well as the benefits, of French Liberalism. The differences between one province and another in France under Louis XVI were as nothing compared with those that divided southern from northern Italy, and yet it was accepted Liberal doctrine that all Italians, whatever dialect of the national language they might speak, would be far happier if only they were subjects either of the same republic or constitutional monarchy. The ideal of one government for the whole peninsula was adopted by a small but influential number of Italians who had travelled abroad, but it was of little interest to the great majority of their countrymen, for whom life was an unending struggle to obtain sufficient food either from the soil or from the sea to feed their prolific families. To them it seemed that all governments required the payment of taxes and the more effective a government tried to be the more it needed money to spend. For this reason there were more anarchists in Italy than anywhere else, and in Sicily the *mafia* made anarchy a way of life.

The Congress of Vienna had left Italy divided, but into fewer parts than in the previous century. Turin became the capital of the royal house of Savoy whose heterogeneous dominions included Piedmont, Genoa and the malarious island of Sardinia. Milan and the prosperous province of Lombardy were, with the former republic of Venice, placed under the Habsburgs. Central Italy was dominated by the grand duchy of Tuscany and the papal states, and the south by the Bourbon 'kingdom of the Two

Sicilies' with its capital in Naples. Various societies such as the Carbonari and the Association of Italian Youth founded by an anti-clerical republican named Mazzini in Marseilles began plotting to expel the Austrians. Mazzini made himself very popular in London, where his nationalism received sympathy and his republicanism was ignored. The plotters were disunited; most agreed that Austrian rule, which had been accepted in the previous century, must be ended. In its place some wanted a federation of states under the papacy, but Pius IX could not countenance a war between Italian and Austrian Catholics.

The idea of a constitutional monarchy appealed to few, but in 1848, when there were revolutions in Paris, Berlin, Frankfurt, Vienna, Prague and Budapest, a constitution

Dobrente castle, built by the Hungarians against the Turks at the end of the middle ages, was pulled down by the Austrian army after the unsuccessful Hungarian revolution of 1848

was promulgated in Turin by King Charles Albert. A successful rising in Milan encouraged the Piedmontese to invade Lombardy. The Austrians, after being expelled from Milan, retired into four fortress towns from which they sallied out to defeat the invaders and to recover the whole province. Charles Albert abdicated in favour of Victor Emmanuel. At the end of the year of revolutions the Roman mob murdered the pope's minister, and Mazzini became head of a Roman republic with a tall, blond guerrilla fighter named Garibaldi at his side. Both men hated the Church and organised a fierce but vain resistance to an army sent by the president of the new French republic, Louis Napoleon, to restore papal power. After much destruction and loss of life Garibaldi escaped into the hills.

Italy was not the only country where Liberal doctrines proved faulty. In every other capital except Paris, revolution also failed, because the mobs behind which Liberals hoped to make their way to positions of authority could not face trained soldiers directed by conservatives determined to restore law and order. Yet Liberals continued to employ high-sounding euphemisms, propagated in a 'free' press and paid for by the politicians whom they benefited. Newspapers carried their thinly disguised incitements to riot and war swiftly from city to city along the new railway links.

The chief minister of the Turin government in the 1850s was Count Cavour, one of the younger generation of politicians who deliberately played on Liberal idealism at home and abroad in order to carry out nationalist policies. Before entering politics he had made a fortune applying foreign methods on his family estates. Victor Emmanuel, the new King of Sardinia, was a good judge of character, and, having found in Cavour one of the ablest men in Europe, left work to him and occupied himself with women. A Piedmontese contingent was sent to fight with the British, French and Turks against the Russians in the Crimea (1854-1856) and by this means Cavour won a seat at the peace conference in Paris. There the possibilities of glory to be found in a conspiratorial mixing of liberalism with nationalism appealed to the Emperor of the French, Napoleon III. He and Cavour met secretly and agreed to provoke a war in which a combined French and Piedmontese army should turn the Austrians out of north Italy. On the outbreak of hostilities in 1859 neither side showed any military skill and after two battles in Lombardy, at Magenta and Solferino, Napoleon made peace; Lombardy was annexed to Piedmont.

Victor Emmanuel thought this treaty sensible, since French casualties had been very heavy. Cavour, who was not consulted, resigned because Venetia had not also been liberated, but it was not long before he was back in office intriguing with Garibaldi to send a small army of volunteers, a number of them English, from Genoa to Palermo as a first step towards overthrowing the Bourbon king in Naples. To cover this plot he carried on negotiations for an alliance with the southern kingdom. Garibaldi sailed for Sicily with a thousand 'redshirts' in three small steamers. With the helpful neutrality of the British navy this novel form of international crime took Europe and Palermo by surprise. An American wellwisher sent three more steamers with more volunteers and a vast quantity of arms and ammunition. The Sicilians, eager to forestall any possible reconquest, also did much, after the capture of their capital, to help Garibaldi launch an expedition across the straits of Messina. He was soon within striking distance of Naples. Cavour, having received much verbal encouragement from London, which cost the Liberal government there nothing, declared war and sent an army overland to join Garibaldi, now so unexpectedly in a position to set up an anti-clerical republic which would frustrate plans for a constitutional monarchy. When Victor Emmanuel met the redshirts, he persuaded Garibaldi to hand over Naples to him. Together they rode into the city. There was still much fighting to be done before all Neapolitan garrisons in the south surrendered. Rome and the papal states, defended by a French army remained, with Venetia, outside the new Italy. Garibaldi refused all rewards; he knew that his followers had hoped for much more; and so, taking leave of them, he retired for a time to Caprera, his island home on the Sardinian coast, taking with him a sack of seed-corn for his farm. The poverty-stricken south simply exchanged the oppression of its old masters for the neglect of the new. Cavour died the following year at the age of fifty-one, also without seeing his dream for Italy realised. His fellow ministers and admirers had to wait for Prussia to defeat Austria and attack France before Romans and Venetians could sit in an Italian parliament.

Bismarck and the Second Reich

Prussia, in 1815 an authoritarian but well-organised monarchy, suffered many humiliations between 1848 and 1850. The King, Frederick William, was both romantic and conceited. He aspired to be a liberal and consitutional ruler, but without surrendering his prerogatives. In 1848 he became alarmed at the violence of the Berlin mob. When the army was sent in to restore order, Bismarck was one who watched with satisfaction. As a youth, after an idle period at Göttingen University drinking and duelling, he had travelled abroad and become a good linguist. His father, a junker or country gentleman, had fought in the cavalry against Napoleon's armies. The son, elected to the Bundestag in Frankfurt-am-Main, an assembly of representatives from the various states of the German confederation set up in 1815, became well-known and popular among those Germans who found the Austrians concerned only to prevent change. The British minister Disraeli, who first met him in 1862, said, 'Take care of that man; he means what he says'. Bismarck had revealed his intention to provoke war between Prussia and Austria by 1866. With this in view the Prussian army was reorganised and re-equipped without the consent of the Prussian parliament. Bismarck, as Chancellor to the elderly King William I, found himself bitterly attacked by Prussian Liberals, but there was no constitutional necessity for him to resign.

In 1864 a border dispute with Denmark led to a brief war in which the Prussians were successful but suffered heavy loss against an enemy protected by trenches. They annexed a large part of Schleswig-Holstein, and Bismarck, who had received many futile protests from the British government, commented that he had always previously believed that Britain was a great power. In 1866 came the premeditated attack on the Austrian empire, delivered across the Bohemian border. One Prussian victory brought the war to an end. The Austrians withdrew from the German confederation, and Bismarck began to plan the destruction of Napoleon III, who with empty pretension posed as the protector of the south German states where Prussian aggrandisement was feared.

When the Spanish government invited a Hohenzollern prince to take the vacant throne of Spain, Paris newspapers worked up an absurd scare that a Prussian in Spain would threaten French security; Bismarck hoped that Napoleon would be goaded into a declaration of war, and when this came in July 1870, the French mobilisation was so slow that the Prussians were inside the French frontier before any battle took place. Within three weeks the emperor and an entire army was surrounded at Sedan and forced to capitulate. In Paris Napoleon's ministers resigned, and a provisional government was set up. When the Prussians advanced on Paris, this government took refuge in Bordeaux, and the capital was soon cut off from the outside world. The chief republican leader, Gambetta, escaped by balloon and attempted to raise a fresh army, but this project was abandoned in view of the hunger and risk of disorder in Paris. Envoys were sent to meet the Germans at Versailles. There in the Hall of Mirrors on 18 January 1871 the King of Prussia was acclaimed German Emperor in the presence of the princes who had joined him in the war. The imperial constitution provided for a Reichstag elected by universal manhood suffrage, and, as a concession to Liberalism, Bismarck frequently addressed its members, but he could not be dismissed by them. The generals now dominated policy and insisted that the French must surrender Alsace and Lorraine and pay a heavy war indemnity. These terms were accepted; and the Germans saw no great danger in them, provided that they continued to keep France isolated. Bismarck had taken care that she should have no allies in 1870. To please the Russians he had refused to join diplomatic protests against their suppression of a nationalist revolt in Poland in 1863, and to please the Italians, he had forced the Austrians to hand Venetia over to them in 1866. Rome became the Italian capital because the French garrison, needed at home during the war with Prussia, had been withdrawn.

The Emperor William I lived on until 1888, when he was over ninety. His heir,

Jews of Russian Poland teaching a child The Law

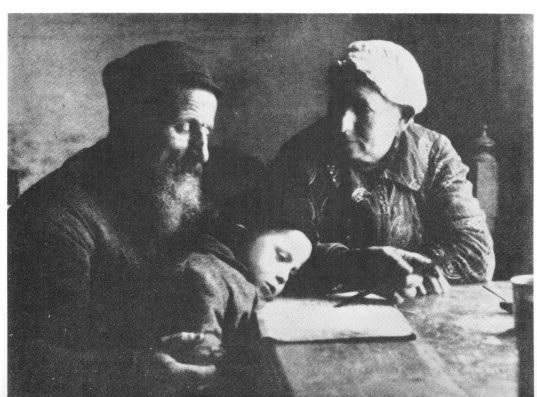

Frederick, a son-in-law of Queen Victoria, who was known to favour Liberal policies, was dying of a throat cancer and reigned for less than four months. He was succeeded by his son William II, but Bismarck, to whom William I had entrusted the whole field of government, remained Chancellor. In old age he had grown irritable and dictatorial, and two years later William II, who was eager to play a spectacular part at home and abroad, found reasons for dismissing him. No other chancellor with his skill and foresight was ever found.

The French Impressionists

Paris in the 1860s and 1870s, though the capital of a country torn by revolution and war, was also the birthplace of a new movement in the art of painting, that of the Impressionists. Parisians sitting in cafés, enjoying the opera and ballet, boating on the

'*Les Parapluies*', *painted by Renoir about 1879*

Seine or walking through the forest glades of Fontainebleau, were their subjects, but the bright colours, delicate tones and jesting spirit of their work were at first severely criticised.

Without forming a school of painting in the academic sense or observing the same rules, they were happy to find that friendship and admiration for each other's work drew them together. They did not choose the name Impressionist; it was taken by a critic from the title of a painting by Claude Monet shown in their 1874 exhibition, 'Impression: Sun Rising'. Thirty artists were invited to contribute, including Pissarro, Sisley, Renoir and Degas. The critics at once recognised the beginnings of a new era.

Pissarro was ten years older than Monet, and his landscapes had been frequently accepted for the Salon, an annual exhibition organised by the academic painters of the day. During the Franco-Prussian war he, like Monet, took refuge in London, and the Germans turned his house at Louveciennes, a suburb of Paris, into a butcher's shop and used his canvases as mats in the garden. Only forty of the pictures he had left behind survived. Later he and Sisley, who also lived at Louveciennes, painted many winter scenes of town and country cloaked in snow.

Monet, who was a grocer's son from Le Havre, came to Paris when he was a young man and very poor. There he made the acquaintance of Edouard Manet, whose father, a well-to-do magistrate, did not wish his son to be an artist, but paid him a generous allowance. Manet had studied the paintings of Velasquez and Goya in the Louvre, and adopted their glowing colours and dramatic poses for his own work. When a Spanish ballet company came to Paris in 1862, Manet borrowed the studio of an English artist, Alfred Stevens, which was near the theatre, and painted a full length portrait of Lola de Valence, which delighted some and shocked others. The novelist Zola was an ardent admirer. The Emperor Napoleon III called one of Manet's best pictures obscene.

Not until the 1880s did the work of the group begin to attract enthusiasm of the kind that viewers now show. To use one's eyes afresh, to see new beauty in familiar scenes and everyday surroundings was not revolutionary, however much it seemed to be so, and now both the happiness and the melancholy of their painting pervades every gallery in Europe fortunate enough to possess examples of it.

The Prevention of War

Most of the delegates to the Congress of Vienna in 1815 had personal experience of revolution and war and, being men at the height of their careers and of a conservative disposition, they made the prevention of war their chief objective. It was an incontrovertible fact that the Napoleonic wars had been the result of the French revolution, which in turn had sprung from liberal doctrines concerning the need to consult 'the people' by means of elections and parliaments. Liberalism was, in the eyes of Metternich and the Tsar Alexander, the enemy; and Liberals, regarding riots and rebellions as justifiable in countries without elected parliaments, deserved their reputation as troublemakers, for the French revolution had shown how men of the highest ideals could bring a whole nation into anarchy within a few months. Metternich, who knew how serious was the danger of fresh revolutionary outbreaks, once remarked that Europe was faced with the consequences not of the French revolution but of the Reformation, meaning that by 1815 the Liberals, having lost faith in Protestantism, had made a religion of their political beliefs. He therefore hoped by holding frequent congresses to deal with each threat to peace as it arose.

In 1823 the king of Spain, Ferdinand VII, was forced by a Liberal revolt to flee from his capital and a congress agreed that the army of Louis XVIII should invade Spain and restore him to power. This proved an easy operation since Spanish Liberals were suspected by the majority of their countrymen of wishing to attack the Church and were too few in number to offer any opposition.

Soon after this a congress met to discuss Greek affairs. The people of the Peloponnese and the Aegean islands had rebelled against their Turkish governors. Since most influential people in western Europe had received a classical education, the Greek cause aroused passionate sympathy. Arms were dispatched and volunteers set out, including the poet Lord Byron, who died on campaign. Even the new Tsar Nicholas I, to whom rebels of any nationality were anathema, felt obliged to contribute a squadron of warships to the fleet that the British and French sent to 'observe' events. There had been a series of atrocities and reprisals, and at the Sultan's request the Egyptian army and navy had sailed to the Peloponnese and was massacring the population and burning their villages. The allied sailors at anchor in the bay of Navarino watched the smoke rising. Shots were exchanged and a battle developed in which the whole Egyptian fleet was sunk. From this point the British and French lost interest in Greek independence. In reprisal for Navarino the sultan expelled all Greeks resident in Constantinople and for this reason the tsar declared war. His armies came within a few miles of the Turkish capital before the Turks sued for peace. They agreed not only that the southern part of Greece should be an independent state, but also that Rumania should have governors appointed for life and not subject to Turkish interference in internal matters. The tsar, an upright and hard-working autocrat, received no gratitude from the French or British Liberals, whose governments had done so little; on the contrary, they continued to abuse him throughout his long life.

No sooner had peace been established in Greece than a Polish revolt began. In 1830 a Russian general had been mistaken for the Grand Duke Constantine, the tsar's viceroy in Warsaw, and murdered. For a few months Polish patriots were masters of the capital and, though quarrelling among themselves, tried to gain concessions from the tsar. When a Russian army of 150,000 men appeared at the gates of Warsaw, all resistance collapsed. Many rebels fled to London and Paris where they made ceaseless propaganda against the tsar.

While these events were taking place hostilities broke out in Belgium. In 1815 the whole of the Netherlands had been formed into a single kingdom under the house of Orange, but the Dutch incurred the hatred of the French-speaking population of Belgium. After a riot in Brussels in 1830 the Dutch army fought with Belgian volunteers, of whom 600 were killed. The threat of British and French intervention prevented war. After long negotiations France, Prussia and Britain agreed that Belgium should be separated from Holland and made into a kingdom ruled over by Leopold of Saxe-Coburg.

They also undertook to regard Belgium as neutral territory in any future war.

The Congress of Vienna settlement, damaged in 1830, was even more thoroughly undermined in 1848. For a time the entire Austrian empire seemed to be disintegrating. Metternich resigned and the imbecile Emperor Ferdinand was hurried out of Vienna. For some months revolutionary regimes in Vienna and Budapest attempted to establish parliamentary constitutions. In Prague a provisional Czech government planned to unite the Slav races of the empire. Against all these opponents the imperial Austrian army proved completely victorious. In Hungary it had the assistance of a large Russian force and much bloodshed resulted. Among the other races of central Europe the Hungarians were hated for their arrogant ways, but the Liberals of western Europe ignored this fact and expressed as much sympathy for them as they had previously done for the Greeks.

The next threat to peace came in 1854. A dispute between Russia and Turkey about the Holy Places led to firing on Russian positions across the Rumanian border. The Russian Black Sea fleet then attacked and sank the Turkish fleet at Sinope. At this news the press in London and Paris worked up anti-Russian feeling. Napoleon III, seeking some inexpensive glory for an empire which, he had publicly declared, 'meant peace', undertook to make war. A British and a French army landed in the Crimea, but no supreme commander was appointed. Battle casualties were severe and they were equalled by losses from exposure to winter cold and a cholera epidemic. The Russians besieged in Sebastopol set the place on fire before retreating. The allies then made peace, having escaped a great disaster through the enemy's inefficiency in failing to concentrate their forces in time. Military prestige, the objective for which the two sides had entered the war, had eluded them both. Little permanent good resulted from the treaty, but the Danube was made an international waterway.

Twenty-one years after the Crimean war the Russian imperial army once more invaded the Turkish empire. The pretext for this aggression was the cruel treatment of Bulgarian guerrillas by irregular troops of the Turkish army. Though the Russian advance was held up for a time at Plevna, the Turks again sued for peace and consented to the establishment of a nominally independent Bulgarian state stretching from the Danube to the Aegean coast. The Russians appeared to be within reach of an ice-free port. The British, who had been loud in their complaints against the Turks before the war, were equally alarmed after it by the southward advance of the Russians. Within Russia a general enthusiasm for expansion had been aroused among the mass of the population, and the disappointment when the treaty with the Turks was called in question by a European congress in Berlin in 1878 was intense. Bismarck described his part as that of 'an honest broker'. The Russians were forced to restore to the Turks that portion of Bulgaria that lay between the Balkan range and the Aegean. The Austrians were allowed to occupy Bosnia and Herzegovina. These and other humiliations deprived the Tsar Alexander II and his administration of the popularity which successful war had brought them. Russian Liberals became involved in a series of plots. Government officials were murdered and Alexander twice escaped bombs before he was murdered by Nihilists in 1881 while driving in St Petersburg.

The Liberals were shocked at this result of the agitation. The revolutionaries responsible for the murder were hunted down and executed. One was a student, the son of a minor official from Simbirsk and brother to Vladimir Ulyanov, who became known later as Lenin. The new Tsar, Alexander III, was a man of iron will and great physical strength, but limited in outlook. Plots against his life began and the government's precautions caused much discontent. University students went on strike. On the other hand trade and industry flourished in the 1880s and 1890s. The new factories, which were often much bigger than their counterparts in the west and could draw on immense reserves of men, land and minerals, began to create a dangerous imbalance in Europe. The United States of America was the only other country in the world with untapped wealth to compare with that of Russia, and in America free enterprise and state divisions prevented the national wealth from being mobilised and concentrated in any one direction. The new German empire, though industrially more advanced, and politically compact, was in potential riches much inferior and became increasingly fearful of Russian policy. This fear grew when, on the death of Alexander III, he was succeeded by his weakling son Nicholas II. The father had been his own prime minister; the son had neither the strength of character to rule nor the intelligence to choose able ministers. Yet Russia by tradition required strong government from the centre. It was a country in which Liberal ideas proved sterile. The emergence of a national leader of the kind both needed and wanted by the majority could not wait upon the parliamentary play of political parties. To the general apprehension caused by the sheer size of the Russian empire was now added uncertainty about her motives and intentions. The seeds of the first world war were already germinating.

CHAPTER TWELVE

The Twentieth Century

Nations in Arms: The Liberal Period

The European conflict of 1914 to 1918, though now called the first world war, arose from the internal troubles of the Austro-Hungarian and Russian empires, and Europe was the scene of all the major battles. Most countries had developed compulsory military service on the Napoleonic pattern. In Britain the Liberal government, which opposed conscription on principle, was forced to resign in 1916 to make way for a government that imposed it. The highly complicated plans for mustering trained reserves, collecting them at railway stations, and transporting them to pre-arranged positions on or near the frontiers had been worked out with great precision in Germany and France, but for political reasons could not be rehearsed in peace time. The order for mobilisation had become more important than a declaration of war, so eager were the generals on

Mobilisation of the French army, Paris, 1914. Reservists on their way to regimental headquarters where they received uniform and equipment

both sides to put into practice the Napoleonic doctrine of the knock-out blow. All feared a drawn-out war.

The German ultimatum to Russia, which expired at noon on 1 August 1914, demanded that the mobilisation of the Russian army should cease. This was a formality; the German armies were already moving towards the west, not the east, on the presumption that the Russians would not be ready to fight for about a month, by which time the French would have been beaten. German troops were beginning to take over the Luxembourg railways on which the invasion of France depended when von Moltke, their Chief of Staff, who was still in Berlin, received a summons to the imperial palace. Kaiser William II, as Supreme Commander, ordered him to cancel the planned attack on Paris. The Ambassador in London, the Kaiser said, had been promised that the French would, at the request of the British, remain neutral. Von Moltke explained that the whole German army would be thrown into confusion if mobilisation, timed to finish on 16 August, were stopped. A single army corps required 180 railway trains for its transport, and nearly 1,000,000 men, seven separate armies, each numbering from 200,000 to 300,000, were moving across the Rhine on a front extending from Aachen through Metz to Mulhouse.

Later that night a personal message from the King of England to the Kaiser assured him that the Ambassador was mistaken and that France would certainly not remain neutral; the violation of Luxembourg and Belgian neutrality continued and so Britain declared war. A British expeditionary force of 100,000 men went into battle at Mons, but the whole Anglo-French line was driven back to the Marne. There, after a month of retreat and terrible losses, the allies were victorious. Both sides fanned out to the north-west and began a race for the Channel ports. The allies saved all the French harbours but not those in Belgium. The hastily constructed lines of trenches stretching from Alsace to the sea shifted this way and that for four years, but were not broken until August 1918, when the British, having invented the tank, the only weapon capable of breaking the deadlock of trench warfare, pierced the enemy line. The allies then kept up their advance until, under the terms of the armistice of 11 November 1918, the Rhineland was in their hands.

Before the armistice was signed the Kaiser had abdicated, the German navy had mutinied, and a socialist republic had been set up in Berlin. During the fighting commanders-in-chief on both sides had been recalled and heads of government in Berlin, Paris and London dismissed. Millions of young men had been killed in action and millions more crippled for life. Town and countryside had been devastated. From start to finish nothing had gone according to plan. The policy of 'the nation in arms' had been a catastrophic failure.

On the eastern front the Central Powers were also unsuccessful in reaching a quick decision. On 28 June 1914 terrorists belonging to the Black Hand, a secret organisation based in Serbia, murdered the Austrian Archduke Ferdinand in the streets of Sarajevo, the Bosnian capital. The Austro-Hungarian government decided in the most reckless manner to invade Serbia; conquest, which was assumed to be easy, could not be achieved without provoking war with Russia, where Pan-Slav feeling strongly favoured action on behalf of Serbia. To deal with this danger the Austrians relied on their German allies, but took no steps to consult them or to organise a joint command. After the Russians had ravaged parts of east Prussia they were met at Tannenberg by a German army under the command of Field Marshal Hindenburg, who had been recalled from retirement.

(above) German cavalry in a Russian village, February 1916
(below) Russian motor-transport supply column, February 1916

The Russian artillery, by tradition so efficient, found the German guns overwhelmingly superior and their army was cut to pieces. Tens of thousands surrendered, and their commander shot himself. The way to Warsaw was open, but the Germans were driven back from the suburbs, and in south Poland the Austrians were decisively beaten. Such successes, however, cost the Russians too much in lives and materials, and their industries could not keep up the flow of food and ammunition. After ten months of war 150,000 men had been killed or wounded; all Poland had been lost. Further fighting in the summer of 1916 led to an Austrian retreat during which their Czech troops began to desert in thousands. On the other hand news from 'the home front' undermined the morale and discipline of the Russian soldiers. The utter corruption of political and business life in Petrograd, formerly St Petersburg, and other big towns could no longer be concealed. Army contractors had been involved in outrageous profiteering. The weak-willed tsar, before whom the cheering crowds had kneeled for blessing in 1914 when 'the war to free the Slavs' began, was unable to take any action without consulting his wife, and she in turn relied for advice entirely on the renegade monk, Rasputin, who had been able to save the life of the haemophiliac heir to the throne when doctors despaired. Rasputin, enjoying the complete confidence of the Tsar and Tsarina, was more powerful than many heads of the government had been, appointing and dismissing ministers in a wholly frivolous way until he was murdered by a royal prince in December 1916. It was then no longer possible for the monarchy to recover its reputation.

In March 1917 a general strike in Petrograd sapped everyone's will to work. Disaster at the front and scandals at home had so weakened the regime that it collapsed. The Tsar abdicated and a socialist, Kerensky, became head of the provisional government. The old Liberal formula for universal suffrage and a parliament was adopted. Elections were held and a constituent assembly met in October. Earlier, in the spring sunshine, amid endless demonstrations and orations, the towns enjoyed, for the first and only time in Russian history, freedom of speech and of the press. A mood of unreasoning and unreasonable exultation pervaded all classes. Yet the Germans were still advancing; the prices in the shops rose higher and the bread queues grew longer. For this revolution Liberalism was not enough.

When the Tsar abdicated, Lenin, the middle-aged Bolshevik leader, had been abroad for many years and knew little of conditions in Russia, but he was in no doubt about his own theoretical remedy. As a Marxist, he believed in the forcible expropriation of landlords by the peasants, wholesale desertion by the soldiers and the control of civilian food supplies by the state. Land, peace and bread was his slogan, and the Germans willingly transported this conspirator from the comfort of Switzerland to his native land. At the same time another Bolshevik in exile, Trotsky, set out from New York. By November the army had disintegrated and the peasants had driven out their land-lords. The Bolsheviks gathered in the capital found themselves strong enough with the aid of a mutinous garrison to carry out a coup d'état, now called 'the Russian Revolution'. The constituent assembly was dispersed; the elimination of non-Bolsheviks began; peace talks with the Germans were started, and a vast surrender of territory agreed. By March 1918 enough German troops had been transferred to Flanders for a last offensive, which nearly succeeded. But the Bolshevik virus with which the Germans had hoped to inject their enemies spread to their own soldiers and sailors. The red flag was hoisted at Kiel, and only the self-discipline and patriotism of the famished population prevented the spread of class war and the total dissolution of the state.

The break-up of the Austro-Hungarian empire preceded that of the Second Reich. The aged Emperor Francis Joseph, who had been placed on the throne during the 1848 revolution, died in 1916 and his successor Charles desired to end the war and create 'a Liberal empire'. At that time the Germans still believed that they could win the war and keep their conquests. They therefore prevented the new emperor from leaving the alliance, and by the autumn of 1918 he was forced to abdicate because the stronger races of his empire set up independent states, while the weaker Ukrainians and Ruthenians were once more partitioned. The new republics of Poland and Czechoslovakia sprang from conspiracies hatched in Russian prisoner-of-war camps before the peacemakers had met in Paris to recognise their existence. The Rumanians attacked Hungary and took much of her former lands. The peace treaties ostensibly based on 'the national will' ascertained by plebescite were in reality the application of the old saying *vae victis*.

The Czechoslovak republic was largely the creation of Thomas Masaryk, the son of a Slovak coachman. He had become a university professor in Prague and married an

President Masaryk of the new republic of Czechoslovakia enters Prague, December 1918. He is seated in the car behind the driver

American student. During the war he escaped to London, where friends enabled him to win the support of the Foreign Office and the American State Department. By visiting prisoners of war held by the Bolsheviks and the immigrant Czech communities in Chicago and New York he made himself so well-known and popular that in 1918, while he was still in the USA, he was proclaimed President of Czechoslovakia.

Another prisoner-conspirator was Joseph Pilsudski, a Polish Socialist who by 1920 had created a national army and rashly led it as far as Kiev before being forced back to Warsaw by the Bolsheviks. Russian sympathy for oppressed nations never extended to the Poles, but Pilsudski received aid from the French, who sent General Weygand and a party of staff officers. Under their direction the Poles cut Russian communications and drove their beaten army beyond the Niemen. Later Pilsudski set up a military dictatorship in Warsaw. Lenin, who had been convinced that every 'imperialist' state in Europe would, as Marx had predicted, collapse, was deeply disappointed; the Bolsheviks had hoped to link up with the German Communists and establish themselves from Siberia to the Rhine.

In Hungary the Bolsheviks also miscalculated. Bela Kun, a Hungarian socialist captured by the Russians during the war, had, after training in Moscow, been sent to Budapest in 1919. Unlike the Czechs and Rumanians, the Hungarians had been on the losing side in the war and were surrounded by enemies. For a few months Bela Kun was able to fly the red flag in their Catholic and conservative capital but he was deposed.

To compensate Serbia for her sufferings in the war the southern part of the Austro-Hungarian empire, with its mixture of Serbs, Croats and Slovenes, was assigned to her. This enlarged kingdom, renamed Yugoslavia, never attained internal harmony; the Serbs, regarding themselves as victors, behaved with arrogance to the Roman Catholic Croats, who had in the past supplied the Habsburgs with some of their best troops. Vienna was, as a result of this wholesale re-drawing of the frontiers, left isolated at the heart of the German-speaking lands of the lost empire. Even the railroads leading to the great capital were broken. Yet the allied peacemakers in Paris feared to strengthen the new German republic by the addition of Austria, where a small socialist republic began, with international help, to save the lives of hundreds of thousands of families financially ruined either by the war or by the terms of the peace. Such were the political blunders of diplomats who ignored the hunger and misery left by the war and, in order to fulfil the Liberal dream of national self-determination for each race, altered every frontier, flouted countless traditions and so fragmented Europe that the parts were too weak to sustain the independence to which they had aspired.

The empire of the Ottoman Turks, who had fought on the side of the Central Powers, was dismembered at the same time as that of the Hohenzollerns, the Habsburgs and the Romanovs. In their Arab territories the British and French formed satellite states while their lands in Europe were assigned to Greece. In 1921 the Greeks, thinking that the Turks were powerless, undertook a campaign to deprive them of the Greek-speaking sea-coast of Asia Minor, but the Turks no longer relied on the weak Sultan in Constantinople. A new leader took command against the Greeks, driving them back to Izmir, where a general massacre of all Greek residents took place and the town was burnt. The victor's name was Kemal Ataturk, the Ghazi, or Raider of the Christians. The presence of British troops in the area stopped a pursuit into Europe, and an international rescue operation transhipped over a million Christian refugees to the Aegean islands and Greek mainland. Kemal Ataturk was allowed to reoccupy Constantinople, renamed Istanbul; he was the first dictator to discover that the dreadful experiences of 1914 to 1918 had left the British and French so weak and exhausted that they would endure almost any affront to avoid another major war. In 1927, after abolishing the Sultanate and the Caliphate, he declared: 'Sovereignty is acquired by force, by power, by violence. It was by violence that the sons of Othman acquired the power to rule over the Turkish nation and to maintain their rule for more than six centuries.'

Art in Russia

To be sensitive to approaching change in the direction of men's thoughts and emotions is as much part of the artist's function as it is of the sailor to prepare for a shifting wind, and it was in Russia during the last years of the Tsarist regime that the first flowers appeared of what is still called 'modern art'. In St Petersburg a magazine, edited by the ballet impresario Serge Diaghelev, made known to the rich cosmopolitan society of the capital the revolutionary changes current among young painters, encouraged by the more enlightened of their seniors, who admired the work of the French Impressionists. They were in revolt against the over-decorated houses of the middle class and the drab apartments and monotonous streets of new industrial suburbs; recognised a hunger for new colour, drama and poetry in the surroundings of everyday life; and wished to break down the traditional view that painting was exclusively a matter for the directors of art galleries, museums and expensive shops.

Some of the millionaires of Moscow, notably Tretiakov, were already keen collectors of the work of living French artists, especially Matisse. They were also admirers of what was described as the 'Impressionist' music of Debussy and in 1904 invited the composer to Moscow for a concert arranged in his honour. Diaghelev, who was in the audience, later used one of his tone-poems, l'Apres-Midi d'une Faune for a ballet. With them was a young artist, Michael Larionov, an enthusiast for cubism and futurist philosophy. After the concert Diaghelev asked whether it would be possible to see the work of a woman artist, Natalia Gontcharova, who had caused a sensation in recent exhibitions, and Larionov offered to take him to her studio. The place was in darkness when they arrived but they lit a candle and carried it from picture to picture. Diaghelev, astounded at the variety and range of her work, at once commissioned a stage décor, something that she had never previously designed. It was for the first performance of Coq d'Or, to be given in Paris the following year. The curtain went up on an unlit stage, a device invented by Gontcharova. As light slowly flooded the scenery, the audience quickly realised that a decorative art had been born, drawing its inspiration from popular Russian religious painting, but in a free and joyous spirit that gave the movements of the dancers not only space but a world of new colours.

Larionov, whose home was in a village near Odessa, had won a gold medal at the Moscow Academy of Art and already completed his compulsory military training. He

168

Backcloth for the ballet Les Contes Russes *by Michael Larionov*

too was asked to design stage sets and masks for the Diaghelev ballet company. When war broke out in 1914, he went to the front and was invalided out of the army. He was then able to join Diaghelev in Florence, and continued to work for him.

Two other artists whom Diaghelev made famous were Leon Bakst and Picasso. Bakst created the costumes and sets for *L'Apres Midi d'une Faune* and another Debussy ballet, *Jeux*, and Picasso those for *Le Train Bleu*.

The Bolsheviks of 1917 disapproved of almost all the artists of their day except Tatlin, the inventor of Constructivism, whom they adopted with enthusiasm, because of his use of steel and glass in place of traditional materials, and his belief in the social function of art. His theories were opposed by Malevich, who upheld the essentially spiritual nature of art, and established the first painting in Europe to rely solely on geometric forms and simple colour harmonies. He was at work from 1915 to 1920, but when the Bolsheviks tightened their censorship of literature and art, originality like his withered away.

Nations in Arms: The Fascist Period

The first fourteen years of the twentieth century had not been peaceful. No year passed without a war or a war scare and almost every state was plagued by strikes, bomb throwing and anarchist murder plots. The King of Spain, Alfonso XIII, and the English princess who was his bride, were bombed as they drove through the cheering crowds to their wedding. They were unhurt, but many round them were killed or injured. It was one of five attempts on the king's life. In other countries less violent, but more socially damaging, action was taken by trade unions inspired by the doctrine of the class war. How was it possible that, in a continent more prosperous than it had ever been, and from which over a million migrated every year to taste the still greater prosperity of America, the sterile slogans of Marxism proved so attractive? For the first time the poor, instead of being urged to economise, were being invited to spend. Cheap newspapers and magazines advertised inexpensive food, clothing and household goods and the dearer periodicals published glittering invitations to buy motor cars, steam launches, houses and foreign holidays. From every street corner hoardings recommended wines and spirits, furs and cosmetics. Journalists refused to allow the newly rich to inhabit a world apart, but described their private lives for the benefit of all. Socialists could not have been presented with a better target; having inherited the puritan traditions of the Reformation without its respect for Christian charity, they urged 'the expropriation of the expro-priators'. With unthinking haste the teachers of economics, noticing how effective the organised envy of the Socialists had become, made the equalisation of incomes the objective of all their proposals for governing industry and managing the fiscal system. Since Liberalism had not produced the millenium by means of universal suffrage, socialism would do so by the redistribution of wealth.

War-time inflation between 1914 and 1918 benefited manual workers; their wage rates rose more steeply than prices; and the employment of women to fill, for con-siderably less pay, the posts vacated by men serving in the armed forces, raised the total income of many households. For four years the mirage of better living 'when the boys come home' attracted every worker, especially in the countries that claimed victory. But one country, Italy, was neither victor nor vanquished. Out of gratitude to the German empire for making possible the possession of Venice and Rome, the Italians had been expected to fight on the side of the Central Powers, but after remaining neutral until 1915, and then joining Britain and France, they became involved in Alpine warfare with the Austrians. At Caporetto they suffered a dissatrous reverse. Only the transfer of British troops from France saved the situation. One officer, Benito Mussolini, wounded in the fighting, never forgot this disgrace and when at the Paris peace conference Italy was not awarded all the Italian-speaking Alpine villages that she considered were her due, his hostility to the allies was confirmed.

Mussolini's career as a politician began in Forli, where his father was a blacksmith. In 1911, when he was twenty-eight he organised a strike there in protest against the war which Italy was waging on Turkey. This won him the editorship of *Avanti*, a Socialist newspaper in Milan, and its circulation figures leapt up with every fresh call to strikes and violent demonstrations. The failure of the Socialists to prevent the outbreak of war in 1914 by calling for general strikes changed Mussolini's views; the Socialists were in-capable of action; he would found a party that could do everything, a private army trained and strictly disciplined to overawe opposition. He named his followers *Fascisti*, having in mind the symbol of the old Roman senate, the rods of punishment carried in procession before the magistrates. His special bodyguard, the *arditi*, wore black shirts and jackboots. Old soldiers, tired of unemployment and the continual strikes organised by the Communists, gladly joined this 'movement' and loved its magic of parades,

170

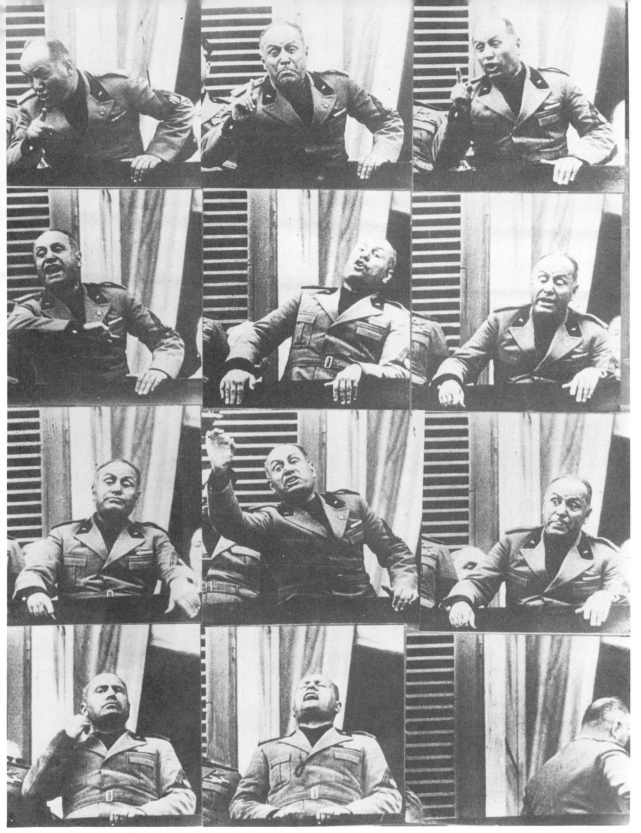

Benito Mussolini (1883–1945). These gestures are not extraordinary, but the normal techniques of Italian oratory

marches, demonstrations, black banners, patriotic slogans, Roman salutes and marching songs, all so different from the dreary round of strikes, lockouts and unemployment in which the Communists dealt. On 30 October 1922 the blackshirts converged on Rome from all quarters. Mussolini followed and a frightened king handed over to him supreme power. Soon millions were wearing the smart *Fascisti* uniforms, provided free, and attending, in the spirit of a *fiesta*, every rally and march. Newspapers carried photographs (chosen by Mussolini himself) showing him in splendid military uniform standing aloft on some palace balcony in studied pose that concealed his lack of height and exaggerated the strength of his lower jaw. Great public works were initiated, malarial marshes drained, and across the new fields *Il Duce* would drive the first tractor in person. Civil servants, soldiers and sailors felt a new pride and a new efficiency pervading all ranks. The crucifix, removed from state schools by a zealous Liberal administration, was restored. Vast sums were spent on rehabilitating Roman ruins. The trains ran on time. Such miracles, achieved by a carefully disguised State Socialism that brought discipline and leadership to a nation that loved ease, sunshine and laughter, had their price. Behind the scenes, blackshirt gangs, unreported in the press, unpunished in the law courts because no witnesses dared appear, beat up and sometimes murdered political opponents or transported them to remote islands. The press was censored, and the minds of the people prepared for a complete reversal of foreign policy. Soon warships, tanks and aircraft, all of new design, were being built and plans made to dominate the Mediterranean.

In Germany the rise of the *Fascisti* was watched, and their methods carefully imitated, by another ex-soldier, a lance-corporal called Adolf Hitler, who first made himself known by his right-wing oratory at about the time of the march on Rome. His political testament, *Mein Kampf*, written about 1923, but not widely read until ten years later, declared: 'Our world is moving towards a great revolution, and there is only one question at issue: Will that revolution be the salvation of Aryan humanity or will it be merely another source of profit to the eternal Jew?' Since a number of ministers in the new German Republic and the editors of some famous newspapers were Jews, Hitler eventually aroused a storm of anti-Semitism, but two unexpected catastrophes occurred to add colour to his speeches.

The Treaty of Versailles, signed by the Germans under protest in 1919, required, among other things, a war indemnity (reparations) of 6,600,000,000 marks; it also restored to France the provinces of Alsace and Lorraine, where the Germans had developed the manufacture of steel in conjunction with that of the Ruhr coalfields. For three years, 1919 to 1923, the Germans put off the payment of reparations and the French army therefore occupied the Ruhr. Occupation was, in German eyes, invasion, an affront to their pride. The Socialist government was abasing Germany, Hitler cried; he and his brown-shirted jack-booted National-Socialists (Nazis) would raise her up. He already had powerful friends, including Field Marshal Ludendorff and a number of business men. An attempted Nazi coup d'état in Bavaria was crushed after some fighting in the streets of Munich. Hitler was imprisoned, but, owing to his popularity, released before he had served his full sentence.

172

Barter trade during the German inflation, 1923; shoe repairs in exchange for sausage meat

The German government, to ease the payment of reparations, attempted a controlled inflation of the currency, but this rapidly became uncontrollable. Paper marks could not be printed fast enough. Shops selling food resorted to barter. The French government fell and its successor recalled the troops from the Ruhr. The middle classes in Germany had been ruined; hundreds of thousands were bankrupt. In bitter resentment against a guilty government many joined the Nazi Party. At this juncture foreign capital from Britain and America began flowing into Germany; the factories were re-equipped; and in four years an astonishing prosperity returned. Support for Hitler had begun to wane, when an Austrian bank failed. Speculators on the New York stock exchange panicked; business throughout the world was seized with a creeping paralysis that spread slowly to almost every capital except Moscow. By 1932 the Nazi Party was the strongest in Germany and Hitler was made Chancellor by the senile President, Hindenburg. The *Fuehrer*, as Hitler called himself, not having an over-all majority, proceeded to eliminate all his rivals by legal means. His ruffian comrades, accustomed to street fighting and secret murder, called him 'Legality Adolf', and before the people of Germany and their neighbours realised what had happened the civilian population, but not the armed forces, were in the hands of a government of gangsters.

In spite of the disarmament clauses of the Versailles treaty limiting the German army to 100,000 and forbidding the organisation of a navy and air force, all three services had managed in secret to keep their officer corps, had studied the errors of judgement leading to the 1918 defeat, and had devised means of winning a war of revenge. Air force men practised gliding, naval men trained in light, unarmed launches. Next time there must be no long war; no simultaneous fighting on two fronts; no battle of the Marne; no shortage of food or munitions. The Schlieffen plan, made by the chief of staff in 1905 and followed in a vague way by Field Marshal von Moltke in 1914, had been hidden away

M

in the archives to prevent its use as evidence of German war guilt. It was taken out and reconsidered. Here was a man of the right sort who said openly that, to knock France out, Dutch as well as Belgian neutrality must be ignored. Marching on foot the 1914 army had reached the Marne exhausted; the new army must have tanks, motorised transport and bombers to terrorise the civilian population and send a flood wave of refugees through the enemy lines. The navy men prepared with equal zeal. Next time the submarines must hunt in packs, and fast new 'unsinkable' cruisers and battleships must operate as commerce raiders.

Step by step, with Mussolini leading the way, international law was undermined. Abyssinia was conquered by the Italians in defiance of sanctions imposed by the League of Nations, the permanent organisation for peace set up under the Versailles treaty. When in 1936 civil war broke out in Spain between the Communist-dominated government of the Republic and the army, which found a political leader in General Franco, Italian ground forces and German bombers were sent to Franco's aid. In the same year the demilitarised zone in the Rhineland was re-occupied by the German army. Two years later the Austrian Chancellor was murdered and the Republic annexed. The persecution of German Jews, started in 1933, became suddenly more open and violent. Czechoslovakia, whose frontiers Britain and France were pledged to defend, was threatened with invasion on the baseless pretext that the Sudeten Germans under Czech rule were being persecuted. War was narrowly avoided after the prime ministers of France and Britain had persuaded Hitler to be content with the annexation of the Sudeten lands. The following spring his troops seized Prague. In September 1939 Warsaw and Danzig were bombed and Poland invaded by Germany and Russia. Britain and France regarded this as a *casus belli*. After a brief campaign the outnumbered Polish army surrendered and Poland was partitioned. The French defence system, known as the Maginot Line, was manned and a large British army mustered in France, but until May 1940 little land fighting took place. Nor were any bombing raids made by Germany westwards. Naval warfare on the other hand began at once, the Germans sinking merchant ships with mines, torpedoes and gunfire from September 1939.

The British intelligence service knew that Hitler had plans for the invasion of the whole western coast of Europe from Norway to the Pyrenees and for the conquest of Britain. Russian intentions were more doubtful. After the death of Lenin in 1924, a Georgian named Joseph Stalin, operating as secretary of the Communist party, had exiled Trotsky and liquidated (the euphemism was of Russian origin) every colleague likely to be a rival. Peasants who refused to surrender their land to the government were massacred in thousands in order to prepare the whole of Russian agriculture and industry for war. Armament factories had been built in Siberia, but when, in 1939, Hitler offered Stalin a pact and a large part of Poland, a further respite for preparation was welcome. Communists throughout the world were shocked to find their new Jerusalem so unprincipled. To Stalin it was more important that the Red army was not ready, owing to his recent execution of seven of its best known generals for alleged plotting with the Germans. Nor could he be sure that the western allies would fight with resolution after having for so long attempted to appease the Nazis.

Appeasement had been a policy welcomed by the majority of all parties in Britain and France because memories of the first world war and its slaughter were still keen, whereas in Russia human life had so often been sacrified for purposes of state that its preservation was not taken into account. In the west Communists, operating through trade unions in war factories, could slow down or speed up production almost at will. Before the outbreak of war their propaganda had been strongly anti-German and anti-Italian. The Russo-German pact and the partition of Poland brought about a sudden change in their views; the war with Hitler was denounced as 'imperialist', and France never recovered from the paralysing doubts and disaffection spread by Communists in the factories and the army.

Stalin's crude plans for the defence of the USSR did not stop at the annexation of eastern Poland. No Communist country needed educated Roman Catholics, and so some 4,000 of the captured Polish officers were separated from their men and shot. From Finland, Estonia, Latvia and Lithuania, all independent republics on former Tsarist territory, the Soviet government demanded, under threat of invasion, naval bases. The Finns courageously fought a winter campaign, forcing the Red army to withdraw. The other three Republics, relying on Russian promises that there would be no interference with their internal affairs, did not resist. By the summer of 1940 all had been Sovietised; their politicians removed to Siberia; and their German minorities handed over to Hitler.

The Germans, feeling themselves to be secure in the east, and having sent their spies and agents into the three Scandinavian kingdoms, suddenly attacked Denmark and Norway in April 1940. A small British force sent to assist the Norwegians was quickly expelled. Sweden remained neutral. The moment had come for the Schlieffen plan to be executed. The Netherlands and Belgium were quickly overrun and a large tank force penetrated the Ardenne forest, split the British and French armies apart and advanced on Paris. The British retreated to Dunkirk, where they were rescued from the beaches by an improvised fleet of destroyers, paddle steamers and small pleasure boats. Of the 338,226 men who reached Britain 139,097 were French. The last boat left on 4 June; on 14 June the French capitulated and signed an armistice, giving up the whole of western and northern France including Paris to the Germans. The Third Republic, set up in 1870, was at an end, and a new government, headed by the aged Marshal Pétain, made Vichy its capital.

After the fall of France preparations for the invasion of Britain began. The operation could not be undertaken without command of the air over southern Britain, but the German bombers and fighters suffered such heavy losses that in September invasion was postponed indefinitely. The winter was spent preparing for the conquest of Russia by a quick summer campaign. The conquered territory was to be emptied of its inhabitants to make living space for the Germans. This was called Operation Barbarossa in memory of the Emperor who founded the First Reich. On 22 June 1941 an army of 3,000,000 men attacked along a 2,000-mile front. The Russian army and air force was taken completely by surprise. Within two months the Germans had captured 665,000 prisoners. By the autumn they had advanced to the Black Sea and the outskirts of

Leningrad and Moscow. Then came rains, roads impassable from mud, transport immobilised by ice and snow, thousands of men, lacking overcoats and snowboots, frostbitten. Hitler ordered operations to stop, but the Russians brought up a hundred fresh divisions equipped for winter warfare. A long war of attrition began. Two vast armies, each controlled by a political party that disregarded both military and civilian casualties, turned most of the area between the Caspian and the Baltic into a battleground. The sufferings of the homeless civilian population, and of the millions of prisoners taken by each side, were bitter beyond description.

In the Far East the Japanese army and navy, which had long controlled foreign policy through secret societies, now decided, with a paranoia equal to that of the Germans, to strike simultaneously at the British, Dutch and American colonies in the Pacific and in Asia. For a time they were victorious everywhere, but their destruction of the American fleet in Pearl Harbour provoked an instant and nation-wide response in the United States. Hastily trained soldiers, sailors and airmen were soon in action against both Japanese and Germans. The Italians, in spite of massive assistance from the Germans, had by the autumn of 1943 been driven out of all their African colonies and an Anglo-American force had taken Sicily. The Italians thereupon deposed Mussolini, but were unable to eject the German forces from their country. When an allied invasion force attempted to do so, the Germans resisted and were not finally defeated until 1945. At the end of the campaign Mussolini was captured by Italian Communists and hanged.

In June 1944 a large allied force landed in Normandy under an American Supreme Commander, General Eisenhower, and by September most of France and Belgium had been liberated. In the following spring Germany was invaded from both west and east. Hitler committed suicide just before the Russians captured Berlin.

The German surrender was followed by a division of the country into four zones of military government, American, Russian, British and French, which had been decided on by the allies during the war. In the American zone alone there were, at the time of the surrender in May 1945, 6,400,000 'displaced persons'. By the end of July 4,000,000 had been sent back to their own countries (1,600,000 to Russia and 1,500,000 to France), leaving 300,000 Poles, and 500,000 Russians, many of whom did not wish to return to Communist-dominated territory. There were also 300,000 Italians and 20,000 stateless persons, mostly Jews who had escaped extermination. To reunite broken families the International Red Cross and the Salvation Army created a vast card index of lost persons. It seemed to some observers that economic life in Europe could never recover. The total war of which Hitler boasted had resulted in total collapse. The Nazis and the *Fascisti* were wholly discredited and offered no post-war resistance. After other conflicts it had been customary for the victors to make territorial claims and to ratify new boundaries by treaty, but after 1945 such deep divisions arose between the Russians and their allies that no peace treaty was ever signed. A new line of demarcation began to appear, the border between the Russian zone of occupation and the rest. Stalin had no intention of withdrawing his forces; he meant all Europe east of this border to be Sovietised. The western allies had fought to liberate Europe; the Russians, having at vast sacrifice expelled an invader, put their own security before every other consideration.

Moscow: monument to Soviet space exploration. It is made of granite coated with titanium. A statue of Constantine Tsiolkovsky (1857-1935), a pioneer of aeronautics, a man deaf from childhood, stands in the foreground

Scientific Progress

Leibniz, the seventeenth-century German philosopher and mathematician, once remarked: 'If man were able to travel through the air, it would no longer be possible to curb his wickedness'. Less than a century after his death men did fly, by balloon. The Montgolfier brothers in 1783 were the first to launch an unmanned one; it made two ascents, one in their home town and one in Paris, where many of those who watched the huge globe being taken through the streets to the starting place were so filled with dread that they knelt down to pray. After flying 24 kilometres the monster burst and fell. Villagers attacked the torn envelope with pitchforks and guns, thinking it the work of the devil. The government had to issue a proclamation declaring balloons harmless and adding: 'It is to be hoped that one day it will be possible to make use of them in the service of mankind.' Two years later the first manned balloon rose over Paris, and another carrying Blanchard and Jeffries crossed from Dover to Calais. Flying in heavier-than-air machines had to wait for over a century after this, that is, until the development of petrol engines for road transport provided an engine of the right ratio of power to weight. The first aeroplane flight was made in 1903 by the Wright brothers in North Carolina, who then flew no more than 246 metres. This caused little interest, few even believing their claim or thinking it important, yet before the outbreak of the first world war pioneers of many nations were flying light aeroplanes. These were faster and more manoeuvrable than large engine-powered airships of the type manufactured in Germany by Count Zeppelin, but did not have their combination of range and load capacity. Until the 1930s only airships were capable of lifting enough passengers and fuel for commercial transoceanic flight. When their inflammable gas-filled hulls proved too dangerous, flying boats were developed since the take-off run, always dangerous on land with fuel for long flights, could be prolonged, but flying boats had not established any regular transocean run before the outbreak of the second world war in 1939.

During the war the Germans developed two new sorts of engine, using both for unmanned aircraft, that is, flying bombs and rockets. The rocket engines used new liquid propellants and after the war Russia and the USA increased the power of rocket engines for intercontinental ballistic missiles and for the exploration of space.

In 1957 scientists planned an International Geophysical Year in which simultaneous observations were to be made all over the world. The Americans proposed to put into orbit an earth satellite capable of transmitting various measurements, but the launching rocket failed. The Russians, who had not revealed any intention of doing so, launched a

The surface of the moon, photographed by an unmanned satellite

satellite weighing 184lb. No man-made object had ever penetrated so far into space before. The 1957 triumph of Sputnik I, which transmitted signals for 21 days, was followed four years later by the first manned space flight, that of Major Gagarin, who made one orbit of the earth in a flight lasting nearly two hours. From this point rivalry between the Russian and American governments over space flight continued throughout the 1960s and culminated in the first moon landing by the Americans. In both countries popular excitement during television reports on space missions was intense, and grief when crews were lost through mechanical failures was not confined to their home country. National pride had found an outlet different from anything previously experienced in peace time; the astronauts were heroes, undergoing unpredictable physical and psychological stresses. They were seen, not by a few thousands in a sports ground, but by tens of millions, in action against a background so vast and awe-inspiring that war and revolution seemed for the first time earth-bound and petty.

As at the time of the Renaissance a whole galaxy of men became known simultaneously for their talents in art, science and scholarship, so in the twentieth century space flight was no solitary triumph. The breaking of barriers between physics and chemistry resulting from the researches of Rutherford at Cambridge and Einstein in Berlin during the first two decades of the century not only benefited all branches of engineering, but pioneered new techniques of measurement. To observe the internal structure of atoms and molecules required apparatus that was adapted to the investigation of the structure of living cells in the human body. A method of manufacturing synthetic penicillin in large quantities was discovered in 1939 and enabled physicians to save innumerable lives and to develop a great range of new drugs. The demands of space travel stimulated the construction with the aid of satellites of a telecommunications system capable of providing live coverage of a single event in all parts of the world simultaneously. None of these achievements considered in isolation would suggest that former international fears and suspicions have withered away, but the frontiers of knowledge have been moving forward so fast and far in the last two decades, and have been seen to move even by young children, that it can be justly concluded that future generations will find in international projects for the exploration of space, and in the better understanding of those cosmic forces that act upon man's natural environment, objectives worthy of the concentration of mind and will formerly devoted to national self-assertion.

A Declaration of Independence

At the end of the second world war the factories, ports, railways and bridges of Europe were in ruins and millions were without houses. The main part of the American forces were demobilised, and there seemed little likelihood that the democratic Europe for which they had fought would emerge from the general chaos. The US Secretary of State, General Marshall, therefore proposed that the countries of Europe should each assess their needs; his government would finance the export of the goods required. There were many criticisms of this scheme; one American senator described it as the greatest boondoggle in history; vast resources were wasted or misappropriated; but its main objective was achieved. In 1948 economic life in Western Europe began to recover.

It had at first been intended that the benefits of the Marshall plan should be extended to central and eastern Europe, but there everything hung upon the will of the aged Stalin, and his order was given for the overthrow of the Czechoslovak government that had accepted the American offer. He had acquired in youth, as a conspirator against Tsarism, a suspicious and brutal attitude of mind that never left him; while he lived Europe must be independent of America but, to be so, it must submit to the only rival world power, Russia.

The American government, which had been one of the founders of the United Nations Organisation after the war, and had been convinced that Stalin might be converted by kindness into the semblance of a Liberal statesman, learnt in 1948 that Soviet troops had cut Berlin off from West Germany. The city's western sectors were only saved by a massive British and American airlift of supplies, an operation which took the Russians by surprise. After this the Americans could no longer deceive themselves. The subversion by degrees of every non-Communist state in Europe was Stalin's aim; and Russian armed forces would advance westwards whenever a pro-Soviet government was in danger. To meet this threat the western allies set up the North Atlantic Treaty Organisation, a military alliance of an unprecedented kind in which integrated land, sea and air forces underwent the training required to meet any threat to the political security of a signatory to the treaty. This was concluded in 1949 by Belgium, Canada, Denmark, France, Iceland, Italy, Luxembourg, the Netherlands, Norway, Portugal, the United Kingdom and the USA. Greece and Turkey joined in 1952, and West Germany in 1954, when military occupation ended.

A simultaneous economic alliance was a natural growth from the Marshall plan. Three organisations, called 'communities', were set up by Belgium, France, West Germany, Italy, Luxembourg and the Netherlands, one for iron and steel, a second for the development of nuclear power stations, and a third for making their territory one vast free trade area under the terms of a treaty signed in Rome in 1957.

Budapest and its Danube bridges

The prospect of a better life in the west produced a steady stream of refugees from the Communist countries, and this continued even when Communist border guards fired on illegal migrants moving westwards. The spectacle of success in the west also stirred up great discontent in Hungary. A revolt in 1956 was suppressed by the Soviet army with fearful bloodshed, but even the Russians could not prevent the mass migration of 100,000 people. By 1968 the European Economic Community (EEC) set up by the Treaty of Rome was showing such good results that the Communist government of Czechoslovakia proposed that socialism there should put on 'a human face'. To end such erroneous ideas a Russian army of 600,000 men invaded the country. The Soviet government alleged that this was necessary in order to prevent an American takeover. Nothing was less likely, for the EEC had made Europe economically independent of the USA. The six nations could claim that their statesmen had achieved a more lasting settlement by a trade agreement than any of their predecessors by a political treaty.

Throughout the 1960s the advantages of belonging to the EEC were becoming so plain that the British began negotiating for admittance to the community. Norway, Denmark and Eire, with whom Britain had a free trade agreement, also applied. They were refused entrance, mainly on the initiative of General de Gaulle, the President of France, who appeared to believe that the British would be a disruptive influence. The British applied a second time in 1967, when a Labour government recommended membership in view of 'the long-term potential for Europe, and therefore for Britain, of the creation of a single market approaching 300,000,000 people'. President de Gaulle was still in power and the British were again rejected, but a third application made by a Conservative government after the president's resignation, was accepted, and the House of Commons agreed by a majority of 112 votes to accede to the Treaty of Rome on 28 October 1971.

Hostility to the development from the Moscow press and radio was continuous. There was no recognition that France and Germany had laid aside their ancient enmity; only the old allegation that the manual workers in the west were ill-treated and underpaid. It was as though the former Europe with its age-long hatreds had found a new advocate in Russia, the very country that had suffered most from the racialism of Hitler. Yet the united states of Europe had made their declaration of independence, and their frontier, now standing on the Elbe, may one day reach as far east as the Urals.

The frontier between the Federal Republic of Germany and the Communist-controlled German Democratic Republic. The poster reads 'Peace for the World'; in the distance is a watchtower and machine-gun post; both are on the Communist side

INDEX

Aachen 39, 43, 63
Abelard, Peter 59
Agincourt 97
Aegean 18
Alaric 35
Alberti, L. B. 103
Albertus Magnus 71
Albigensian Crusade 71
Albrecht of Hohenzollern 111
Alexander IV, Pope 66
Alexander Nevsky 78
Alexander the Great 15, 23
Alexis, Tsar 125
Alfonso X, King 80
Algarve 80
Alsace 156
Alva, Duke of 117, 120
Anne of Austria 126
Antwerp 111, 117
Aquinas, Thomas 71
Archimedes 24
Aristotle 22, 23, 72, 130
Arius 34, 37
Armada 118
Arnold of Brescia 64
Arquebus 107
Ataturk, Kemal 168
Athanasius 34
Augustine, St 39
Austerlitz 149
Autun 38
Avignon 81, 89

Barcelona 38
Bastille 126, 143
Batu 70
Belisarius 36
Bergen 78
Berlin, Congress of 160; Decrees 149
Bernard of Clairvaux 58, 65
Beyazit I 94
Bismarck 155
Blenheim 135
Bonaparte, Napoleon 140, 145, 148; Joseph 149; Josephine 149
Boniface 39
Bordeaux 81, 143
Borodino 151
Bosnia 160
Brahé 120

Breitenfeld 123
Bremen 79
Brétigny 83
Bridget, St 98
Bruges 78
Brunelleschi 104
Byzantium 34

Caesar, Augustus 25; Julius 24, 35, 65
Calais 83, 97, 177
Calendar, Julian 24
Calvin, John 112
Campanilismo 152
Canossa 50
Canute 46
Capet, Hugh 62
Caprera 155
Caravels 102
Carbonari 153
Carthaginians 24, 35
Casimir, King 85
Catherine, Queen 119
Catherine of Siena 90
Catherine, Tsarina 139, 146
Cavalry 15, 39, 66, 83, 98, 122, 151
Cavour, Count 154
Charlemagne, Emperor 38, 43, 44, 63
Charles V, Emperor 108, 109, 110, 114, 115
Charles VI, Emperor 140
Charles V of France 84; IX 119
Charles XII of Sweden 133
Charles Albert, King 153
Charles Martel 38
Chartres 72, 83
Christ 27
Christina, Queen 123
Cîteaux 58
Clare 69
Clovis 36
Cluny 47, 50, 52
Colbert 127
Coligny 118
Columbus, Christopher 102
Commodus, Emperor 34, 48
Conrad III 60, 63
Conscription 148
Constantine, Emperor 34

Constantinople 34, 35, 38, 42, 45, 50, 52, 94, 130, 159, 167, 168
Copernicus 120, 131
Cordoba, Gonzalo de 108
Cracow 85, 120, 147
Crécy 81
Crimea 160
Croats 45, 130, 167
Crossbowmen 81
Crusade, First 50
Cyprus 61, 89, 96

Dante 76
Darius 19
Democracy 18, 22
Denmark 40, 46, 78, 84, 111, 132, 175, 180
Diaz, Bartolomeo 102
Diderot 138
Dimitri, Prince 88
Dinis, King 80
Diocletian, Emperor 31
Dominic 71
Doria, Andrea 108
Dogs 14

Einstein 179
Elba 151
Eleanor of Aquitaine 62
Elizabeth of Bohemia 122
Elizabeth, Tsarina 141
Erasmus 110
Escorial, Palace of 115
Esztergom 44
Eugène, Prince 135
Euripides 21
European Economic Community 181
Evangelists 27
Eyck, Jan van 99
Eylau 149

Falaise 52
Fascisti 170
Ferdinand, Emperor 121
Ferdinand VII 159
Feudalism 55, 62, 113
Florence 93, 104, 109
Flying Bombs 178
Francis Joseph, Emperor 166

Francis I 108
Francis of Assisi 68, 71, 93
Franks 36
Frederick of Bohemia 122
Frederick Barbarossa, Emperor 61, 63, 75
Frederick II, Emperor 75, 77
Frederick the Great 139, 140, 146, 149
Friedland 149
Fronde 127
Fuggers 108, 110

Galileo 130
Gama, Vasco da 103
Gambetta 156
Gagarin, Major 179
Garibaldi 154
Gaulle, Charles de 181
George I 136
Geneva 111
Ghibelline 76
Gibraltar 37, 136, 142
Giotto 69, 91
Gokstad ship 41
Golden Horn 94
Goths 35, 40
Göttingen 155
Greeks 11, 14, 17, 20, 24, 88, 104, 106, 159, 167, 180
Gregory VII, Pope 48 50; IX 69, 71, 76
Guelf 76
Guerrillas 149, 160
Guescelin, Bertrand du 83, 97
Gunpowder 107
Gustavus Adolphus, King 122
Gutenberg, Johann 104

Hannibal 24
Hanseatic League 77, 84
Henry II of England 63, 66; V 96
Henry II of France 118; III 119; IV 119, 126
Henry III, Emperor 47; IV 49, 50; V 62; VI 75
Henry the Lion 66
Henry the Navigator 101
Herodotus 19
Hildebrand 47
Hitler, Adolf 172
Horde, Golden 70, 90, 98
Horse collar 16
Horse shoe 16
Hospitallers 61, 76, 89, 109
Hungary 113, 140, 181

Huss, John 98, 109

Ignatius Loyala 112
Impressionists, French 157
Indulgences 110
Inflation, German 173
Innocent III, Pope 68, 71
Iron Smelting 16
Isabella of Castile 102
Ivan III, Tsar 98

Janissaries 87, 90, 94
Jena 149
Jengis Khan 70
Jesus, Society of 112, 139
Jews 11, 24, 27, 37, 64, 79, 85, 124, 146, 172
Joan of Arc 97
John, Don 117
John II 83
Justinian, Emperor 35, 94; Digest 62

Kalman the Booklover, King 45
Kepler 120, 130
Kerensky 165
Kiev 42, 70
Koran 38
Kosciuszko 147
Kun, Bela 167
Kutusov 149
Kyffhauser Mountain 67

Lafayette, Marquis de 142, 144
Lagos 101
League of Nations 174
Lechfeld 44
Legnano 66
Leipzig 151
Lenin 161, 165, 174
Lepanto, Battle of 109
Levant 51, 60, 76
Leyden 117
Leo I, Pope 35; III 39
Leonidas 20
Leopold I 159
Lithuanians 86
Lombards 39
Longbow 81
Lorraine 47, 97, 100, 156, 172
Louis VI of France 62: VII 62; IX 72; XI 99; XIII 126; XIV 127, 129, 135, 140; XV 140, 142; XVI 144, 151; XVIII 151, 159
Louis of Hungary 114

Lübeck 66, 77, 85, 122
Luther, Martin 110
Lützen 123

Magdeburg 123
Magenta 154
Magyars 44
Mahomet 37
Mahomet II 94
Malta 109
Marathon 19
Marcus Aurelius, Emperor 31, 34, 48
Marengo 148
Maria Theresa, Empress 140, 146, 149
Marie Antoinette, Queen 142
Marie Louise, Empress 151
Marshall, General 179
Masaryk, Thomas 166
Maurice of Nassau 118
Maximilian, Emperor 100, 108, 114
Mazarin, Cardinal 126
Mecca 37
Medici 104, 131
Meissen 136
Metternich 158
Michael, Tsar 124
Miltiades 19
Minden 141
Mohacz 114
Montesquieu 138
Moscow 70, 86, 87, 98, 122, 124, 132, 151, 168, 176, 181
Moslems 37, 61, 76, 79, 87, 89, 94
Mussolini, Benito 170

Nancy 100
Nantes, Edict of 118, 119, 128
Napoleon I—see Bonaparte
Napoleon III 154, 155, 158, 160
Navarino 159
Nationalism, Spanish 149
Nazis 172
Nero, Emperor 29
New Testament 27
Nicaea 34
Nicholas I, Tsar 159; II 161, 165
Nicopolis 90
Nihilists 160
Nile, Battle of 146
Nördlingen 124
Normans 41, 50, 52, 75, 97
North Atlantic Treaty Organisation 180

183

Novgorod 41, 42, 70, 98, 124

Odin 40
Olaf, King 46
Olaf the Saint 46
Olga, Princess 42
Oratorians 112
Orthodox Church 34, 86, 87, 96, 99, 125, 133
Ostrogoths 36
Otto, Emperor 43, 44

Padua 92
Painters, Russian 168
Palermo 64, 76
Paris burnt 41; Parlement 126
Parma, Duke of 117
Parthians 15
Paul of Tarsus 27
Pavia 65, 108
Peipus, Lake 78
Pericles 18, 23
Persia 17
Pétain, Marshal 175
Peter, Tsar 125, 132, 137
Pheidias 21
Philip II of France 61, 63, 68, 73; VI 81
Philip II of Spain 114; IV 126
Philip of Macedonia 15, 23
Philip the Good 97, 99
Pilsudski, Joseph 167
Pisano, Giovanni 92
Plague, Bubonic 83
Plato 21, 22
Pliny 29
Poitiers 38, 84
Poland 85, 146, 159, 167
Pompey 25
Poniatowski 146
Printing 104
Protestants 111, 114, 118, 120, 121, 128

Rainald 65
Ramillies 135
Rasputin 165
Red Cross 176
Redshirts 154
Renaissance, Italian 103, 106, 120, 179
Rhine Palatinate 121
Richard I 61, 63
Richelieu, Cardinal 122, 126
Riga 78
Rockets 178
Roger II 64

Roland 11, 16, 39
Rollo 41
Romans 11, 14, 24, 27, 40, 104, 106
Rome, Sack of 108; Treaty of 180
Rousseau, J-J 139
Rumania 159
Rurik 41
Rus 41
Rutherford 179

Saddle 15
St Petersburg 133, 160, 165, 168, 176
St. Sophia 94
Salic Law 81, 140
Salvation Army 176
Sanction, Pragmatic 140
Schism, Great 90, 97
Schleswig-Holstein 155
Scots 123
"Sea Beggars" 117
Sedan 156
Semaphore Telegraph 145
Serbs 87, 88, 163
Seven Years' War 141
Sforza 100, 104
Shamans 90
Sicilian Vespers 76
Sigismund, Emperor 98
Silesia 140
Skanderbeg 94
Sluys 81
Sobieski, John 128
Socrates 21
Solferino 154
Spartans 19, 20
Sputnik I 179
Stalin, Josef 174
States-General 126, 143
Steel 16
Stephen, King 44
Stephen, St 28, 44
Stirrups 15
Stuart, James Edward 135
Suleiman the Magnificent 109, 114
Sully 126
Suvarov 146
Sweden, 40, 46, 78, 85, 98, 111, 122, 124, 128, 133, 175
Switzerland 13, 90, 100, 111, 149, 165

Tacitus 29
Tamerlane 90, 94
Tartars 69, 98

Templars 61, 76, 88
Tenchebrai 62
Tertullian 31
Teutonic Order 78, 85, 111
Themistocles 20
Thermopylae 19
Tiers État 143
Tilly, Marshal 123
Trafalgar, Battle of 149
Trajan, Emperor 29
Trent, Council of 112
Troitsa Monastery 88
Trotsky 165, 174
Tulip 96
Turks, Seljuk 50; Ottoman 86, 88, 94, 167
Tyrol 150

United Nations Organisation 180
United States of America 142, 161, 180
Urban II, Pope 50
Utrecht, Peace of 136

Valhalla 40
Vandals 35
Versailles 143, 156, 172
Vézelay 60
Vichy 175
Victor Emmanuel, King 154
Vienna, Congress of 151, 158
Vinci, Leonardo da 103, 108
Visby 78, 85
Visconti 104
Visigoths 36
Vladimir 42
Vladislav the Dwarf 85
Voltaire 139

Wallenstein 122
Warsaw, Grand Duchy of 149
Westphalia, Peace of 124
William of Orange 116
William the Conqueror 52
William I, Emperor 155; II 157
William III of England 128, 135
Wittenberg 110
Worms 111
Wyclif, John 98, 109

Xavier, Francis 113
Xerxes 19, 21

Yugoslavia 167

Zeppelin, Count 178
Zwingli 111